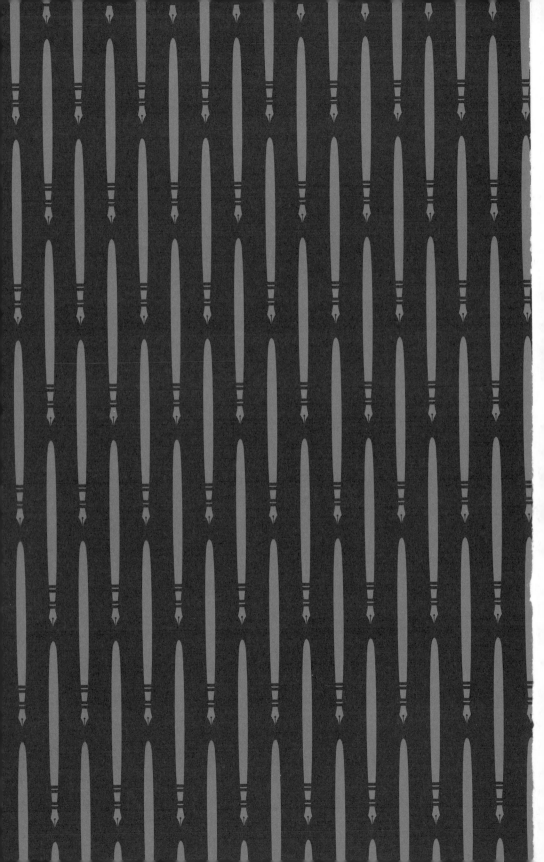

BEING
ELISABETH ELLIOT

BEING
ELISABETH ELLIOT

ELLEN VAUGHN

B&H
PUBLISHING
BRENTWOOD, TENNESSEE

978-1-0877-5099-6

Published by B&H Publishing Group
Brentwood, Tennessee

Dewey Decimal Classification: B
Subject Heading: ELLIOT, ELISABETH / MISSIONARIES /
WOMEN AUTHORS

Cover design by B&H Publishing Group. Cover photo used with permission of Elisabeth Elliot Foundation; photographer unknown. Flap
photo: Courtesy of Buswell Library Archives & Special Collections,
Wheaton College, IL. Cover decorative ornament © Vector Market/
Shutterstock. Author photo by Jonathan Whitten.

1 2 3 4 5 6 7 • 27 26 25 24 23

*"If the book we are reading does not wake us,
as with a fist hammering on our skulls, then why do
we read it? Good God, we also would be happy if we
had no books and such books that make us happy we could,
if need be, write ourselves. What we must have are those
books that come on us like ill fortune. . . . A book must
be an ice axe to break the sea frozen inside us."*

—Franz Kafka, quoted in Elisabeth Elliot's
journal, October 30, 1978

In memory of and gratitude for
Lee Vaughn

March 29, 1958–July 20, 2022

"The LORD gave, and the LORD has taken away;
blessed be the name of the LORD."
(Job 1:21 ESV)

Contents

Foreword by Joni Eareckson Tada   xi

Part One: Bedrock

Chapter 1: Certainty   3

Chapter 2: An Irregular Stone   7

Part Two: Being

Chapter 3: Elisabeth Elliot and the Psychedelic '60s   15

Chapter 4: New Construction   19

Chapter 5: *Playboy*, Filene's Basement, and Writer's Block   29

Chapter 6: Immaturity Cannot Tolerate Ambiguity   35

Chapter 7: The Heart of Human Experience   43

Chapter 8: The Runaway Tricycle   49

Chapter 9: Forcible Shakings   55

Chapter 10: Haunting Doubts   63

Chapter 11: A Return to Ecuador   71

Chapter 12: The Way Forward?   79

Chapter 13: The Biographer's Burden   87

Chapter 14: The Unredeemable Elisabeth Elliot   95

Chapter 15: "I Am Hopelessly Vulnerable"   99

Chapter 16: The Writing Conference   105

Chapter 17: The Six-Day War   111

Chapter 18: Jerusalem the Golden   117

Chapter 19: 1968   123

Chapter 20: Things as They Are   129

Chapter 21: "I Simply Boggle"   137

Chapter 22: Take Me!   145

Chapter 23: Domesticity and Complexity   153

Chapter 24: Reprieve   167

Chapter 25: "Is It Cancer?"   173

Chapter 26: *Selva Oscura*   177

Chapter 27: "Oh! If Only . . ."   185

Chapter 28: Thy Will Be Done   193

Chapter 29: Does the Road Run Uphill All the Way?   199

Chapter 30: A Paper Streamer   207

Chapter 31: Men in the House   215

Chapter 32: Boarder Crisis   221

Chapter 33: Walking MacDuff   233

Chapter 34: Depression Lurks   237

Chapter 35: Keep Me from Tears   243

Chapter 36: It's Too Much   251

Chapter 37: The Fence   259

Part Three: Believing

Chapter 38: Who Was She?   267

Epilogue: The Truth *Is* Love   277

With Gratitude   279

Notes   281

Foreword

*I*t is no secret that I adore Elisabeth Elliot. After a broken neck nearly did me in, her no-nonsense way of living and robust theology of suffering mercifully yanked me back from the edge of despair. She taught me how to wake up in the morning, sit up in my wheelchair, and face life with courage.

In some ways, our stories parallel each other. My quadriplegia fettered me to the dark companion of suffering and like Elisabeth, I wrote extensively on the subject. One of my earliest books included a list of the thirty-five good biblical reasons as to why God allows affliction and how you can benefit from it—a refined faith, a deeper prayer life, and compassion for others, to name just three. I asked Elisabeth to offer an endorsement, which she did. But in her reply, she confessed that although the book was very satisfactory, it was a bit technical. And slightly mechanistic.

I was crushed. I remember thinking, *She's written so much on suffering; how could she not laud its benefits?* After another decade of paralysis I saw what she meant. Searing, jaw-splitting pain was added to the mix, making my disability feel like a walk in the park. I realized then there was far more to Christian growth than having confidence in God's reasons for suffering. Life was more complex and mysterious than I thought.

Perhaps in her reply to me, this is what Elisabeth was getting at. She was the elder conveying to the younger that life is never neatly packaged. That suffering will squeeze you like a lemon, spurting out the true stuff of which you are made, stuff that surprises and shocks even you. That life is a flow of feelings, frailties, and failures and that only by confessing our brokenness do we truly engage with our suffering Savior. That the strongest saints are weak and needy.

You will discover this when you turn the pages of *Being Elisabeth Elliot*. Our hero of the faith was not a bronze statue, impervious to fissures; nor was she an airbrushed paragon of virtue, untested by the things that thwart and frustrate us all. Elisabeth owned her flesh-and-blood shortcomings and would bristle whenever people insisted on putting her on a pedestal.

Yes, after tragedy upon tragedy, she became a hero to us all. But as with any hero worth her weight, she would set people straight who idolized her, pointing them to the only hero who will never let us down, Jesus Christ.

My good friend Ellen Vaughn has been charged with the daunting task of showing us this side of Elisabeth Elliot. It's a painfully poignant side. Relatable and approachable. There aren't many authors skillful enough to write honestly, yet gracefully about such a beloved Christian stateswoman as the remarkable Elisabeth Elliot. But Ellen takes the prize. This *New York Times* bestselling author has written numerous books with Chuck Colson, with Greg Laurie on the book, now film *Jesus Revolution*, a powerful biography of Mama Maggie—the Mother Teresa of Egypt who cares for the poor in the garbage slums of Cairo, as well as many other beautiful books.

Relying on Elisabeth's private journals and never-before-published letters, Ellen takes us beyond the life of Elisabeth the young idealist and opens our eyes to the warm-hearted disciple of Jesus who was honest enough to acknowledge how much she did not understand.

This is why this book touches me so. I've lived more than half a century with immense suffering and with a constant need of Jesus, yet I still do not have life figured out. I am forever being tested by things that thwart and stalk us all. I have lain awake at night and thought, *Lord, is this how I am to do life, is this right?* The older I get, the more I deal in the realm of the unknown, and like Elisabeth, the more I am certain of just a few things—God's unfathomable grace and the astonishing delight of Christ toward His people.

Turn the page and discover how a young seer of suffering, fresh-from-the-mission-field, learned the art of *Being Elisabeth Elliot*. Delight in the "impenetrable mystery," as she put it, of the complex and beautiful enigma God has willed for you and me. And if He has dealt you a bewildering hand, play your cards with courage. God will show you what life is all about.

Joni Eareckson Tada
Joni and Friends International Disability Center
March 2023

PART ONE

Bedrock

CHAPTER 1

Certainty

*"The Christian realizes that his true identity is a mystery
known only to God, . . . and that any attempt at this stage
on the road of discipleship to define himself is bound to be
blasphemous and destructive of that mysterious work of
God forming Christ in him by the power of the Holy Spirit."*
—Elisabeth Elliot

I feel perfectly certain that I shall never marry again," Elisabeth Elliot
declared early in 1956.

It had been nine days since her muscular young husband and his
four fellow missionaries had been speared to death by members of a
remote tribal people in the Amazon jungle.

"No doubt all new widows make that statement," Elisabeth continued. "But I feel sure in my heart."[1]

But "perfect certainties," even among the most disciplined and
celebrated of God's saints, sometimes shift in the face of His surprises.

After Jim and his colleagues died, Elisabeth remained in Ecuador
for seven more years. Improbably, she trekked deep into the jungle
with her tiny daughter and a colleague and lived among the Waodani[2]
people who had killed her husband and friends. Many of the Waodani
embraced a new way of living. News reports called her a "missionary hero," a brave widow carrying the gospel to those who had never
heard it.

But this brave widow struggled. A lot. Painful personality conflicts
with her fellow missionary compelled her to leave the Waodani. She
worked among the Quichua people for a time, living in the house that
her late husband had built in a mission station called Shandia. Her
days advanced like a series of photos on a screen.

But in mid-1963, the setting of those images changed. The green eastern jungle of Ecuador became the White Mountains of New Hampshire. Little Valerie Elliot no longer frolicked naked in the river with her Waodani friends; now she wore plaid jumpers and rode a yellow school bus to elementary school each day. The grass hut in the jungle, and the mildewing wooden home that Jim built in Shandia, gave way to the house that Elisabeth designed, a streamlined structure with an enormous picture window overlooking Mount Lafayette. The days of translating the New Testament into Quichua or lounging in a woven hammock with Waodani women—puzzling over their indecipherable language and swatting flies—became a life of hunching over a typewriter, swatting interruptions and struggling to get English words on a page for a publisher's deadline. The missionary who had written a few books now purposed to be a "serious" writer who used to be a missionary. It was hard work.

There was no more *chicha* drunk by the campfire from a common, hollowed gourd among the tribal people. Now Elisabeth's tribe was the laconic New England laborer who cleared her field and dug her well, the wool-clad neighbor who taught her to ski, and the erudite crowd at New York cocktail parties, sipping gimlets. The small jungle campfire, with its background chatter of equatorial birds, became a crackling blaze in her own stone fireplace, the acres of woods beyond her window cloaked in a silent shroud of snow. Rather than running through the jungle at night, the lay midwife called to attend crisis births, now Elisabeth flew on Boeing jets toward speaking engagements at conventions and seminars, a sought-after public figure.

Eventually, the loneliness of a passionate woman who dreamed in the jungle of her lost lover Jim became the surprise of a new love that swept her right off her feet. Her earlier "certainty" about remarriage melted. A middle-aged Elisabeth Elliot, the financially independent writer and speaker, now shivered to the touch of Addison Leitch, the university professor, theologian, and writer with whom she had fallen desperately in love. They married on the first day of January 1969.

But the story, like Elisabeth's married life with Jim Elliot, would not end on that happy note.

The death of a loved one can come fast or slow. The sudden loss is devastating, a free fall through space where the mind cannot catch up with the physical reality of the death. With the gradual loss, perhaps the mind has time to "get used" to the idea of the loved one's departure before it occurs. The problem is, we never become accustomed to death's cruel theft of the one we love, whether it is a sudden robbery, so to speak, or a long, slow, embezzlement.

Once stunned by the joy of new love, now she was widowed again. Another death. But her widowhood would not define her, particularly since she would marry a third time in 1979. Her life rolled on, decade by decade, until her own death in 2015.

Her earlier years, related in *Becoming Elisabeth Elliot*, traced the transition of a young woman who dealt in "certainties" to the older woman who dealt, far too often, in the realm of uncertainties and the unknown. Now, *being* Elisabeth Elliot increasingly meant understanding how much she did not understand. She was certain of very few things—the good and holy character of God, His redeeming love, and merciful faithfulness. She sought her reference point beyond her own experiences, always pondering what she called the "impenetrable mystery" of the interplay between God's will and human choices.

It is that strange mystery which shaped the next portion of her startling life story.

CHAPTER 2

An Irregular Stone

"Here, then, is as much of the truth as one biographer
could discover about a [person]. Let the reader find
as much of its meaning as he [or she] can."
—Elisabeth Elliot, in her biography
of missionary Kenneth Strachan, 1968

I first met Elisabeth Elliot's cheerful daughter, Valerie, when Val and
her husband, Walt, drove a pickup truck several hundred miles from
their home to mine. The flatbed overflowed with boxes, cartons,
photo albums, and crates of an ancient invention called cassette tapes.
We hauled it all into my home office.

We laughed, talked, and ate pork tenderloin, asparagus, and
roasted red potatoes. Then Val and Walt had to hit the road, bound
for the home of one of their eight children. I left the dishes for my kind
husband and crept into my office, pulling open the boxes as if it was
Christmas morning.

Here were Elisabeth Elliot's journals, stacks of them filled with
her firm, flowing handwriting, recounting her days from her childhood through the next six decades. Her baby book, reams of personal
correspondence written with faded blue ink and a flourishing script,
carbon copies of typewritten letters, dozens of notebooks filled with
monthly expenses. There were lists of Christmas gifts given and
received each year, books read, and shopping lists. There were notes
for speeches, notes for seminary classes she taught, personal devotion-
als, scrapbooks with flaking, yellowed pages, and loose photographs,
the glue that had once held them to the page long gone. And here was
Jim Elliot's Bible, and his hand-drawn maps of the great eastern jungle
of Ecuador. Here were the famous black-and-white photographs taken

after Jim and his fellow missionaries were killed. I had seen them all before, of course, in books and magazines. But these were the originals. I laid it all out, wearing gloves like an archeologist, on six-foot Costco tables I'd set up in my office. Heaps of buried treasure.

As I picked through these treasures over the weeks and months that followed, Elisabeth's strong voice spoke from the past. She often made me laugh. She sometimes surprised me, and as I later questioned her family and friends about some of those surprises, I heard stories I had not expected. There were hidden realities that would mar the shiny surface of a tidy story, ripples of ruptured relationships, difficult dysfunctions: in short, the disorderly challenges that face real people in the real world. It's just that I hadn't expected they would be part of the life of Elisabeth Elliot, a woman renowned for her sense of order and decorum.

Her life was full of paradoxes. A spiritual rebel when she returned to the United States from her time in Ecuador, she later became a conservative evangelical standard-bearer, though she was no prude. She regarded both heterosexual and homosexual attraction full of compassion. This might surprise those who might assume she would shriek and judge any temptation or behavior aside from a life of unsullied purity. A fiercely independent woman, in her third marriage she yoked herself to a definition of marital submission that many of us would question. In her older years, this woman known for her diffidence and monosyllabic personal interactions with strangers at speaking events and book signings, became a beloved "mother figure" to thousands who had never met her. Her advice heeded by tens of thousands of radio show listeners, she made some surprisingly sad personal mistakes.

Did any of this disqualify my interest in Elisabeth Elliot? Far from it. I loved her as a fellow pilgrim on the trail. Her story echoed parts of my own, and I found it all to be redemptive.

So, as an earnest but doomed biographer, I had a choice. I could write a victorious, "inspirational" white-washed story, always a popular option in many Christian circles. Or I could tell it straight. I thought about the Bible. Surely its authors would have produced a far less puzzling book if they had omitted certain stories, the ones that we just don't tend to read to our children. Some Old Testament protagonists were masters of duplicity. Sarah, Rachel, and Tamar: clever and deceptive. Noah singlehandedly saved humanity from the global flood, and then got drunk and naked on his own new grapes. Some kids—well, forty-two of them—made fun of the prophet Elisha's bald head as he walked down a path, and he basically called forth judgment upon them. Two female bears obligingly emerged from the forest and mauled them all.

There are also forthright accounts of agonizing human frailty and brokenness. Eve and Adam disobeyed God and lost Paradise. Just as we would. Jesus's friend Peter, who had lived with Christ for three years, denied that he even knew Him just before the crucifixion.

If Scripture had been made up to support a humanly engineered religion, it would have been far glossier and more palatable to human readers. Its very scandals—most notably, the scandal of the Cross—offer evidence of its authenticity. It is a real book about a supernatural God mysteriously invading the stories of real people. Outside of radical revision, the Bible would not make it as a cheerful Hallmark movie.

As Elisabeth wrote in 1968, "Possibly there is no better model for biography than the Bible. There it is perfectly plain that a true understanding of the world is not to be gained by pretending that things are other than what they are. If there is good, let it not be exaggerated. If there are evils, let us see what they are, and, if we will, let us bring to bear upon them the light of a Biblical faith, but let us not operate as though they simply did not exist and therefore needed no redemption."[1]

There is great virtue in truth, told with love. Flawed and relatable protagonists showcase the supernatural power of God. We all resonate with them, as opposed to the dull and caricatured folk of fake religiosity.

This is just a biography. It's not the Bible. I saw pieces of Elisabeth's story that had not made it into her public speaking, nor her books about families, men and women, and faith. I wish she had included them; the story would have been all the richer, brimming with God's grace. She was a human being, after all, not some flawless, gleaming captain in the army of God. I puzzled over some of the broken relationships, the falsehoods that had been perpetrated, not deliberately, but by assumptions that had rolled onward for years with an energy all their own. The story was made more difficult to tell, too, because some of her meticulously numbered journals and key pieces of correspondence were missing. I did not know why.

I began to realize that I should warn my readers: If you want the expected version of Elisabeth Elliot's story, don't read this book. Find another, more predictable version.

I do not want to create a melodrama, with one-dimensional saints and villains. I do not want to titillate with a tell-all. I do not want to offend, or smear, or gush, or get it wrong. I do not want to write this book, partially because I know I will need to insert more of my own voice in the account.

Elisabeth's early years, the subject matter of Volume 1 of this two-part biography, lent themselves to a discernable narrative arc. That story had a beginning, middle, and end, and Elisabeth's years in Ecuador brimmed with color and drama.

Her later years were no less dramatic, but they were more psychologically complex. In the 1960s Elisabeth articulated views that would likely shock some of her followers of the 1980s and '90s, while they might relieve some of her critics.

As with a film, it's all a matter of the editing and what one leaves on the cutting room floor, so to speak. I could choose scenes and writings from Elisabeth's life that would present her one way. Or I could choose other selections and spin it the other way. We could all say, ah, yes, Elisabeth Elliot, she was *this*. Or *that*. Choose your tag line; post your tweet.

Miserable with the responsibility of it all, I was strangely comforted by Elisabeth's one novel, published in 1966. It was not particularly popular. *No Graven Image* evoked the idols we so easily establish in our lives, particularly the religious constructs that codify God and resist any complexity and mystery. We presume to speak for God, the god we assume shares not only our political and social views, but our *taste*. The god of the bumper sticker, the hashtag, the slogan. The one who is on our side. Never mind if we are on God's side.

It's nothing new that we tend to do this with the Almighty. The concurrent problem, of course, is that we do it with each other. It is so easy to divide the world into "Us" and "Them," and to demonize the other side. As long as there is an enemy, we can raise money and gain adherents for our cause. As long as we see people as one or two-dimensional, we can typecast them. Ah. He was a great hero . . . but then the statue—the graven image—topples, and he was just a villain. We look up to someone as a spokesperson for our movement . . . but then the secret sin emerges, and we don't know where to look. We admire someone, and it turns out she hated golden retrievers, and it's all over. We long for heroes without complexity, heroes without aspects that we just don't like and can't admire. We want images, the noble, gleaming statue without the pigeon poop.

But among human heroes, these just do not exist.

There is a movement today that seems to suggest that perfect virtue is possible, and that any human being with any flaws must be dragged down. Given those standards, the movement itself cannot stand; utopian views about human nature always prove untenable in the end.

There is only one Hero who does not disappoint. As for the rest of us, we must be strangely content to see people as they are, courageous and terrified, noble and petty, discerning and blind. In it all, among the best of our lot, there is plenty to admire and plenty to strive for; the rest is simply cause, as always, to look to God and praise Him for His amazing grace that He would save "wretches like us" as the old hymn says. Our legacies as individuals are not so much about the trophies we win in our short lives, because that so easily leads to pride. Rather, the legacy of our brokenness and need for Christ highlights His eternal, golden mercies.

Martin Luther is one of those complex figures who changed the course of human history. We all know he was famously flawed. Brilliant, stubborn, in love with God and His Scriptures, fond of ale, subject to depression, anger, and the source of scurrilous, horrifying hate speech against certain people groups. What do we do? Cancel him?

Luther thoughtfully provided the key for the rest of us: his dying words. *We are all beggars.* Elisabeth Elliot would shout out an "amen to that, brother," if she was the sort of person who shouted amens, which she was not. But we are all poor, restless, needy people, right down to the end of this perplexing life. We have no merit on our own, no wealth of good deeds in our pockets that God counts up and, mollified, lets us in. No, we're all beggars. Vagrants. Bums. Yet what awaits us is the great Feast of grace God offers on the other side, where Martin Luther and Elisabeth Elliot and a host of other imperfect heroes sit today, passing the platters and praising the Lord.

Early in my research process, I visited the North Shore of Boston. Elisabeth had lived for many years in Magnolia, Massachusetts, in a cozy home overlooking the cold, gray sea. At the time her third husband, Lars Gren, still lived there. I had various visits, both puzzling and friendly, with him, as well as rich conversations with Elisabeth's younger brother, Tom, various close friends, and other relatives in the area. I had much to sort out.

One afternoon I drove to the church where Elisabeth had worshipped during her older years, the First Congregational Church of Hamilton. It had been established in 1713, sixty-three years before the signing of the Declaration of Independence, a little parish church in the tiny hamlet that eventually became Hamilton, Massachusetts.

I parked and walked across the road to the church's graveyard. It was a glorious, sky-blue day. Sunshine filtered through the soaring, old trees above me; small American flags fluttered in the breeze. The grave markers were all different sizes and shapes. Some marked the lives of those who had fought in the Revolutionary War; other stones commemorated men and women, boys and girls, who had lived their lives and died in the centuries since.

I had looked up the location of Elisabeth Elliot's grave and walked toward the rear of the long cemetery. No one else was around.

The gravestone was a big, irregularly shaped, smooth boulder with Elisabeth's name and one of her favorite verses engraved upon it. "When thou passest through the waters I will be with thee." She is buried with Addison Leitch, whose inscription reads, "loved husband and best friend of Elisabeth." This is interesting, given the fact that she was married to Addison for less than five years and to Lars for more than three decades. I decided to think about that later.

I sat down, my back against the sun-warmed stone. I thought of the flawed saints who have gone before us, all those biblical characters and men and women of faith down through the ages. I leaned on that boulder and thought of the irregular shapes of all our stories, how God redeems us all, and that somewhere in heaven, so close and yet so far, all is calm, and all is well. My mind drifted in the breeze, up toward the dappled light. *So, then, God,* I prayed, *how do You want me to tell Elisabeth's story?*

He did not audibly answer. Neither did Elisabeth Elliot, her bones underneath the green sod and the big stone on which I leaned. Presumably, they both had better things to do.

I breathed deep, stretched, and got to my feet. My eyes fell on the gravestone behind Elisabeth's. I don't know why I was drawn to it, as its back side was facing me. But I walked a few paces, knelt, and pulled away the long grass that was obscuring the inscription near its base. I read the deep-carved words.

"The truth, in love."

That was all.

I took it as a message, a guiding principle, as I began the journey of writing these biographies about the life and death of Elisabeth Elliot. *Tell the truth, in love.*

So that is what I have endeavored to do.

PART TWO

Being

CHAPTER 3

Elisabeth Elliot and the Psychedelic '60s

"Modern man is hung up on his identity. The Christian realizes that his true identity is a mystery known only to God, and that any attempt at this stage on the road of discipleship to define himself is bound to be blasphemous and destructive of that mysterious work of God forming Christ in him by the power of the Holy Spirit. Certainly the Christian does not define his identity by his actions: that is the very ultimate in anti-Christ, for it is in effect saying that I am my own creator."
—Michael Marshall, quoted by Elisabeth Elliot[1]

*"I deplore those above the knee skirts.
No one is flattered by bare knees."*
—Elisabeth Elliot

When Elisabeth Elliot first sailed to Ecuador in the spring of 1952, she was an idealistic, dedicated, single missionary in her mid-twenties. When she returned to the United States for good in the summer of 1963, she was a widow with a seven-year-old daughter, earnestly committed to Christ, but idealistic no more.

During Elisabeth's dozen years in Ecuador, life had of course gone on in the world beyond the missionary station and the Amazon jungle. But social changes in America had not had a huge effect on Elisabeth's daily life in the distant, isolated jungle.

When she and Val moved to Franconia, New Hampshire, in the summer of 1963, Elisabeth's new life in small-town America continued to be fairly insulated.

These years of radical transitions in American life and thought fomented philosophical forces still reaping profound changes in the world we inhabit today. And even if Elisabeth Elliot did not march in the front lines of '60s civil rights protests, or burn her bra in the nascent women's movement, or demonstrate against U.S. involvement in the conflict in Vietnam, these social convulsions—and many more—made up the increasingly turbulent times in which she and Valerie transitioned into their new lives in North America.

In 1963, President John F. Kennedy and his glamorous wife, Jackie, dwelt in the White House. A month before Kennedy's inauguration in early '61, a communist and insurgent coalition called the Vietcong threatened the existing regime in faraway South Vietnam. Concerned about a domino effect in Southeast Asia, with countries tumbling to communist rule one by one, the Kennedy White House quietly increased the U.S. presence in Vietnam . . . which would mushroom over the years.

In 1962, the Soviet Union's Nikita Khrushchev put the charismatic young President Kennedy to the test. On October 14, 1962, an American spy plane photographed a Soviet medium-range ballistic missile being assembled for installation on the island of Cuba, just ninety miles from the coast of Florida. A nuclear missile launched from Cuba against the United States could mean the death of eighty million Americans within ten minutes.

The Cuban Missile Crisis brought America to the brink of nuclear war with the Soviet Union. There seemed no way out until, thirteen days later, the USSR agreed to remove its missiles if America agreed not to attack Cuba.

It was a reprieve, but no one knew for how long. There was little cause to feel confident about lasting peace in the tense, Cold War world.

The United States also had deep problems at home. Though the Supreme Court had ruled against racial segregation in public schools in 1954, segregation was still legal in 1963. Alabama's new governor, George Wallace, had famously proclaimed in his inauguration speech, "segregation now, segregation tomorrow, and segregation forever!" In the spring of '63, the Reverend Martin Luther King Jr. was arrested in Birmingham during a civil rights protest for "parading without a permit." King then wrote his masterful *Letters from a Birmingham Jail*. In August, the civil rights leader made his "I Have a Dream" speech before 250,000 people at the Lincoln Memorial. In September,

Ku Klux Klan members bombed a predominantly black Baptist church in Birmingham, Alabama, killing four young Sunday school girls. Segregation would not officially end until the Civil Rights Act of 1964; its awful legacy continues today.

In 1963, the population of New Hampshire was roughly 660,000 people. Ninety-three percent of them were white. The most popular show on the clunky TV set that Elisabeth Elliot did not own was *The Beverly Hillbillies*, about a backwoods family that strikes it rich and moves to Hollywood, shocking the locals with their homespun ways. *Cleopatra*, an epic starring Elizabeth Taylor and Richard Burton, was the number one film at the box office. The first James Bond film was released. A movie ticket cost 85 cents.

The average cost of a new house was about $12,650. The standard wage was about $4,400 a year—roughly 84 bucks a week. A loaf of bread cost 22 cents, a gallon of gas, 30 cents. Cars were large and shiny, with big fins, happily guzzling all that cheap gas. A failing car company called Studebaker was the first to offer new devices called seat belts as standard vehicle equipment. The U.S. Postal Service introduced its own new idea: zip codes.

Beatlemania had not yet hit America. Billboard's top song for '63 was a cheery balled called "Dominique," recorded by a habitual musician known as "The Singing Nun." A new vaccine for polio was introduced; since it was delivered via a sugar cube, schoolchildren had no problem ingesting it. Coca-Cola introduced its first-ever diet drink, a foul concoction called TaB. It was sweetened with cyclamate, which was later banned for causing cancer in calorie-conscious rats.

There were other drugs at work as well. The decade that began with the black-and-white conformity of the 1950s, now blossomed into a bodacious bounty of flower-power pop art, neon peace signs, skies full of diamonds, and visions through kaleidoscope eyes— enhanced, of course, by marijuana, hashish, and the sixties' favorite trip advisor, LSD.

Along with the drugs—and aided by the drugs—the biggest upheaval of the psychedelic decade would be the sexual revolution. Rejecting the double standards or cloistered sexuality of the 1950s, the young people of the '60s happily rode a tide of free love and sexual experimentation, immeasurably helped by the introduction of the birth control pill in 1961.[2]

There would be a musical revolution as well, led by the Beatles, the Rolling Stones, the Doors, the Who, Jimi Hendrix, Pink Floyd, the Kinks, Creedence Clearwater Revival, the Beach Boys, the Byrds, the Grateful Dead, Bob Dylan . . . the list, like the beat, goes on. And on.

Much of the music mirrored what was happening in popular culture, even as it led the way. "I want to hold your hand" became "Why don't we do it in the road?" "Love, love me, do" became "I'd love to turn you on." If George Harrison was into Eastern religion and the Maharishi and sitars, next thing you knew, everyone was singing about Vishnu and checking out transcendental meditation. When John Lennon said in 1966 that the Beatles were more popular than Jesus— with a wide backlash from angry pastors with crew cuts—most people under thirty just shrugged and agreed with John.

The bumper-sticker philosophy pasted on flower-festooned Volkswagen buses said it all. Harvard professor Timothy Leary, an LSD enthusiast, famously urged young people to "tune in, turn on, and drop out." They did. "Make love, not war." They did. "Don't trust anyone over thirty." They did not . . . until a year after their twenty-ninth birthday. And then there was the zeitgeist of the day: "Question authority." They did.

For her part, Elisabeth Elliot did not exactly consider Dr. Timothy Leary an authority by whose injunction she would question authority. She was in her mid-thirties by now. She did not use hallucinogens, groove to rock and roll, embrace free love, join a commune, or march in the streets. But in one respect, Elisabeth Elliot was a 1960s rebel. For if her often-painful faith journey in Ecuador had taught her anything, it was indeed to question authority. Not divine authority. She took God at His Word. But she questioned the human authority of those who so often purported to speak for Him.

CHAPTER 4

New Construction

*"They were cosy and comfortable in their little house
made of logs, with the snow drafted around it and the
wind crying because it could not get in by the fire."*
—Laura Ingalls Wilder, *Little House in the Big Woods*

While she was still in Ecuador, the enterprising Elisabeth had pur-
chased a plot of land in Franconia, New Hampshire, overlooking the
White Mountains. There were thick, pine-scented woods, a natural,
unforested knoll on which to build a house with rolling, open views of
the mountains in the distance, and a valley below dotted with farms,
ski resorts, a village, and a public school for Valerie.

Elisabeth contracted with a home-building franchise called
Techbuilt, first introduced in the United States in 1953 by a Harvard
architect who taught at MIT. Characterized by simple lines, pitched
roofs, overhanging eaves, cedar siding, and the extensive use of glass,
these homes were created from factory-made modules for the walls,
floor, and roof panels and delivered by truck. The idea was that a
construction crew could put it up in a few days. The result would be
a sleek, modern home that could be erected for much less cost than a
conventional "stick-built" house.

Elisabeth wrote to her family that she loved the "lovely, simple
lines, semi-rustic appearance, and good quality materials." Regarding
décor, she wanted "nothing distinctive, identifiable, individual, original, or whimsical . . . I wanted the very best quality materials, and
had to sacrifice style and individuality in order to suit my budget."[1]
The house, presumably, would be a backdrop for life, not the focal
point. She would name her new home *"Indinyawi,"* a Quechua word
drawn from Inca traditions. It meant "Eye of the Sun." The home was

no Machu Picchu, but its southeastern exposure meant that sunlight would flood its front windows most of the day.

Though the shell would go up quickly, it would take time for the rest of the house to be completed. Elisabeth observed that plumbers and other contractors tended to "come only when they feel led." She and Val temporarily settled into Gale Cottage, the Howard family property that had shaped the happy summers of Elisabeth's childhood. It had been built in 1889 by her uncle Will and aunt Annie, at a time when any house where people of means spent the hot season was called a "cottage," including enormous summer homes complete with servants' quarters, multiple chimneys, great stone fireplaces, and wrap-around porches.

Gale Cottage, far less grand, was a simple wooden lodge. There were two large rooms downstairs, two large and two small chambers upstairs, and two servants' accommodations in the attic. As a child Elisabeth had loved reading by its fireplace, hiking in the endless woods, swimming in the frigid Gale River, and fishing with her father. On rainy days she'd explored the dusty trunks piled in the attic. They held treasures such as a music box, a furry mechanical bear, and a mummified child's foot, brought from some ancient tomb in Egypt when Elisabeth's uncle Will was searching the world for artifacts for the then-new Metropolitan Museum in New York.

Now, the adult Elisabeth inhaled the smells of her youth: old wood, old leather, old books, scents of pine and balsam and wood smoke. At night there were the sounds of the wind in the white pines, the river flowing over the cold, smooth stones. Elisabeth and Val would snuggle under a feather quilt and read the books Elisabeth had loved as a child. They made their way through Laura Ingalls Wilder's *Little House in the Big Woods*, with its wholesome family of late-eighteenth-century American pioneers. Their setting felt like the Elliots' cottage, with one exception. Little "Laura and Mary shivered and snuggled closer to [their father]," Elisabeth read to Val. "They were safe and snug on his knees, with his strong arms around them."[2]

"She was enchanted with the coziness of the story, the warmth of the family life," Elisabeth wrote to her family. She asked Val, "What made the characters so happy? What is the most important thing in a home?"

Elisabeth was thinking of "love," but Val cut to the chase: "A daddy."

Val had started school in early September. She was thrilled to clamber onto a school bus and carry a lunch box and learn in a classroom with other kids. Remembering her own awkward days as a child, Elisabeth was mystified and delighted when the bouncy, blonde

Val went "skipping right into school" on the first day. Val seemed to have inherited more of her dad's "life of the party" genes than her mother's socially awkward DNA.

With Val happily settled into their new life, Elisabeth breathed easier, stared at the silent woods, and wondered just how to commence her endeavors as a serious writer. Her days spread before her like blank pages; a prime time for creativity. Eleanor Vandervort—Van—her close friend, confidant, and support system during those last months in Ecuador, was visiting with family and friends, and would return after Christmas.

Elisabeth need not have been alone. After all, she had received a marriage proposal while still in Ecuador. An "odd little Czech" kept turning up at her home in Shandia. He'd arrive at lunch time just about every day with a worn gunny sack flung over his shoulder, his cheeks and chin stubbled with whiskers. He was about a foot shorter than Elisabeth and retained just enough teeth for her to almost understand what he was saying. It had something to do with food . . . and her house . . . then he finally screwed up the courage to make his intentions known and asked for her hand in marriage.

Elisabeth did not need to pray about God's will on this one. She told him no, and to please not visit her anymore. His face fell, his shoulders slumped, and he slunk away.[3]

Now Elisabeth sat in solitary, silent splendor in Gale Cottage and pondered writing. She had a contract with her publisher, Harper's, to write a new book on the topic and in the genre of her own choosing. It was like a blank check . . . but Elisabeth's *brain* was also blank. She had wisps of ideas, yes, but nothing she could capture and organize into a book. Instead, her mind overflowed with a thousand domestic details regarding floor tile, paint colors, and cabinet knobs.

Most of the choices were not easy. She anguished over whether to install a submersible pump or a multi-stage centrifugal jet. "I feel like the private who didn't want to sort potatoes," she wrote to her family. "Those DECISIONS."[4]

She escaped from the decisions by meeting the locals. The Howards had worshipped during the summers at a local Baptist church called Sugar Hill; Elisabeth's mother was anxious for her to now be involved there full-time. A group of Sugar Hill ladies invited Elisabeth to tea. She was grateful, but found the conversation "deadly boring—allergies, diets, dogs, Harvard, horses, maids, houses in Palm Beach, etc."

A woman from the tea invited Elisabeth to a dinner that was much more fun. There were elegant hors d'oeuvres, and a dinner including two Maine lobsters for each person. After dinner one of the hosts read aloud from a humorous novel, and then they played charades.

The church invited Elisabeth to sing a solo during the worship service. The visiting pastor was "about 4'11"," with "tiny little hands and a soft little voice." Before she stood to sing, he introduced her as "Mrs. Saint," as in the widow of pilot Nate Saint, who had been killed with Jim.

"I sang anyway."

Later she had lunch at a local club with a non-church couple who actually knew her name. "It's a strange bunch of people—definitely clique-ish, everybody 'darlings' everybody else, but all were most cordial to me, offered me some of their drinks and smokes which they had brought along, since the club serves only hamburgers in this season. (I just had hamburgers.)"[5]

She kept trying with the Sugar Hill church people. They came to her home for a prayer meeting. "The Bible study was pretty pathetic, unfortunately. [The pastor] is a nice guy . . . but just mouths platitudes, I fear, which really mean very little to him or anyone else. Fundamental—oh sure, but where is the life? Where the honesty? I am in a quandary as to what to do about the church situation. Does one go to a church just to 'encourage the poor struggling little group'? I am not at all sure this is required."[6]

Predictably, Elisabeth's mother was worried about Elisabeth's spiritual health. Why couldn't her daughter just settle down and go to that nice Baptist church and be happy?

"I feel terribly when these great chasms seem to yawn between us," Elisabeth wrote to her mother. "The more life goes on, the further I feel from all the old ties—rather like Abraham, leaving kindred and lands—and perhaps this is what God has to do to each of us, in some measure, in order to isolate us for Himself. But it is never an easy thing to know that one is hurting those he loves. I do love you, Mother, and thank God for you, for your constancy of love, and for the humility of spirit which enables you to seek to understand your offbeat children, rather than condemning them and crossing them off."[7]

The workmen Elisabeth met were far more colorful than the church people.

A local character told her stories about his boyhood in the area. Elisabeth wrote up his story in her journal: "Used to trap mushrat along heah—got seven dollahs one time for a pelt, but nowadays don't believe they'a wo'th anything. Only thing's wo'th anything now is a mink.'" He pointed "to a farm by the Connecticut River, 'See that fam theah? Man by the name of Reynolds lived there. Look on the mailbox—don't that say Reynolds?'"

"It says Runnels," the ever-particular Elisabeth observed.

"Yeah," the handyman responded. "*Reynolds*. His daughter lives there still. Well, that man was the meanest man ever lived. The whole town hated him. One time his hired man—he was an old man—come a little bit late and he beat him till they had a put him in hospital. Finally, that town got so mad at him they all ganged up and tied him hand and foot and throwed him in the river.

"They never found him till next spring. Had the whole state police, FBI and everybody out here trying to figure out who did it. The whole town done it—so no one would talk. They never did find out who done it, so they ruled it suicide."

Not to be outdone, the man digging in her backyard told her about the time he did some work at a nudist colony.

"Is that like going to a Bible camp?" Elisabeth asked facetiously.

"Hell," the man responded. "You'd probably learn just as much.

"Guys walking around with their teapots out," he continued, shaking his head. "When a man introduces you and says 'this is my wife,' and she ain't got no clothes on, by golly you gotta be careful" about shaking hands.

The man was part of a team drilling an artesian well, necessary in a geographical situation when the water is confined under pressure below layers of relatively impermeably rock. After two days of drilling, the crew struck two gallons of water per minute, at 293 feet. "They had hit 'ledge' (Yankee for solid granite) at 98 feet, and from there on down it was solid rock, hence the standard charge of $7 foot," the frugal Elisabeth wrote to her family. (Seven dollars a foot in 1963 would be approximately $60 a foot today.)

"Oh well," she continued, "I could have had a nervous breakdown and all that jazz, standing there watching that immense rig grinding away, but then I figured God knew where that water was, the money was His anyway, and He could just as easily have made them hit water at 50 feet if He'd wanted to save Himself some money, but we've got to learn that His ideas about [money] are not ours."[8]

Elisabeth strode around her property wearing boots and a plaid skirt, chopping down smaller trees with her jungle machete. Now, instead of Amazon critters, she wrangled with raccoons on her front porch and chipmunks in her garage. A porcupine lumbered past a window; a woodchuck scuttled near the front door.

Meanwhile the contractor laying ceramic tile in the master bathroom muttered and sputtered to himself because the tub had not been placed properly. He comforted himself by smoking cigars, one after the other. Other workers tracked mud throughout the house, which "smelled like a subway" and looked like a bad dream to the meticulous Elisabeth. She could not just put it out of her mind, retreat to

Gale Cottage, stir up the embers in her cold imagination, and create great works of literary art.

"For your information," she wrote to her family, "I'm not writing a book on anything else just now. I can't put my mind on anything except concrete (tomorrow they're to pour the garage) and such."[9] She had no idea what she was going to write to fulfill her contract with her publisher, but did succeed in having this unknown book's deadline pushed back from June to December 1964.

Valerie told her mother that the other kids at school, or their parents, would sometimes ask her what her mother did.

"What do you tell them?" Elisabeth asked.

"Oh," said Val, shrugging. "I just say she doesn't do anything. She never works."

Meanwhile, at least Val was writing. She sent a pencil-scrawled poem to her "Gradma."

"There once was a rat/Who sat on a mat/He was fond of a rat/Who wore a big hat."

Soon after this opus, the house was finally completed. Elisabeth loved every inch of it. She spared her family few details of its design and latest in '60s decor. The "house is L shaped," she wrote, "50 feet long north and south, 36 feet wide at the wide end, 24 at the narrow. Ten-foot picture window in the front. Living room, dining room paneled in wood, with oak floors and a stone fireplace at the east end, built-in bookcases flanking the fireplace, white handwoven Ecuadorian rug on floor."

The kitchen had dark walnut cabinets, wallpaper, and the latest in white and gold Formica counters. There was a guest bath with "fawn-colored" tile, with towels in sand, fawn, and coral. The hallway was "French blue with natural woodwork" and a cork tile floor. Val's room had lavender and orchid wallpaper with a white background; Elisabeth had sewn white ruffled organdy curtains and a dust ruffle for Val's new white canopy bed with its lavender spread.

The guest room had gold walls and the latest in gold wall-to-wall carpet, while Elisabeth's white room had a blue and purple bedspread, a new rock maple bed and dresser, and a bath done in ceramic blue tile with aqua accents. The outside of the house, stained a deep brown, had white trim and a bright turquoise door, with a flagstone walk winding down from the front door to the driveway, and a post lantern on the side.[10]

There were only a few mementos from Ecuador: Waodani spears like the ones that had killed Jim, the coffee table he had built from jungle hardwood, and the white rug in the living room.

The Elliots moved into their new home mid-November 1963. "The sheer luxury of this house is at times overwhelming to me," Elisabeth wrote her family. "God alone knows how grateful I am. To waken at night on a foam rubber mattress, deliciously warm under your blanket . . . between new, smooth sheets, and to hear the wind whistling around outside and know that snow is falling but we are sheltered from it all—well, it's just such a contrast to the past I can hardly get over it!"[11]

It was a far cry from sleeping in a dirty hammock in the mud of the Amazon jungle.

Soon after Elisabeth and Val moved into their new home, on November 22, 1963, Val was at school, and President John Kennedy was campaigning; riding in a fin-tailed, open-topped black limousine in Dallas, Texas. The waving crowds, craned to get a view of JFK and Jackie, so elegant in her pink Chanel suit and her matching pillbox hat. She carried a bouquet of blood-red roses as she and the president waved to their fans.

A businessman named Abraham Zapruder, his state-of-the-art 8 mm Bell & Howell Zoomatic movie camera in hand, stood on a narrow four-foot concrete abutment on the parade route as he filmed the colorful procession.

Texas governor John Connally and his wife, Nellie, rode in the limo seat in front of President Kennedy and the First Lady. Nellie turned around. "Mr. President," she called above the crowd noise, smiling big, "you can't say Dallas doesn't love you!"

A few seconds later there was a rifle shot, unnoticed in the roar of the crowd. Then another. The president and Governor Connally were both hit, though not mortally. Then came the third shot, the one that Abraham Zapruder's film captured taking off the top of the president's skull, blowing a pink mist in the air and spewing part of his bone and brain matter onto the back of the limousine. There was Jackie Kennedy, crawling in that primal moment of horror onto the trunk to retrieve it; a Secret Service agent threw himself into the car and it screeched toward the hospital as Jackie cradled her ruined husband in her arms.

Elisabeth Elliot did not own a television, but she devoured everything the print media published about the tragedy. She quoted a *New Yorker* editorial about the national experience: "It was as if we slept from Friday to Monday and dreamed an oppressive, unsearchably significant dream, which, we discovered on awaking, millions of others had dreamed also. Furniture, family, the streets, and the sky dissolved; only the dream on television was real."[12] She poured over *Life* magazine's November 26 issue, which featured still shots of Abraham Zapruder's chilling video.

Elisabeth related with JFK's wife, suddenly widowed by unthinkable violence. She wrote to her family, "The movie footage reproduced in Life last week is terribly moving, isn't it? Just what do you suppose Jackie was thinking when she crawled over the trunk of the car? The captions say, 'a pathetic search for help.' I doubt that. I doubt that she knew—or would remember even now—what she was doing. What a thing. I can still scarcely believe it."[13]

Thanksgiving 1963 was five days after the president's death. Elisabeth and Val went to New York's Thanksgiving Day parade at Central Park. There were Donald Duck and Popeye balloons that were a block long. "It took about 45 men, holding on for all they were worth to the guy lines, to keep the monsters from taking off over the skyscrapers." They celebrated Thanksgiving in the Philadelphia area with family friends, then returned to New York on their way home.

Val was part of a Christmas pageant with other kids from her school. Elisabeth baked pies and filled her mantel with pungent pine fronds from her woods. Snow fell. Thrilled about the concept of sledding for the first time in her young life, Val climbed confidently on her new red Flexible Flyer, her head facing downhill, lying on her back. Elisabeth had to set her straight. Meanwhile their new puppy, Zippy, barked frantically and leapt through the drifts. Elisabeth had gotten him for free from an acquaintance in town. He was "part Walker hound (whatever that is), part Collie, and I don't know what else. He is very roly-poly and cute, mostly white with very badly arranged black patches."

Though not a genius, Zippy Elliot would be an enthusiastic companion for Elisabeth and Val, always ready to explore the woods, his snout vacuuming the narrow trails, quivering with excitement. He accompanied Elisabeth everywhere, waiting in the car while she shopped in town, lying next to her chair by the fire at night after Val went to bed. She tolerated in him what she did not accept in humans, forgiving his untidy behaviors. He would pull paper from her trash can and chew it to bits. Even though he knew she did not "like to have my wastebasket emptied thus," she wrote that "he does it so unobtrusively and humbly, he knows he can get away with it." Occasionally his sins were more flamboyant, as when he ate a tassel off the new guest-room bedspread . . . or when he pulled down and devoured Elisabeth's roast pork and baked potato one night when she left the table to take a phone call. She loved him anyway.

On Christmas morning, 1963, as Elisabeth and Val celebrated in the white snows of New Hampshire, Elisabeth's parents, Philip and

Katharine sat at their breakfast table. Philip seemed distracted. He anxiously looked over his left shoulder as if someone were behind him. Again. After the second time, his wife asked him what was wrong. No response. A moment later he looked over his left shoulder again, wide-eyed, and gave no recognition of having heard Katharine when she asked him what he was doing.

Worried, Katharine called some friends—a Mr. and Mrs. B.—they had planned to visit later that day. They arrived within minutes. They sat down together, and Mrs. B. read the Bible out loud. Philip continued to look over his left shoulder. Mr. B. walked him around the house to show him no one was there.

Later, Philip recovered sufficiently for the guests to return to their home, and later Phil and Katharine made their way there to open Christmas presents together. Suddenly Phil looked over his shoulder, turned in a tight circle, and fell to the floor, convulsing, groaning, and vomiting. As they flurried to help him, Mrs. B. heard Katharine whisper a frantic prayer: "Oh, Lord, take him quick, and take him easy!"

At the hospital, Philip stabilized, so Katharine returned home to welcome Christmas guests, who would accompany her back to the hospital . . . and during that interim, her husband passed away. He had gone quick. And easy.

Later, Mrs. B. told Katharine she had had a vivid dream early that Christmas morning. In it, she asked, "Why is this Christmas so different?" An unknown voice answered her. "Because there has been a death in the family."

Later that afternoon, of course, she discovered what her dream had meant.[14]

After the flurry of the funeral, Elisabeth wrote to her mother with empathy. She'd been a widow for eight years now and knew the shock of sudden loss.

"I know that you loved Dad, and your life was happy together, and I know too that now that God's time has come for you to be alone, He will be your portion as He promised, and you will find a new kind of life with Him.

"Remember that word about our 'light affliction'—it is working for us a far more exceeding and eternal weight of glory. I don't know what this means, but I know it must be wonderful.

"Do not waste any time or energy in self-reproach for what you didn't do for Dad, or what you might have said which you now regret, etc. This is a natural reaction, but useless and probably results from a distorted view.

"I love you, Mother, and trust God to prove His own love to you.[15]

CHAPTER 5

Playboy, Filene's Basement, and Writer's Block

"Walking in the woods Hemlocks bowed with snow,
rabbit tracks crisscrossing in every direction,
and such utter silence! How I love it here."
—Elisabeth Elliot's journal, winter 1964

*E*arly in 1964, Elisabeth finally settled down to write her new book, her friend Eleanor Vandervort—or Van—now with her. Van had been a friend of Elisabeth and Jim's at Wheaton. At age twenty-four she had gone to South Sudan as a Presbyterian missionary. She worked among the Nuer, a primitive people who had never heard of Jesus and had no written language. Van worked for thirteen challenging years developing a written form of their tongue, and then translated the New Testament into it.

Like Elisabeth, Van was not afraid to ask hard questions about commonly accepted missionary methods, means, and mindsets; what did it mean, really, to communicate the gospel to people whose culture is different from your own?

In early 1963, Van had been abruptly informed by the new Sudanese government that she, like other missionaries, must leave the country. She made her way to Ecuador to visit her old friend Elisabeth Elliot, and the two women—being similarly affected by their missionary experiences—found a deep connection in their views on life, faith, and the world. For Elisabeth, Van had been a welcome relief from the deep loneliness she'd felt since Jim's death; at last, someone who understood how she felt and thought.

"The joy of being with Van goes on and on, day after day, like a pure stream, and still it is hard for me to believe the love God had for us both in working this out. To think of Him . . . contemplating two lonely women, and biding His own time, and then finally saying 'Now!' and sending her across the world so we could be together! It's marvelous to think of how He knows our needs and longings, and He meets them in His own way, far above our imaginings. There are times when we must learn to satisfy ourselves with Him alone, but there are many other times . . . when He freely gives us with Himself, all things."[1]

Elisabeth introduced Van to Mel Arnold, her editor at Harpers. After hearing Van's story, he offered her a contract to write her own book, an account of her grueling years among the Nuer.

Van moved into Elisabeth's new gold-and-white guest room. She helped Val with her homework and Elisabeth with the housework. She was handy with a wrench or a screwdriver. When Elisabeth traveled for speaking engagements, Van stayed home with Val.

It was a great setup. The two missionary oddballs, kindred spirits, and gifted thinkers would now write their respective books in Elisabeth's hilltop retreat. But for Elisabeth—and Van as well—the creative juices just were not flowing.

"Since September, I have tried to write a book," Elisabeth ranted in her journal. "Lived at [Gale] cottage then—too cold, too occupied with floor tile and foundations, paint colors and countertops, jet pumps and heating systems, to concentrate on a book."

She kept telling herself that as soon as she moved into her new home, the writing would flow.

"Then it was draperies and furniture. Then Christmas, Dad's death, Florida . . . 'Oh well—January will see the grand opening!'" she had thought.

January passed. As did February. "Still no form. Plenty to say—how to contain it in a book? Novel? Journal? Essay? Not a line on paper so far."

What was the thing inside of her, burning to be expressed?

"Pray for clarity of vision, for the ability to put it down, for truthfulness in the inward parts," she begged her family. "This is always a hard thing for me as I write—I keep feeling my own inadequacy in perceiving the truth and in actually formulating it on paper. One wonders if one's soul is really big enough for the task. I keep thinking of old John [the apostle], seeing that tremendous vision, and being told Write what you see. None of us can do anything else in honesty—we must write what we see, not what someone else sees, not what we may think we ought to see, not what we wish to see."[2]

Elisabeth felt that most of her life had been in the context of people seeing what they felt they ought to see, expressing the "right" answers, having the "right" reactions. The "oughts" had been a staple all her life. It was hard now, to say the least, for her to write about life without the subtext of a mission agenda. In her growing up years, she'd been surrounded by people who saw no value in art or literature unless it pointed people overtly to the "plan of salvation." Now she believed that literature itself, in showing—not "telling"—the truth about life, human beings, sin, death, and relationships, could itself redemptively evoke the design of the Divine in His creation. But was *she* capable of doing this?

The quiet days and nights passed.

"11:30 p.m. by the fire. Zip asleep on the white rug at my feet. Peace. Van and Val both asleep."

She was reading Isak Dinesen's *Out of Africa*, an "exquisite gem of twentieth-century writing . . . Should the book be a novel? Am I that capable of creativity??"

And who in the world would read her novel, she wondered. The people she knew who read missionary books frowned on novels. The people who read novels had no interest in missionary books. She was doomed.

She kept reading *Out of Africa*. "Such dignity and grace, such truthfulness and brilliant imagination."

"It is painful in the extreme to find myself incapable of putting a single line on paper," she wrote in her journal the next day. "I sit, in a perfectly silent house, no phone ringing. Valerie in school, no Indians at the windows, no housework to do, no interruptions of any kind. I read, I think, I read some more—the Bible, *Playboy* magazine (first copy I've ever seen—bought in Boston because someone mentioned that now and then they print some excellent literature. I wanted, too, of course, to see what sort of women the 'Playmates' are). Then I think some more. Nothing profits."

While in Boston, besides buying *Playboy*, Elisabeth had visited Filene's Basement. Though she was having trouble writing her book, she had no difficulty describing the mad scene at Filene's in a letter to her family.

"They get all sorts of fabulous bargains from the country's best stores (Neiman-Marcus of Dallas, etc.). They are automatically reduced 20 percent after 10 days, 40 percent after 20 days, and then they are given away after 30 days."

"It was a screaming bedlam. Whole families with babies and tots, tough fishwives determined to get the gold opera slippers for $2.99, Mom with the beehive-haired teenage daughter who need coats for

Easter, [elderly aunt] types scrambling for corsets. You are not allowed to try anything on, and to this end everything is sewed together. Never mind that. Women come equipped with scissors, snip open the stitches, peel off their dresses in the aisles, try on anything and everything, drop things they don't want on the floor where they are promptly trampled. . . . I could hardly stand it for the half-hour or so we were there, but in that time I got a wool suit for Val for $7.99, a $15 black patent purse for myself for $5, Van got some beautiful kid gloves and a suitcase."[3]

Back at home, she was less productive.

"Yesterday felt on the verge of actually writing something down, all day. . . . A day spent in hope—and it was hope deferred. Nothing comes <u>clear</u>. Panic that what I write be not true—in the truest sense (i.e., fiction may be true—in that it truly represents life and the human being who encounters life). Fears of what fellow missionaries will feel as they recognize themselves; cowardice at being thought ill of; misgivings again that I am not really capable of evaluating my experiences justly and portraying them honestly—with perspective and understanding. God help me. God give me the insight. Reveal, Lord, <u>reveal</u> what I'm to do. This fruitlessness is <u>agony</u>. I feel guilty when I am not producing. Oh help me, Lord."

She commenced a vigorous dialogue with herself; Fretful Elisabeth and Faithful Elisabeth went at it about her fears that she was incapable of giving birth to a new book.

How can I write?

(Shut up—God has given a gift.)

How shall I pay the bills?

(They're paid, aren't they, for a year or so?)

Yes—but what then?

(Don't fret about the future. Be thankful for the present.)

But I'm not producing anything.

(But gestation is prerequisite.)

Suppose I'm kidding myself about this gestation business? Suppose it's all a fake—only a tumor or something?

(But you have something to say.)

What good is that to me if I can't write it?

(You will. Tho' the vision tarry, wait for it.)

How long is this going to go on?

(That's not your concern. Trust a little. Wait patiently—"for the Lord.")

But I'm meant to work, am I not?

(Not if you're meant to wait.)

God—I've been "waiting" since September.

(But the time isn't wasted. You're learning, ruminating, formulating—this is part of the process.)

"Alack," concluded Fretful Elisabeth. "I'm going to quit for the day. Glad I have to go to the kitchen now and start the corned beef cooking. Always nice to have something immediate that one simply <u>has</u> to do. Anything rather than think!"

CHAPTER 6

Immaturity Cannot
Tolerate Ambiguity

". . . doubt wisely; in strange way
to stand inquiring right, is not to stray;
to sleep, or run wrong, is."
—John Donne, from Satire III

Since her thinking and writing seemed to be creatively constipated, it was a paradoxical relief for introvert Elisabeth to travel to speaking engagements. Because of her books and well-known personal story, each day's mail brought invitations to address missions conferences, women's meetings, church gatherings, or some other group. Some of the hosts seemed fairly confused about just why they wanted her to come. Months after initially issuing an invitation, one host wrote to her again, now wondering if by any chance Elisabeth might be the same Elisabeth Elliot who wrote some book and was a missionary to the Waodani. *Why had she invited me in the first place*, Elisabeth wondered. Another host gushed about how much Elisabeth's late husband's fine "work in Africa" had meant to her.

Elisabeth was not sure what to do about all these opportunities. "I don't feel that I can further the 'cause' of missions much, if that is what they want, but I could tell them some personal things the Lord has showed me . . . But I feel, too, that that is what I should be <u>writing</u>."[1]

She was invited to speak at the King's College, a Christian institution in New York. Its president, a well-known evangelical leader, had never met her before. Elisabeth was put off by his instant familiarity and backslapping enthusiasm, which felt contrived to her. He escorted her to the chapel, where 400 students waited. There was a rousing hymn and then the type of introduction Elisabeth had heard many times . . . "Author, missionary to the savage Waodani who martyred" her husband and four other brave missionaries, but God used it to bring a great harvest for the Kingdom.

The president continued. "And now we're happy to have Mrs. Elliot, who I know has a real burden for soulwinning and for getting you young people stirred up for the mission field."

Elisabeth stood, not feeling very "stirred up" herself. She wasn't sure she could emotionally induce young people to sign up for missions.[2] She believed she was there to talk about what she knew to be true, what she had experienced in Ecuador, and what she had learned about God in those hard situations. No spin.

"I fear," she told the students in her precise and dispassionate way, "that your esteemed president has invited the wrong speaker for chapel. I want to talk simply about knowing God."

"[The president] hadn't a clue what I was getting at," Elisabeth told her family later. He "said 'Amen' at inappropriate intervals, thanked me at the end, handed me a check, and said goodbye."[3]

She went from the college chapel to a women's luncheon for 400, with a lovely spring hat fashion show before her talk. An evening or two later she spoke at a church meeting that the acerbic Elisabeth deemed "dreadful. Hollow mockery, the show, the missionary machine, the Gospel business, the introduction of me, the total lack of comprehension of what I was saying, the sheer phoniness of everything about it. Van and I came away appalled."[4]

A week or two later she traveled to a Christian school called Barrington College in Rhode Island to speak, along with others, at a "vision-vocation conference."

She dreaded it.

"It was jammed, to my surprise, and I felt that it was the most eager, attentive, and intelligent audience to which I had ever spoken. It was a great pleasure, indeed, after the kind of church audiences I have faced."[5]

She showed color slides with scenes from her time among the Waodani. She spoke on knowing God, using Isaiah 43:10 as her base, and the passage from Exodus that had been so meaningful to her in Ecuador. In it, God told Moses to do something that was in fact doomed to failure. "I will send you, I will be with you, but Pharaoh will not listen to you."

What does faith look like, Elisabeth asked, when the "results" of obedience cannot be seen? How do we understand ministry apart from impressive statistics and victorious stories?

"Several told me they had never heard anything like it," Elisabeth said later in the same letter to family. "The attitude of students and faculty alike was one of earnest seeking for truth, an openness and willingness to listen to something new which I simply have not found in churches—there seems to be such intellectual sterility, such insufferable bigotry in the churches."

Elisabeth spent several nights at the school, which was housed on a former estate from the early 1920s, with heavy stonework, bleak rooms, sweeping lawns, and pools with dolphin statues. It reminded her of *Wuthering Heights*. But each speaking session buoyed her. A faculty gathering made her feel that "there were still a few people in the world who are on my wave-length! And naturally one cannot help feeling that those who see his point are exceptionally intelligent," she joked in a letter to her family. "I have never had so many kind expressions of appreciation, and the people there treated me like a human being, instead of a commodity, which is the feeling I usually get."[6]

She spoke on the book of Job, an ongoing theme in her study and contemplation. She was fascinated by Job's honesty before God, and the fact that, far from condemning Job for impertinent questions, God commended him for that honesty. Elisabeth spoke about "the dishonesty in mission representation, our false sense of what it means to believe God, our mistaken idea of what it means to serve God."

To Elisabeth, Job's friends who had assumed that God could only act in certain ways, and therefore Job must have sinned in order to bring such suffering upon himself, were like modern-day Christians who put God in a box. She was "disturbed by the tendency of missionary speakers to sidestep their real questions and try to defend the Gospel which they don't really understand themselves."

God was mysterious. The universe was not so predictably dictated by cause and effect. When Job's poor friends equated Job's suffering with God's judgment of sin in his life, they "were up against something far too big for them, something their categories did not cover. So, rather than admit to ignorance, they resort to oversimplifications, snap judgments, easy cliches—which amount to lying."

There was a question-and-answer session at a reception after Elisabeth's session at Barrington College. It, too, was refreshing. There were none of the joshing, "You're not a *widow*, are you?" kind of superficial questions she'd received elsewhere. The queries ran the gamut:

"What place do you give [people's] intelligence and reason in the will of God?"

"Jim seems to have practiced a form of self-discipline that approached asceticism; what value do you think this had?"

"Is there <u>anything</u> in terms of language that can be said without fear of equivocation?"

"How much does a missionary try to change cultural patterns?"

"If someone had said to you the things you've been saying to us, would you have gone to the mission field?"[7]

Elisabeth grinned when she heard the last question. She knew she could not have said the things she told the students *unless* she had gone to Ecuador. Would she, could she, have internalized such advice if it were given to her by another? It was unknown. God works as He wills for His own mysterious purposes that echo in eternity. The "what if?" questions were intriguing, but useless in the practical scope of things. And Elisabeth Elliot was a very practical person.

Around the same time, Van and Elisabeth went to an evening performance of "Luther" in New York. "Very moving indeed," she wrote. ". . . the soul-searching Luther went through before making his break with the Church."

Elisabeth was no Martin Luther. But in her own way, at the time, she was making a break with the church as she had known it in the past. She felt like a packaged product, a cog in the wheel, expected to play the part of the "heroic missionary" who never felt pain or perplexity, only victory and assurance. She was interested in talking about knowing God, not selling His stuff.

Why was Elisabeth Elliot so perturbed by what she experienced in many of her speaking engagements? Why did the hospitality at the King's College, for example, irritate her so? Why did she recoil from the effusive "welcome, sister, I'm sure we'll be blessed by what the Lord has led you to share with us" familiarity so common among Christian backslappers of the day? Was it just that she was put off by hearty personality styles so different from her own?

That was likely part of it. There seemed to be, in Christian circles, a habitual familiarity that grated against the more formal Elisabeth's sensibilities. But her aversion went deeper than personality differences. And though she could sometimes sound snarky in her critiques, she was reacting against what she perceived as the false piety and easy certainties that she had rejected in Ecuador.

Also, Elisabeth grew up in an environment that she later rejected as, if not legalistic, then at least more concerned with appearances than with truth. Her growing up years, schooling, and season of missionary work were all within a "bubble" of a worldview that was articulated in a particular way and could not be questioned. That view now drove her crazy. Not the Christianity; Elisabeth Elliot fiercely embraced her faith in Christ. But she rejected a religious subculture that bifurcated the world into secular and sacred, worldly and spiritual, "them" and "us." It was an unquestioning acceptance of mores that did not allow doubts, questions, or critical thought.

A weekend in New York in late 1963 highlights her discomfort with her former institutions.

Elisabeth and Val had spent the night on the upper East Side with a friend named Mena and her husband. Mena had been a graduate student at Wheaton when Elisabeth was a senior there. She was now an accomplished editor and writer. Mena and her husband hosted another well-read couple for a little dinner party; the husband taught at Columbia, the wife at Rutgers.

The conversation that evening, Elisabeth told her family, was a discussion of "spiritual famine. None of them believe in God, but seemed quite fascinated with the idea that the wealthiest communities (e.g., Scarsdale) suffer from the most acute spiritual poverty. No one had any remedy to suggest. Mena asked me a few leading questions about the Waodani, and it was apparent that no one else had ever heard of them or of the five fellows."

Mena "is a beautiful woman—tall, honey blonde, with exquisite hands and perfectly marvelous eyes," Elisabeth went on. "Her apartment is exactly to my taste, down to the last detail, as are her clothes, her manner of thinking and everything. She spoke of Kennedy with tears, and of her belief that possibly there is ultimate meaning in the universe, but [people] cannot possibly have any part of it. Her experience at Wheaton . . . repelled her—to find so many 'little' people, articulating these deep mysteries with such assurance. I found myself unable to answer her."

Elisabeth's description of this scene says more about her own thinking at this point than that of the beautiful Mena. In that exquisite Manhattan apartment, uncharacteristically speechless in the face of her urbane friend's comment, she found herself astride two worlds, her roots in one and her inclinations in another. She had believed since her childhood that there is indeed "ultimate meaning in the universe." She believed in a God of power, love, justice, and mercy who had broken into human history in the person of Christ.

But, like Mena, she was repelled by Christians who blandly articulated His deep mysteries, as if they needed to defend God and could do so with a proof text or a catchphrase. She loathed the way so many Christians she knew shrank from "worldly" people, unless of course they encountered them on some foreign mission field, and then the goal was to save their souls and for God's sake get them to put some proper clothes on. They didn't develop friendships with anyone except safe Sunday school friends, and then spoke to one another in a strange dialect of "victory," "soul-winning," and phrases like "God laid it on my heart" to tell you such and such, usually something you did not want to hear. Meanwhile they looked askance at any of their number who confessed fears, anger, doubts, pain, or depression. Such human emotions showed a lack of faith. Period.

There were no mysteries. Only certainties, which could be delivered with a memorized Bible verse, often out of context, or a formula or pat phrase to make one's point. *The Bible says it, I believe it, that settles it.* End of conversation. She doubted that anyone "in the world" would likely be "won for Christ" by such tactics.

Few loved the Bible more than Elisabeth Elliot. But she was appalled when Christians used it as a weapon to clobber or distance themselves from people who were different from them. Or to distance themselves from suffering, mysteries, and difficult questions.

"Immaturity cannot tolerate ambiguity," Elisabeth thought later. "It's either black or white. And if you make your system your god, you'll soon be telling lies in order to remain consistent."[8] Such people were stuck. Static.

In contrast, as Elisabeth wrote to her mother about a friend who'd grown up in the church, "she seems to be in a constant state of learning and changing, which to me is the most encouraging sign in a person. When we stop changing, we're dead. And how sad to see dead people walking around trying to convince others they have life. That's what so many Christians do. God will not be bound or pigeon-holed or defined or categorized."[9]

She railed against this in her journal, citing with sardonic regularity the comments of those who codified their faith into a system of behaviors. Sometimes the comments were small or inane, but to Elisabeth they all shared a general stance: fear.

One night she had a local pastor and his wife over to play Scrabble. At some point he began talking about the subject of "separation from the world." To him, that meant

> . . . "certain arbitrary taboos. He actually believes that not to smoke is evidence of faith. On and on he went, ad nauseum, and I felt that I no longer can cope with this kind of mind. It is useless to explain. It is painful in the extreme to see such bullheadedness articulating what is supposed to be the truth of God. That God would be far too small.
>
> "O Lord, O Sovereign—how long will You suffer us? When will you lighten our darkness?"

Smoking was not the only sure evidence of worldliness. A Christian friend of Elisabeth's, seeing pictures of Jackie Kennedy wearing mourning clothes at her late husband's state funeral, concluded dismissively that Jackie "must not be saved." Grieving and wearing black at a funeral was "selfish" and meant she did not believe that her husband had the glorious hope of eternal life.

There were other easily-identifiable taboos. Visiting Elisabeth, one of her sisters-in-law worried about her young son playing Monopoly with Val, concerned that the board game might stir up a "lust for money." While reading the children the story of Robin Hood, she took pains to explain to the bemused kids that "we don't approve of ale-drinking!"

When Elisabeth's mother, Katharine, visited, she often raised this question of social drinking—"always as though to drink were synonymous with to be drunk," Elisabeth jotted in her journal. When Elisabeth asked her about it, Katharine cited an example of a man on the mission field in Colombia who "became a Christian simply by reading the New Testament, and the first thing he did was quit drinking."

"This proves," said Katharine, "that it is the Holy Spirit who convicts that drinking is <u>sin</u>."

Elisabeth stared at her mother for a moment. "Why, then, did the Holy Spirit not convict Jesus?" she asked.

That was evidently not the right question. "I don't know," her mother said, picking up a dish towel to flick some invisible dust off an already-dry plate.

One night Elisabeth went to hear an evangelist, author, and speaker who was well-known in the "victorious living" circles she'd grown up in. His theology "no longer speaks to me at all," she said. Her sister-in-law questioned her closely about her lack of enthusiasm, worried about her questions, and told Elisabeth "I must 'enter in,' 'be willing to go all the way,' etc. Now I know how it feels to be 'witnessed to.' Lord, you're not really like that, are You?"

All this was not helped by the plain banality of some pastors she encountered. "A man from [a local] church gave one of the worst messages I've ever heard anywhere," she noted in her journal. "He spoke on the fragrance of Christ overcoming the stench of sin (which 'literally turns God's stomach')—like a <u>spray deodorizer</u>.

"I was so appalled," said Elisabeth, "I didn't know where to look."

CHAPTER 7

The Heart of Human Experience

*". . . I have not done the expected thing. I have not
disavowed Christianity. The pulling and hauling [questioning
of dogmas and orthodoxy] has not convinced me that
God was not in Christ. It has, on the other hand, led me
to suspect that we are involved in something wild and
unmanageable, and in nothing that can be successfully
incarcerated in any dogmatic orthodoxy."*
—Thomas Howard, *Christ the Tiger*

*I*n 1866 a short, fluffy-haired poet named Algernon Swinburne wrote
a piece called "Hymn to Proserpine," in which he mourned the loss of
what he regarded as lusty, dynamic pagan culture. It had been replaced
by a "Christian" culture that he saw as a cloying and anemic Victorian
sentimentality.

"Thou has conquered, O pale Galilean," Swinburne wrote, "and
the world has gone gray with thy breath."

He saw Jesus Christ not as the compelling, central figure of history, God in the flesh, a swarthy, middle-Eastern carpenter rabbi who
loved and laughed and danced at weddings, but the pallid girl-man
of religious art, hair parted in the middle, with passive, ivory hands,
always slightly annoyed that perhaps someone, somewhere, might be
having a good time.[1]

This was what bothered Elisabeth Elliot in her own day. It seemed
to her that churches were putting forth a pallid image of a Jesus without personality, passions, blood, and emotion, an insipid leader whose
chief legacy had been to leave His followers with lists of activities that

were safe and nice, as contrasted with those that were dangerous and worldly.

Elisabeth's brother Thomas Howard would best refute Swinburne's ghostly image of Jesus. In his 1967 book, *Christ the Tiger*, he would write, "I find the Incarnation compelling. For in the figure of Jesus the Christ there is something that escapes us. He has been the subject of the greatest efforts at systematization in the history of man. But anyone who has ever tried this has had, in the end, to admit that the seams keep bursting. He sooner or later discovers that he is in touch, not with a pale Galilean, but with a towering, and furious figure who will not be managed."

This is the Jesus who drew Elisabeth Elliot in the early years of her return to the United States. The Jesus of Truth, not religious dogma. She sensed Him where she had not seen Him before.

Reading the Russian playwright Anton Chekhov, she related to his determination to be a free artist. "He refused "'any of the dogmas that threaten to hinder the task of the observer.'" He knew exactly how to evoke a feeling . . . I am astounded at my present ability to understand and appreciate things (e.g., Chekhov) which were meaningless to me in 1957. This is in one way gratifying—I have a new vision, a far broader horizon—and then again it is lamentable. Why is it that for so long I lived, as it were, in prison? My whole perspective was bound by the four walls of Christian <u>dogma</u>—I do not say Christian truth. God save us all—dogma imprisons. It is truth alone which liberates."

Because of this, she resisted labels. Her mother asked her about her views on the "neo-evangelicalism" of the day. She told her that she'd heard the term but knew nothing of it. "I only know what God seems to say to me, and if someone else wants to label my thinking, he will soon find that the label breaks down somewhere, that no pattern can be found. Jesus said, 'I am the Truth,' not 'This is the Truth.'"[2]

She saw that she had been limited in her ability to see well in the past. She wanted to be what she considered a "real" writer, to be able to organically evoke life in its essence, not some caricature of human experience.

"It has taken me over a year to begin to think of myself as a writer. I never thought of myself as a writer, even though I had written three books, while I was a missionary." She felt she had made only "feeble efforts" to gain any authentic understanding of the world and the people in it. She had lived in a context where fellow Christians tended to see people in terms of *us* and *them*. Now she saw this as "a make-believe world in which the people were merely sinners, in need of redemption, i.e., what I had. O God in Heaven—have mercy on my idiocy."

When she was a missionary, Elisabeth said she was "wholly insulated against trying to understand the world <u>at large</u>. Because of the person I happen to be, I did not succeed in toeing the missionary party line, and I kept trying to understand the Indians. I had no sense of the need to understand <u>life</u> and <u>people</u> and <u>myself</u>, and the urge to get at the truth did not go so far as the urge to put it down (only to a very circumscribed extent). Now I find that I must try to understand, and get at the real feelings which a situation evoked.

"As a missionary I saw my whole responsibility in terms of doing something specific for a certain people—when this theory was proved inadequate in Tewaeno there began the process of questioning and examining and trying to understand which has laid the foundation— very late in life, to be sure—for my writing. And it is only now—[so long after] leaving Ecuador, that the perspective is clearing, and I feel as though I am beginning to know. Of course, I will always be seeking. And I hope I will be able, with this perspective, to deal accurately with the material which is stored up."

She also felt like an idiot because of what she now saw as enormous gaps in her education. She had not until now read Shakespeare and Dostoevsky and Tolstoy and so many others. Nor Flannery O'Connor—a "new friend," Elisabeth wrote in her journal. "O marvelous writing. Humble woman, with terrible clear vision and demolishing wit. And she loved God." Reading these writers, she found her heart leaping with recognition of the authenticity of their portrayal of human life. Such writing was like a movable feast she had not known she could attend.

Contrary to her upbringing, she could now see that "all truth is God's truth," and that He imprinted His creative image even on people who had not yet confessed Him as Lord. A beautifully-rendered novel that cut to the heart of the human experience and evoked the very rhythms of creation, fall, redemption, and restoration, even in the faintest of echoes, spoke more powerfully of the glory of God than the trite "Christian" novel in which the main characters all prayed the "salvation prayer" at the end.

In spite of her mother's fears, Elisabeth had not become a libertine, or a drunk, or "worldly." She was relishing, for the first time, the riches of literature, music, poetry, drama, films, wine, and conversation. If nature and the heavens themselves declare the glory of God, she now saw that any beauty and truth implicit within the best of the arts in fact had been seeded there by the common grace blessings of God Himself.

She would read, at a sitting, sources as varied as *The Secret Life of Walter Mitty*, French author Simone Weil, Deuteronomy, and Ecclesiastes. Then she would think about her own project, "trying to formulate a book. It's the thinking that is by far the most difficult part, and I go through the same deep misgivings with each book—e.g., how arrogant, how fatuous to think I am qualified to write at all. Weil is so enormously erudite (she died at thirty-three) and I have so little educational background. I do have things to say, but how to say them? And who will listen? And have I the courage to say what I see to be true, without fear of opinion? Well, as in any other endeavor, one must simply do it."

The utter honesty of the Minor Prophets appealed to her. "I will take my stand to watch, and station myself on the tower, and look forth to see what He will say to me, and what I will answer concerning my complaint. And the Lord answered me: write the vision; make it plain upon tablets, so he may run who reads it. For still the vision awaits its time; it hastens to the end—it will not lie. If it seems slow, wait for it; it will surely come, it will not delay."[3]

"So this is my role now. To take my stand, to watch, to wait. Then to write—without fear—what I see."[4]

Again, trips to New York nourished Elisabeth's hunger for experience. She spent time whenever she could with her friends, photographer Cornell Capa and his wife, Edie, and their many acquaintances in the arts community in the city.

One night Elisabeth and one of Cornell's friends, a Jewish woman from Poland named Bessie, attended an amateur performance of "J.B.," the modern-day version of the book of Job written by Archibald MacLeish in 1958. Written in free verse, the play "asks the ultimate questions, in a twentieth-century setting, and follows closely, until the third act, the actual theme of the book," Elisabeth reported. "The third set is a let-down, as MacLeish attempts to give a more satisfactory answer to Job's questions than he got out of God."

After the play Bessie introduced Elisabeth to the lead actress and several of the other actors, who invited the two women to stay for a drink. Curious, Elisabeth asked the actress how emotionally involved she becomes in a part like the role of Job's wife. Did it reflect her own attitude toward God?

"No," Elisabeth recorded later in her journal. "Essentially she doesn't react to God at all. A writer who was there concurred; she doesn't consider questions of the origin of man's mind, or of the existence of God as issues at all. They simply do not occur.

"I am baffled anew—these serious people, who can portray so convincingly the basic problems of life, seem unwilling to come to personal terms with them."

Elisabeth and Bessie left the group at about 1:30 a.m. to find it snowing outside. They had a hard time finding a cab, but eventually ended up sharing a taxi with a model and her boyfriend. In true 1960s fashion, everyone was smoking except Elisabeth. They asked her why Elisabeth didn't smoke cigarettes, and she rather earnestly asked the model what she got out of it.

"Oh, I suppose it's simply a socially accepted way to commit suicide, that's all," the young woman responded.

During this period and throughout Elisabeth's life, there were plenty of people in her circle who dealt with sensual temptations. Some missionaries in the field had affairs and were either physically or emotionally unfaithful to their spouses. Unmarried couples slept together before marriage. There were friends, too, with same-gender attraction who struggled with what to do, with their place in God's kingdom, and with the flat condemnation of so many Christians.

A letter Elisabeth wrote in 1964 shows her own opinions at the time as she counseled her mother, who was concerned about a mutual friend struggling with same-gender attraction. (In Elisabeth's teaching, writing, and radio broadcasts later in her life, she clearly held the position that homosexual behavior was "clearly forbidden in God's Word," and that *any* sexual intercourse outside of marriage between one man and one woman was outside of God's ordained design.[5])

"Mother," wrote Elisabeth, "to hope for victory over such a thing as this problem is like hoping for victory over blindness or paralysis. I believe God could do it, He could have given Dad two eyes again. [Elisabeth's father had lost an eye as a teenager after an unfortunate encounter with a firecracker.] But the problem is far more complex than a simple matter of sin. It is not sin in any sense of the word though it is a frame of mind and attitude which presents its own particular kind of temptation. Sin only enters when the law of love is transgressed, if I understand Jesus' interpretation of the law. David and Jonathan clearly had a much deeper love than the usual man-to-man friendship. They met in secret, they kissed one another, and they frankly said it passed the love of women. I'm not building a doctrine on this—I only want to face up honestly to what we are told in Scripture, not ignoring or explaining away any facet of it. Perhaps the truth is that there are no such things as lines drawn, coincident with sex. Love is the great thing. Without love, where does any human relationship stand? For you, in acceptance lieth peace."[6]

At the time, New York was preparing to host the 1964 World's Fair. Its theme, influenced by the nascent space age, was "Peace Through Understanding," dedicated to "Man's Achievement on a Shrinking Globe in an Expanding Universe."

Cornell Capa had been in Peru, photographing members of the Amahuacas, a remote Stone Age tribe. He had gained entry to the tribe through his relationship with Cameron Townsend, the enterprising head of Wycliffe Bible Translators and the Summer Institute of Linguistics, who was well-known to Elisabeth throughout her hard times in Ecuador. Cornell now told Elisabeth that he had heard from Cameron that Wycliffe was "to have a $175,000 pavilion of their own at the fair, with a huge mural depicting the 'conversion' of the Shapra 'chief' Tariri,"—the "converted headhunter," according to Wycliffe's press releases from the time—"and they want to have a clothed Waodani in order to demonstrate (Exhibit A, as it were) what [the ministry] does to civilize" untouched people groups.

Elisabeth was beside herself. The notion of showcasing "a clothed Waodani" to demonstrate the ministry's civilizing success seemed manipulative at best. "But God sits in His heaven," she said. He "sees the truth, and waits. . . . I can find no words for the horror it evokes in me for what has been done to those simple people and to simple people in the U.S. who swallow the report hook, line, and sinker."

"And now, my writing. I am finding it difficult in the extreme to pull myself out, after twenty years, more or less, of denying life, and now trying to learn to affirm it. I am learning, bit by infinitesimal bit, who I am and what it means to tell the truth, and I am glad, very glad, for all of this, but I worry because I cannot get the book written, and [time] goes on apace and I cannot see what I ought to do with it.

"If God will just grant me enough courage to go on in this situation, and enough faith to trust Him for it . . . I do not think it really requires very much of either. Just give it, Lord, if you please . . . "

She was hungry to consume all that she had missed. She wrote of her missionary years, "Eleven of the best years of my life were spent denying myself, negating existence, shunning opportunities to learn, earnestly seeking to limit myself to the one thing (never adequately defined) God required of me. I came and went, without seeking out Quito's cafes and museums, never reading what my contemporaries wrote, listening to no music, seeing no painting, never heeding the voices that cried within me, not daring to live to the hilt.

"And now—I am hungry. I want to learn all of these things, to do everything, to listen to the voices, to see life clearly and whole, and to write about it. I am trying to make up for it all, I am trying to write, in spite of this great zero factor in my development. It is a constant handicap.

"And what does my faith say in response to this?

"I believe. Still I believe God has made with me an everlasting covenant, ordered in all things and sure. But I feel like a bird released after a long imprisonment, confused and unable at once to fly.

"This, too, must be a part of the covenant. As though He had held me quiet in His hand, pinned my beating wings until I subsided then, in the fullness of time, said, 'Now.' And let me go."

CHAPTER 8

The Runaway Tricycle

"And now I stand at the threshold of a new life—
feeling keenly the obligation to close the door behind
me, to go on into truth even if it means a slow and
difficult unlearning of all that has guided me."
—Elisabeth Elliot, journal, 1964

As Elisabeth tried her new wings, she submitted articles and short stories to mainstream periodicals of the day like *The New Yorker*, *Redbook*, and *Ladies Home Journal*. Each submission exposed her to despair. Her daily walk down her driveway to her metal mailbox nailed to its wooden post was fraught with dark peril. Would some urbane, busy editor, half-glasses on his nose in some New York office humming with literary power, accept her piece or not?

Most often, the news was bad.

"Rejection slip today from *Redbook*. I had felt, actually, quite confident when I sent in my piece. Rain. Meadow sodden. No birds at my seed station. No joy in my writing, no words. A morning gone— some Dinesen, some coffee, a few sheets of yellow paper through the typewriter, despair."

She combined such haiku-type moments in her journal with equally glum images in her sleep. "Dreamed of an immense sink filled with lukewarm, gray, greasy water in which I was desperately trying to wash a never-ending stack of dishes. They would not get clean, and more seemed to materialize from nowhere so that the task was patently hopeless. No progress. This is my life as a writer now. It is dreadful."

Elisabeth had decided by this point to write a novel set in an environment she knew well. It would be a story about a female missionary in Ecuador. She hoped to explore the life questions and the lack of easy answers that she had experienced in her own missionary experience. She wanted to paint characters who sounded like real human beings, not Sunday school caricatures. She compared herself to great writers who could evoke great stories, like her hero Isak Dinesen, and found herself lacking much.

The book that Elisabeth birthed, with pain, was called *No Graven Image*. It would be her only novel among her many writings. It also seemed to be a self-imposed test to see if she was able to capture the truth as she saw it through the genre of a fictional story.

Readers' reactions were decidedly mixed as to whether she succeeded or not. Regarding her ability to create fiction, there were debate as to the quality of her writing, her evocation of real characters, and her ability to breathe life into dialogue and the psychology of her heroine.

Further, Elisabeth yearned for an audience that her novel just could not engage. As she had written in her journal near the end of her time in Ecuador, she wanted to write for secularly minded people. She had thought of Paul's words in Romans 1, where the apostle wrote that he had an obligation to "preach the Gospel" to both "Greeks and to barbarians [the cultured and the uncultured]."[1] Elisabeth wanted to reach "cultured Greeks"—people who read *The New Yorker* and went to plays, Ingmar Bergman films, and museum openings.

Yet the specialized setting of Elisabeth's novel held little interest for such people. Why would an urbane materialist—or even a former evangelical like her Manhattan friend Mena—engage with a story about a *missionary*, a person whose motivations held no resonance, who spread a message she might or might not agree with, particularly since these missionaries spoke in an evangelical dialect that was unintelligible to most human beings on the street?

Author and well-known apologist J. I. Packer, a good friend, captured the inherent problem Elisabeth's novel faced: "Christian novelists today have a hard furrow to plough," he wrote in his foreword to *No Graven Image*.

> Secular readers find their vision of life "unconvincing," and Christian readers have been conditioned to a certain type of story built around an easily understandable, edifying formula, usually that someone in terrible trouble turns to God and thus finds blessings and peace. The result, both funny and sad, is that when folk fed on this diet read a genuine novel by a Christian novelist (Graham Greene, say, or Charles Williams, or George Target, or Flannery O'Connor, or Fyodor Dostoevski, or Aleksandr Solzhenitsyn) their appreciation, if any, is overshadowed by regret and puzzlement that the author did not so manipulate his characters as

to produce a straightforward moral tale, clearly illustrating the gospel. No suspicion that the novel is a different thing from the moral tale enters their heads.[2]

Still, our gritty Elisabeth resolutely ground out her story, word by agonizing word.

"I <u>know</u> that it is so bad, such hopelessly bad writing and such a complete failure at saying what I meant to say that I am astonished at myself that I keep going at all," Elisabeth wailed in her journal. "Yet somehow I have the feeling that I am impelled to do so—to keep pedaling, as it were, because my feet are on the pedals and, like a tricycle, I rush downhill and dare not take my feet off though I know full well disaster awaits me at the bottom of the hill.

"Will it be a resounding failure, or will it merely be a point where a new beginning <u>can</u> be made, and the work redone as it ought to be done? I do not know. I do not know what to do, or perhaps it is that I do not know what else to do, and hence I must do this."

The good thing about Elisabeth was that her journal's wails, like the psalmist's, always turned into a prayer. "God, what is it all for? God <u>help me</u>. Thou art my Helper and You know, as no one else knows, how very badly in need of help I am."

Her story was about a young, idealistic American missionary named Margaret Sparhawk. Margaret heads off to her first assignment in Ecuador with high hopes. She is single, unencumbered, and wants nothing more than to help an indigenous tribal people living in the Andes. Their language has never been written down; they know nothing of the gospel. Margaret will translate the New Testament into their tongue, so they can know the Bible for themselves . . . once they learn to read.

Margaret gets settled in a small house in the town below the mountain settlement where the Indians live. She is a likeable, reflective sort who genuinely wants to help the Indians. She just finds it a bit mysterious as to how to really commence her glorious missionary work.

"I could not begin my work until my living routine was established and my house in order, and although I awoke each morning with the thought of going to visit Indian homes, each evening came before the thing was done. During the day I felt triumphant to see the time passing in useful ways, conscious that I was not sitting down and wasting time, but when evening came and I took stock of the day's accomplishments I felt guilty to see that no breach had yet been made in heathenism. Hudson Taylor had made an impact on China, Mary Slessor on Calabar, John Paton on the South Sea Islands, David Livingstone on darkest Africa. Just exactly how had they *begun*?[3]

"It was strange to find the actual daily doing of missionary work so unspecific, so lacking in direction." Margaret thought of the description of her missionary endeavor back in the U.S.: "'Margaret Sparhawk is working among mountain Quichuas.' I could not get away from the image I knew I had projected at home, but here was the other side of the coin. 'Working.' What does she do? Missionaries wrote of 'doing' visitation, of 'reaching' people, of 'witnessing.' I did not need to read any more missionary books, prayer letters, or progress reports in magazines to learn the terminology. I needed to find out what was really basic in the operation, and I went back to the source, the Bible, and read avidly the Old Testament stories of men on a mission."[4]

Eventually Margaret travels to a multi-day meeting in Guayaquil, the port city on Ecuador's coast. She meets missionaries from all over the country. She chafes at their conversation. She hears men talking about "our" work, "our" mission, "our" Indians, "our" tribe, with a certain paternalism, and a certain "hail fellow-well-met" misogyny at work. The men "seemed to see only one another; they acknowledged the presence of women, but without looking any of them straight in the eye."[5]

Margaret feels similarly uncomfortable when she discovers the class distinctions between the people in her new town and the Indians who live in the mountains. The townspeople cannot fathom why Margaret would want to engage with lower-class barbarians. During a festival in which the Indians drink, fight, and drink some more, an Ecuadorian shopkeeper tells Margaret, "They are savages, animals. They ought to be shut up in prison, but then there is no way to that. All of them would be in prison. What is there to do then? *Caramba!* The Indians have no souls! . . . Do you think, señorita, that the Indians are like the rest of us? . . . They are like animals, isn't that true, señorita?"[6]

Margaret gradually begins to get to know an Indian man named Pedro. He is not particularly impressed with her—none of the Indians are—but Margaret persists, and he agrees to serve as her "informant." She will pay him to teach her his people's unwritten language. Pedro and his wife, Rosa, don't understand Margaret's interest in them, but they begin to tolerate, then trust her, and a fragile friendship grows.

Margaret believes that Pedro is clearly God's answer to her prayers. She sees glimpses of his slowly increasing understanding of "God's words." Perhaps, indeed, he might be the inroad for the gospel to spread among these thousands of unreached mountain people! She hums rousing missionary hymns as she treads the path several times a week to Pedro's home.

At the same time, Margaret struggles with less lofty thoughts. One day she comes home praising God for progress in the mission field, and then breaks a fingernail unlocking her rough front door.

"Damn it all!" she thinks, then her face burns that such a response would have been right there, lurking in the recesses of her shallow, superficial mind. She knows that missionaries are just human beings, of course . . . but isn't she supposed to be growing in a higher, richer spirituality? (Upon its publication in 1966, the book's use of this four-letter word alone caused a small tidal wave of shock among evangelicals, with more than one reader appalled that as legendary a figure as Elisabeth Elliot could so casually employ "blasphemy" in her writing.)

Elisabeth Elliot was concerned with a graver sort of blasphemy. She set the tone, and a key, for her book by placing three Bible verses on the first page of *No Graven Image*. All were acute warnings about worshipping God *alone*. The last was Ezekiel 22:28 (RSV): "And the prophets have daubed for them with whitewash, seeing false visions and divining lies for them, 'Thus says the Lord GOD,' when the LORD has not spoken."

This set a severe mood for her story, to say the least. But to Elisabeth, even the most benign of smiling missionary representatives could be guilty of whitewashing God's truth. Her character Mr. Harvey, a cheerful photographer from a fictional U.S. ministry called Millions Untold, arrives in the Andes to document Margaret's work among the Indians. Together, they climb the narrow path to the indigenous settlement. He complains that he might ruin his new leather shoes on the stony trail, but recovers, saying brightly, "nothing's too good for the Lord, eh . . . ? Ought to be glad to wear out a pair of shoes for Him!"

As they hike, Mr. Harvey tries to give some Spanish-language tracts to a group of shy Indian women washing their clothes in the river. They do not speak Spanish, only Quichua or their tribal dialect, and are in fact illiterate, but the photographer assumes he is "spreading the seed of the Gospel." (*This is like planting bananas in Alaska*, thinks Margaret, who is given to irony.)

Later, he snaps photos of Margaret hunched over a Bible painstakingly working on a word-by-word translation with her friend Pedro, whom Mr. Harvey repeatedly and heartily calls "Pablo." He gets a backlit shot of the Indian, with his rope sandals and dark poncho, against the sky.

Margaret thinks of the captions he will probably give the slide for his unwitting audiences back home. "A typical Indian of the High Andes, one of millions still without Christ." Or, if he happened to catch Pedro smiling, then the title would be something like "The light of the Gospel shines in the face of one of the descendants of the Inca sun worshipers."[7]

Either way, Mr. Harvey's pictures, and his few hours with Margaret, were not an honest fact-finding mission. They served only to tell an expected story that would get folks at home fired up about missions.

He "had not come to learn but to document what he already assumed; his preconceptions governed his selection of picture subjects. Propaganda, I thought, demands simplification. Choose the pictures which show the poverty and primitiveness of the Indian, the successes of the missionary."[8]

Mr. Harvey leaves. Everyone breathes a sigh of relief. Margaret's days unfold; she helps the Indians with her limited lay medical skills. One night a young child runs down the mountain to her little home in the town. A woman is dying in childbirth. "Quick, señorita, you must come!" Margaret grabs her medical kit and a lantern and follows the child back to her shack. She finds the mother in agony. Margaret somehow manages to turn the baby from its breech position, and successfully delivers the child and saves the mother.

Now she has cachet among the other Indians. One day Margaret is visiting with Pedro and his wife, Rosa. Pedro has a bad infection in a leg wound. He cannot walk. The pain is terrible. He asks if Margaret has "her needle" with her, and can she stick him with medicine? Margaret has her medical bag and several ccs of penicillin. Rosa stirs up the fire, produces a pot of water, and Margaret boils a needle over the fire to disinfect it.

"Why do you cook it, señorita?" asks one of the children.

"To kill the little things that make sickness," says Margaret.

She carefully plunges the needle into Pedro's leg, injects the penicillin, and cleans up the blood and pus as best she can.

Within just a few minutes, Pedro is mad with itching, shrieking like a madman, filled with nausea, retching. His wife is terrified; Margaret is frantic. Suddenly the word enters her mind: *Anaphylaxis*. Could that be what has happened? Was Pedro allergic to penicillin?

Pedro lay quiet, his hands limp, his breaths shallow. Margaret prayed like never in her life. "We know that You love Pedro, and that if You want to You can make him well. Don't let him die, Lord, please don't let him die. . . . You know how he has helped with the translation of Your word. In order that he may go on serving You, cause him to live."[9]

Pleasepleasepleasepleaseplease!

Pedro lay still. Time went by. Margaret felt for his pulse. So weak. His wife alternately keened with a death wail and screamed that Margaret had killed her husband. His children peered from the shadows of the shack, terrified. Occasionally his hands twitched. His head had fallen back at a grotesque angle and Margaret tried to rearrange it. So heavy in her hands. Pedro's eyelids fluttered, his jaw worked back and forth, and then he gave a deep sigh and was still.

Dead.

CHAPTER 9

Forcible Shakings

"And if you make your system your god, you'll soon be
telling lies in order to remain consistent."[1]
—Elisabeth Elliot, notes on Lectures on Job

We can imagine the Elisabeth Elliot of 1964, writing the appalling scene of the fictional Pedro's death, remembering all too vividly her anguished days in Ecuador among the Colorado Indians in 1953. Even as Elisabeth created the fictional Margaret's story, she relived her own story. She saw herself—a young, earnest, single missionary in a dusty shack, her little medical bag beside her in the dirt, unable to staunch the flow of blood when a young woman named Maruja died in terror. "If God had spared Maruja's life," Elisabeth wrote later, "the whole . . . tribe might have been delivered from spiritual death. In my heart I could not escape the thought that it was God who had failed."[2]

Elisabeth also relived her horror when her own language informant, Macario—the only man in Ecuador who could help her translate the New Testament into his unwritten language—was shot, point-blank, in the head. "Had I come here, leaving so much behind, on a fool's errand? . . . How was I to reconcile His permitting such a thing with my own understanding of the missionary task?"[3]

Unlike her fictional heroine, Elisabeth had not directly caused those deaths, but the horrifying result was the same.

The questions Elisabeth had asked in her own life became the questions of her fictional heroine. Why would almighty God allow such losses? Did He not want to use His workers—His earnest missionaries and converts like Macario and Pedro—to advance His kingdom?

Silence.

In *No Graven Image*, after Pedro's awful death, Margaret slowly makes her way back to her little house in the village. She opens the door and falls on the floor.

"Do You mock me? Why did You let him die? Why did You let me kill him? O God! I came to bring him life—Your life—and I destroyed him in Your name."[4]

There is a knock on her rough door. It is Pedro's daughter. Rosa, Pedro's wife, has invited Margaret to sit with the family at Pedro's wake. She goes back up the mountain to do so. Numb.

In the days and weeks that follow, Margaret is accepted as part of the Indian community. The translation work has ended; she no longer writes missionary prayer letters to supporters.

"It seemed, on the night of Pedro's death, as though *Finis* were written below all I had done. . . . God, if He was merely my accomplice, had betrayed me. If, on the other hand, He was God, He had freed me.

"I find that I can no longer arrange my life in an orderly succession of projects with realizable goals and demonstrable effects. I cannot designate this activity as 'useful' and that one as 'useless,' for often the categories are reversed and even more often I am at a loss to apply either label, for the work, in the end, as well as the labeling, is God's."[5]

As the novel ends, Margaret visits Pedro's rough grave. She thinks of her friend, remembering his worn face, strong nose, and patient, dark eyes. She lies down on the cool ground. High above her, a condor circles, looking down on the tops of the frosted peaks, wheeling high above the lakes and the quiet valley.

After *No Graven Image* was published in 1966, this anticlimactic and inconclusive ending troubled many an evangelical reader. Where was the victory? Where was the affirmation that God's kingdom had triumphed, that His Word *would* go forth like a banner in those frosted mountains? Some Christians were offended, others merely baffled. What in the world had happened to Elisabeth Elliot, martyr's widow, faithful missionary?

Some Christian bookstores refused to stock *No Graven Image*. Some reviewers panned it. It sold well to the publisher's general market audience, while disappointed religious readers wrote to Elisabeth that God would *never* allow such a thing to happen to a dedicated missionary who had so prayerfully dedicated her life to His cause. Others noted that she had not mentioned the Holy Spirit once in her story or shown even one recognizable conversion. (*Recognizable* assumably meaning a conversion accompanied by the right key words or perhaps the "sinner's prayer.") A lovely woman named Angela "objected strongly" to the book, writing to Elisabeth that Pedro should have lived, the missionary, Margaret, should never have sworn or drunk chicha, since "'my conception of missionaries is that they are superior in every respect, and I don't like to have this image marred.'"[6] Many other readers agreed that there should have been a more definitive ending, one that clearly showed how "the main character learned and grew and matured to be a better missionary."

One prominent evangelical leader of the day, perplexed by Elisabeth's heretical message, scheduled a luncheon with her. It was more like a trial in which she was not allowed to testify, according to Elisabeth.

"Lunch with Harold John Ockenga himself," she wrote in her journal.

Harold Ockenga was a noted theologian, pastor, and evangelical leader. He pastored Boston's famous Park Street Church, founded in 1809, from 1936 to 1969. He cofounded Gordon-Conwell Theological Seminary with Billy Graham and was integral in the founding of Fuller Theological Seminary, the National Association of Evangelicals, World Relief, and *Christianity Today* magazine.

"He wanted to examine me," Elisabeth continued, "as regards questions raised about my 'change' in views. His attitude was not one of cautious inquiry. There was no readiness to hear or to admit the validity of my testimony. Arrogance, unimpeachability, woodenness. He raised the question of my novel. Told me—rather jokingly and off-handedly—that it was he who had put his foot down to refuse to allow <u>NGI</u> to be selected by the Evangelical Book Club. Said the book is negative, hopeless, and the scene at the missionary conference is a caricature. When I asked if he had never seen anything like it, he said no, he most certainly never had. 'And furthermore,' he added, 'I've sunk $10,000,000 into this missionary enterprise, and if I thought your book was true I would feel we needed to do some serious rethinking of the whole thing.' I asked if it was possible that his heavy vested interest had blinded him. He was willing to admit this possibility."

"He thought that the book was about the sovereignty of God. Period. Typically blind—once the doctrine is recognized it is checked off and has no further implication in terms of our faith, our understanding of God. He kept showing me how "'experienced'" he is ("'I've been dealing with people with all *kinds* of problems—I could write a book, now!—for 40 years!'") how wise, how sought after ("'Why, you should see the *letters* I get!'")

"Some of the adjectives he used of me, my message, my book— picayune, negative, joyless, rebellious, sarcastic.

"You don't <u>mind</u> my asking you these things, do you?" (I wonder if he would have minded if I had asked <u>him</u> a few questions.)

"I observed that the people who most strongly disagreed with NGI were non-missionaries. No comment.

". . . It is a hard position to be in," Elisabeth reflected later. "[A] nd each time I find myself a target for criticism and misinterpretation I say 'why do I do it?' but each occasion has to be judged on its own merits, and I could say no to any one at any time. The Lord has, I do strongly believe, been my Shepherd up until now—He knows how to show me the path, I'll wager."

Another well-known evangelical leader of the day, Harold Lindsell, was more positive than Dr. Ockenga in his review of Elisabeth's book. The *Christianity Today* editor wrote,

> "She paints what is often an unpretty picture of evangel-
> ical life. The picture could only have come from personal
> experience, and with notable insight she has captured the
> idiosyncratic—the warts and bumps. 'Are evangelicals really
> like that?' everyone will ask. We can only hope that the kind
> she singled out are a minority. Yet surely evangelicals are
> mature enough to face their own shortcomings and to see in
> what the author depicts something of themselves, not simply
> of others. . . . She is driven into despair and introspective
> analysis. How could God let this happen to her? How could
> he allow the death of this Indian to whom she had come to
> minister? And the answer emerges: Men cannot tell God how
> to act; he works sovereignly. We are to worship and serve.
> Results belong to him, not to us.
>
> "*No Graven Image* is one of the better modern Christian
> novels. It says some hard things and says them vigorously.
> There is no padding, no fluff, no wandering from the subject
> at hand. The characters are real. Even the visiting clergyman,
> camera in hand, making a one-day stand to snap pictures to
> activate his congregation at home, crackles with life. . . . It is
> a solid, well-written piece of fiction."[7]

The then-prominent monthly periodical *Eternity* gave a similarly positive review, though author Russell Hitt pointed out that "There is one missing note—the element of Christian joy and the sense of divine victory even when human events are in disarray."[8]

Elisabeth noted in her journal that "Stacey Woods [founder of IV, InterVarsity Christian Fellowship in the United States] writes, 'It is notably deficient in the answers it fails to provide. . . . Perhaps the book's greatest weakness is its failure to spell out a biblical world and life view for Christian missions.'"

"Dear God," Elisabeth wrote, "who can require this of any book, least of all a <u>novel</u>? What are they thinking of? How would Hitt and Woods have reviewed the Lamentations of Jeremiah?"

As Elisabeth had told Dr. Ockenga, many field missionaries nodded at her portrayal of conferences, attitudes, and catchphrases that often characterized their communities. They recognized the spiritual struggles and the hard realities of missions work. Many lay readers also resonated with the story and wrote Elisabeth to tell her so. Elisabeth visited Wheaton College to speak to an anthropology class; faculty there told her that *NGI* was the most talked about book on campus. Billy Graham told his wife Ruth, who told Elisabeth's mother Katherine Howard, who told Elisabeth, that he was "thrilled" with the book. (Not exactly a public endorsement.)

The well-respected Trinity Divinity School professor Walter Liefeld (whom Olive Fleming had married several years after her husband Pete died with Jim in Ecuador), touched Elisabeth's heart when she visited with him and Olive as she was passing through Wheaton. He told her he saw nothing in the book that contradicted the Old or New Testament, and that she "use[d] question and symbol most effectively." He saw, in the book's final scene, a sense of freedom in the image of the condor soaring high above the mountains.

Paul Woolley wrote Elisabeth thanking her "from the bottom of his heart" for writing *No Graven Image*. Woolley, along with Ned Stonehouse and J. Gresham Machen, had founded Westminster Theological Seminar in 1929. Woolley taught church history there for thirty years, and Elisabeth Elliot looked up to him as a senior evangelical statesman. "The dream world in which so much Christianity lives has become a barrier that almost completely isolates it from the realities of present existence," Woolley had written to Elisabeth. "Christianity has to come to direct confrontation with the problems of this present world, and particularly with the question as to how to enter into an intelligible discussion with it. You have made that necessity clear and you have even started to give an answer to the question as to how it is to be done . . ."[9]

The *New York Times* said that "The narrative rings true and the leading character is beautifully realized."[10] It also called the book a "subtle and savage" satire on "fundamentalist missionary customs and attitudes."[11]

Two thought influencers who resonated with Elisabeth's novel, or at least these premises underlying it, were young seminary students named Tim and Kathy Keller.

Elisabeth Elliot gave a lecture at Gordon Conwell seminary after *No Graven Image* was published; she spoke specifically about what

Tim Keller called "her extraordinarily bold" novel's ending. He remembers,

"She went on to explain to us that the graven image, the idol of the title, was a God who always acted the way we thought he should. Or more to the point—he was a God who supported our plans, how *we* thought the world and history should go. That is a God of our own creation, a counterfeit god. Such a god is really just a projection of our own wisdom, of our own self. In that way of operating, God is our 'accomplice,' someone to whom we relate as long as he is doing what we want. If he does something else, we want to 'fire' him, or 'unfriend him,' as we would any personal assistant who was insubordinate or incompetent.

"But at the very end, Margaret realizes that the demise of her plans had shattered her false god, and now she was free for the first time to worship the True One. When serving the god-of-my-plans, she had been extraordinarily anxious. She had never been sure that God was going to come through for her and 'get it right.' She was always trying to figure out how to bring God to do what she had planned. But she had not really been treating him *as* God—as the all-wise, all-good, all-powerful one. Now she had been liberated to put her hope not in her agendas and plans but in God himself."[12]

In short, Dr. Keller said, inexplicable suffering had opened the door to an encounter with God as He is, not a god we have made up, who is, in fact, only an idol: the "graven image" of Elisabeth's title.

As each day's mail brought both scathing and congratulatory responses to her novel, Elisabeth continued to find enjoyment in her daily life. One day in early 1967 she went skiing. Red-cheeked and content, she came home and brewed a steaming cup of cocoa. She stirred up a fire and sat with a book in her lap in front of her hearth, her faithful dog by her side. Zippy's feathery paws twitched as he dozed on the warm wooden floor, dreaming of rabbits.

Elisabeth found, as was so often the case, a kindred spirit in C. S. Lewis. "Nothing but these forcible shakings," he wrote to his friend Owen Barfield in 1938, "will cure us of our worldliness."[13]

"This, in a nutshell, is what *NGI* was about," Elisabeth wrote in her journal.

"Why is it that Christians find it so easy to define worldliness in terms of amusements only? It must be because that sort of thing can be cured by an edict rather than by a fundamental shaking. Those who have been forcibly shaken have found that worldliness is a fundamental thing—a frame of mind, a way of looking at the world, a set of values applied to all of life, and deeper than such trifles as are argued about, condemned, and used as the criterion for judging fellow

Christians. So long as one's conscience can be occupied with matters which can never be more than superficial, it will be untroubled by matters which are really important and basic."

Forcible shakings. Elisabeth had experienced many. She viewed them as earthquakes designed to topple the idols we so habitually construct, whether they are false gods of stone, substances, self, bogus beliefs about God, or whitewashed religion itself. The latter, as Jesus so often pointed out to the Pharisees, are the hardest idols to fall.

Elisabeth stared into her fire, sipping her cocoa. She looked out her plate glass window toward the white treetops and the valley below, framed by the frosty peaks. No condor circled in the gray skies above her snug home. But there was freedom, just the same.

CHAPTER 10

Haunting Doubts

"Whatever befalls us . . . however it befalls us, we must receive
as the Will of God. If it befalls us through man's negligence,
or ill will, or anger, still it is, in even the least circumstance,
to us the will of God for if the least thing could happen to <u>us</u>
without God's permission, it would be something out of His
control. His providence or His love would not be what they
are. Almighty God Himself would not be the same God;
not the God whom we believe, adore, and love."
—E. B. Pusey, noted in Elisabeth's leather
notebook of favorite quotes

*I*n spite of her usual self-questioning within, and the criticisms of
other Christians without, this was a sweet season in Elisabeth's life.
Massive, silent snows cloaked the cozy security of her peaceful home,
with Val at school, Van traveling or busy with her own writing, and
Elisabeth managing her time without any expectations upon her. She
read, wrote, hiked, and thought. "How I love this life! Read <u>Three</u> by
Flannery O'Connor, started Tolkien's <u>Hobbit</u>, read a book on New
York, wrote two stories (submitted to <u>Life</u> and <u>Eternity</u>!), started on
income tax, read Lillian Ross's <u>Hemingway</u>. Days seem wonderfully
long."

Elisabeth was now in her late thirties. She looked older. She often
wore her dark brown hair pulled up and back in a French twist, which
had the effect of making her look even taller than she was. Her blue
eyes were clear, her nose upturned; she had deep dimples, the signa-
ture gap between her front teeth, a network of fine lines around her
mouth and eyes, and two pronounced furrows between her eyebrows
when she concentrated, which was most of the time.

Valerie, however, was a fresh, blossoming pre-teen, a slender, dimpled, elvish-looking lass with shoulder length light brown hair turned up in a hip 1960s flip, and oversized light blue cat-eye glasses.

Val reveled in her new life in New England. She learned to ski, she had friends who came over for slumber parties, she roamed the woods with Zippy, consumed muffins and tea by the fire on Sunday evenings, dutifully practiced piano, and prayed with her mother as Elisabeth tenderly tucked her growing daughter into her lavender canopied bed each night.

"Her beauty is stunning," Elisabeth mused. Here was Val, sitting up in that fluffy bed in a sky-blue nightgown with ruffles at the neck and wrists. Her cheeks glowed, her bright hair shone in the lamplight. Elisabeth had ordered a kit in the mail about growing up, with a little book about menstruation and life changes. "She was simply thrilled," Elisabeth wrote. "'Oh, Mommie, it's so exciting to grow up!'"

"Little girl turns into little lady, then into woman and she is gone. I dread it, I anticipate it, I accept it, and I embrace it all. Live. Live to the hilt."

Val was different from the dutiful young person Elisabeth had been. "Had a bad time with Val over her not finishing her practicing and other before-school duties today. Prohibited her ice-skating this afternoon. Tears. More tears over homework and practicing.

"Then, after playing 'Blue Danube' she looked up and said, 'Mommie, will you forgive me for being bad? I'll try to be sweeter.' I assured her she was forgiven and asked what had gotten into her . . . dear little soul."

Val's gregarious, charming, distractible butterfly brain mystified her mother. "Val is having great struggles with learning to take responsibility," Elisabeth wrote tersely in her journal. "Wastes time, forgets to do assignments, spends hours dressing and undressing, spends money quite thoughtlessly (treated two friends to sodas with money I had given her for meal tickets at school) and yesterday simply forgot to meet me for [a] dental appointment and took the school bus home. How does one instill this very necessary sense of responsibility?"

Meanwhile both Elisabeth and Val enjoyed the local customs, which were as exotic as anything the Waodani had invented, like the early springtime ritual of "sugaring off." Neighbors Zeke and Thelma invited everyone they knew for the annual event. Thelma boiled a huge kettle of maple syrup to the taffy stage; the fragrance filled her small kitchen. Meanwhile Zeke filled two immense basins with fresh-fallen snow and brought them inside. Thelma dribbled the thickened, dark syrup onto the icy surface, where it immediately hardened. Elisabeth, Val, and the other guests twisted it up off the snow with forks, like spaghetti. It was sticky and fun; Thelma had also laid out dill pickles, which everyone consumed to cut the sweetness, so they could eat more syrup, as well as doughnuts and hot coffee.

For further entertainment, Zeke brought out his bongo board, a plank about two feet long, which was balanced on top of a wooden cylinder. Zeke demonstrated that the idea was for the guests—by now half drunk on sugar and pickles—to try and stand still on it without flying off in a sticky heap on the floor.

After the long, cold yet cozy New Hampshire winter, springtime was all the more miraculous.

"Oh loveliness," Elisabeth breathed in her journal, remembering the unchanging jungle landscape of Ecuador. "Who can appreciate it like those who have lived in a one-season country?

"Warmth.

"Sunshine.

"Greenness.

"Soft pale tints of budding trees—mauve, pink, chartreuse, brick red, yellow."

In the beginning of May, Elisabeth, Val, and some friends hiked the Basin Cascade Trail in Franconia Notch State Park.

"It was an absolutely perfect day, warm and sunny, though none of the leaves are yet out, and the flowers are only just beginning to bud. We explored up the river which flows into the basin and came to a lovely falls which spreads over a huge brown slab of granite. The rush and power of that crystal water over the rocks, spraying its freshness into our faces and assailing our ears with its roar was like a cathedral to our winterized souls. The children took off shoes and socks and waded in the icy water. Zip tore around in the woods, beside himself with ecstasy."

"We found dogtooth violet leaves just unfolding, arbutus with buds on it. Stopped at the Cottage [the Howard family's cottage, site of so many of Elisabeth's happy childhood memories] on the way home and went down to the Meeting of the Waters—found False Solomon's seal at the spring, which bubbled clear as always. There is something marvelous about finding certain physical objects in God's creation which never alter—those two huge rocks, and the water which flows past them, the little beach and its smooth blue-gray stone on which Mother used to sit while we played in the water—exactly as they have always been since my earliest memory!"[1]

On one such walk, Elisabeth and Val found an abandoned baby woodchuck. He was a tiny, gray-brown creature with a charcoal nose. They fed him milk and mashed cereal with a doll-sized baby bottle, cradling his miniature body with its little black rubber feet.

He flourished. They named him Chuckles. He surmised that God had put him on the planet to torture the dog.

"Chuckles is shaped exactly like Mrs. Tiggywinkle, considerably broader than he is tall or long, a literal ball of fur," Elisabeth wrote to her family. "He follows Zip pitter-patter along the hall into my room, Zip lies down on the rug and Chuckles begins exploring Zip's entire geography, biting his toenails, nipping his fur, crawling into his ears and over his back, sliding down the other side, etc. Zip is never quite convinced that he enjoys this, and writhes nervously, lifting a paw to tumble Chuckles off, shaking his head and then licking the woodchuck, taking its whole head into his mouth at times, and then placing a protective arm over the little fellow's back. When he can't stand it any longer he gets up, with Chuckles hard on his heels, which makes Zip realize that he really is flattered by the attention, and then he lies down again for more. We just die laughing at them."

Elisabeth spent more and more outside as the glorious spring continued. "Last week I actually slept outside in the hammock in the afternoon—perfume of pine and balsam, song of birds, gentle rocking of breeze in the pines, warmth of sun and utter bliss. Thank God for this home. I think I have never been happier."

On May 30, she wrote in her journal, "Twenty years ago today Jim first acknowledged his love for me . . . breakfast at the Lagoon in Wheaton. Now I sit at the redwood table under the pines behind my house. Song of birds, scent of pine and apple blossom, sparkling of a single solitaire of dew on a grass blade near my feet."

The third human person of the household, Eleanor Vandervort, or "Aunt Van" to Val, made life easier for everyone. Van was now in her early forties, plain, with a large nose, small mouth, short, dark hair, and severe black spectacles that made her look like a 1960s NASA engineer. In addition to helping Val with homework and staying with her when Elisabeth traveled for her many speaking engagement, she taught Val about gardening and opera; she laughed with her, and according to Val, *at* her, a lot. Van sat with Elisabeth in the evenings by the fire, reading aloud from Simone de Beauvoir or Francoise Sagan or Betty Friedan or any number of existentialist and secular writers. "The perspective they provide force me to think outside the mold in which I'm poured," Elisabeth wrote.

Unlike some members of Elisabeth's family, Van did not confine her tastes to only "Christian"—as in "religious"—novels and writings. She not only fit in with Elisabeth's intellectual pursuits, but, almost as important, with her need for order and tidy housekeeping habits. "Van is such an easy, quiet person to live with," Elisabeth wrote to her mother.[2]

Van also worked painstakingly on her book for Harper & Row about her twelve years as a missionary in the Sudan. But she was not a writer at heart, and eventually Elisabeth's writing success, as well as her romantic relationships, would create fissures in the foundation of their friendship as Van perceived it.

But for now, it was a relief to have Van, a kindred spirit, with her when Elisabeth traveled to speaking engagements whose aesthetics chilled her soul. Elisabeth spared little in terms of uncharitable details when she described a church's Mother-daughter Mother's Day banquet in a letter to her family.

"Alack and Alas," she sputtered. "You can just picture the whole thing—church basement, men in shirtsleeves waiting on the tables, smell of coffee and dishwater and wet cement, paper tablecloths, artificial flowers, Maine farm wives and their buck-toothed, pig-tailed daughters, diffident pastor's wife trying to be bright and clever as mistress-of-ceremonies, chicken pie, rolls, Jell-O salad and home-made cake—and the program. Oh, oh, oh.

"One duet by the Bumble sisters, ages 9 and 11, with cousin Mattie at the piano, one poem to Mother read by emcee, one autoharp solo (four numbers in a row) by old Mrs. Harold Hemptweet, the one who won the prize last year for oldest mother.

"Well, the poor, dear soul. I am sure she had practiced faithfully for the past 49 years in her dusty front parlor complete with . . . portraits of American Gothic ancestors and pump organ. She first read the words to one of the hymns in a quavering voice, and it was a good thing she did, for no one could possibly have recognized a single bar. She had a hard time finding the notes, but she kept trying till she did, devil take the timing. Van thought she must be both deaf and blind.

"Then we had to have the cooks bow out of the kitchen, a big hand for them, and the 'waiters' with a big laugh out of the fact that [the men] were having to do the dishes. I spoke upstairs in the 'sanctuary' to perhaps 125 people. Then the same show was repeated Tuesday night of this week, when I drove alone to . . . Massachusetts. Remind me, somebody, not to accept any Mother and Daughter banquet invitations for next year, please."[3]

In descriptions like this, Elisabeth sacrificed kindness for what she perceived as comic effect. She seemed to lack the understanding that such cutting descriptions sounded patronizing. A friend—whose mother, a gracious, cultured woman, was from the Deep South—experienced this when she lived with Elisabeth for a while. One day she was out and her mother called for her; Elisabeth picked up the phone and later delivered the message in full-on mimicry of the older woman's rich

Southern drawl. The daughter felt that the mockery was unkind and realized that Elisabeth had no idea that she was being offensive.

A few days after the dreadful mother daughter banquet, Elisabeth, Val, and Van went to an event more in line with their artistic taste. It was a performance of the Boston Ballet at Dartmouth, including a *pas de deux* by members of the New York City Ballet. "I suppose in the long run it was just like the banquet programs," wrote Elisabeth philosophically. "[E]veryone was doing his very best."

But still—"Oh, those soaring leaps that the men do, and the way the women float and swoop with never a sound of a footfall. Beautiful."

Meanwhile, Elisabeth's continued speaking engagements earned her some reviews that were almost as critical as her reaction to the poor Mother's Day banquets.

After a speech in Detroit, Elisabeth heard via the always-humming evangelical grapevine that an old friend named Bob had written to his mother that Elisabeth was "'melancholic, heavy-hearted, gloomy, [and] controversial.'"

Somehow Elisabeth got hold of actual quotes from his letter to include in her journal. "'It was hard to believe that she was really the author of such victorious books as [*Through Gates of Splendor*] and [*Shadow of the Almighty*],'" Bob continued. "'She was quite withdrawn, did not join the ladies in the tea after the service but sat alone on a pew.

"'Frankly, I believe this wonderful Christian woman needs God's deliverance from something. We all have our problems and personality difficulties but Christ calls us to a life of irrepressible joy and optimism . . . When one thinks of the triumphs of Amy Carmichael and John and Betty Stam and many others, we get the picture that reflects apostolic Christianity in reality. Elisabeth said from the platform that few people understand her. She is so right.'"

It's difficult to know how much of this critique had to do with the natural reserve and diffidence of Elisabeth's personality, and how much related to the writer's understanding of "apostolic Christianity" and what that actually looked like in a person's life. Elisabeth could have made things much easier for herself if she had had, by nature, a more affable and outgoing disposition. But perhaps those qualities were at odds with the intrinsic nature of some of her particular spiritual gifts.

Around this same time, Elisabeth was reading the Old Testament prophets. She noted in her journal their oddities, their conviction, and their courage. She was concerned that she learn to see clearly in order to write truly. "The actual process of writing is a continuous unfolding of truth which I have to deal with somehow. It is so difficult to strip or be stripped of the layers of prejudice and preconception which have inhibited me, and the expose of what one is can't help being painful . . ."

If, in that stripping process, she came across as a person in pain rather than a paragon of spiritual victory, that was all right with her. She wondered if she had been called by God, like the prophets, like her favorite writers, as a *seer*. Seers called spades spades and revealed situations as they were, not as viewers might wish them to be. Seers are rarely popular. Surely religious people in Old Testament times found Amos to be a prickly, odd fellow, and few would have invited weird, dusty-robed Jeremiah over for the evening. Ezekiel lay on his left side for more than a year; Elijah ate bird food. Poor Hosea named one of his kids "Unloved." All of these brave men were following God's specific directions, but doing so did not endear them to their listeners. They were strange.

Her brother-in-law, the straight-shooting, faithful missionary Bert Elliot, told Elisabeth during a visit to New Hampshire that "he thinks me a prophet. Could it be so? This would explain some things—peculiarity, isolation, off-beat vision (inability to see things as others see them). I wonder how seriously the prophets of old took themselves?!"

Elisabeth took Bert's words seriously, though her response sounded unconsciously grandiose. "I must accept the responsibility of a seer. Someone has to see and make others see."

Certainly there was widespread concern regarding what had happened to Elisabeth Elliot. Even the benign *Christianity Today* review of her 1966 novel included a "haunting" question, not about the book, per se, but about Elisabeth herself.

Editor Harold Lindsell wrote, "[Elisabeth] Elliott passed through the fires of testing—her husband was martyred by the [Waodani]. He found deliverance in death, but she remained to seek her own deliverance in life. That it has not come easily is seen in this novel about missionary life."

Lindsell concluded that the novel's main character, Margaret Sparhawk, "finally puts the pieces together and gets an answer, a believable and adequate answer, to her spiritual quest. This reader, at least, was left with the feeling that the author placed the right answer in Miss Sparhawk's mouth, *but he has a haunting doubt whether the author herself has settled for that answer.*"[4]

Elisabeth wrote in her journal, "the revelation of myself which the process of writing entails is hard to accept. But here, for me, is the meaning now of laying down my life. . . . How different a death from Jim's! Yet, for me, as inescapable. Through his death Jim gained a reputation. Through mine I lose one. But this is not so painful a prospect as my writing of it may make it sound.

"Nothing matters; just set forth the truth; let the chips fall."

As time went on, Elisabeth would note that the constant stream of speaking invitations that she'd received from churches since she returned from Ecuador had slowed to a trickle . . . right at the same time that *No Graven Image* had been released. "The simple fact is that I am not asked to speak to churches any longer," she wrote in her journal. "What does this mean? What ought I to learn from it? I am who I am and have always been. God is my witness, my stronghold, my life, my salvation. Let me call this enough . . . was remembering this a.m. [a friend's] advice to me: Never withdraw from people just because they oppose you."

The problem was, Elisabeth Elliot had a publicly withdrawn personality. Even if she was not intentionally withdrawing from people, she *looked* remote to others, sometimes in spite of her best efforts. At a student retreat around this time, she found herself bunking in a broken-down cabin with six college girls and a mouse that ran from bed to lumpy bed. She had gamely tried to engage the kids seated around the campfire one night. "Tried to be chatty, friendly, interesting," she wrote glumly in her journal. "No go. I simply haven't got it, and I wish I had, but there we are."

And because she was tall, austere, and rather formidable, she was an easier target for criticism—of both her views and her behavior—than if she had been short, warm, and effervescent at the podium.

CHAPTER 11

A Return to Ecuador

*"He destroys that he might build; for when He
is about to rear His sacred temple in us, He first
totally razes that vain and pompous edifice, which
human art and power had erected, and from its horrible
ruins a new structure is formed, by His power only."*
—Madame Guyon

When the weather in New Hampshire turned warmer, and the last snow had fallen, the widowed Katharine often visited her daughter and granddaughter for extended stays. Elisabeth loved her mother. But it was difficult for her to maintain her emotional equilibrium—and her intellectual creativity—during these visits.

"How long has it been since you cleaned your refrigerator?" Katharine asked one bright morning, setting off alarm sensors buried deep in Elisabeth's soul.

The question hung in the air. Her mother went off to have tea with a neighbor. Though Elisabeth had writing she needed to get to, the refrigerator haunted her. It was not particularly grimy, even by Elisabeth's own exacting standards. But she cleaned it anyway.

Later Katharine returned from her outing, bustling into the kitchen. "'Well, now I'll clean out the refrigerator if you'll—'"

"I've just cleaned it," Elisabeth interrupted.

"What? You couldn't have. Why, you couldn't possibly . . ."

This sounds innocuous, but it's often the combined weight of tiny domestic annoyances that can create fissures in family relationships. Like when she overheard her mother talking to her daughter as Val ate before she left for school one day.

"Val, have you finished your breakfast?"

"No."

"Well, I wish you'd hurry. I don't like to spend the whole morning with the dishes unwashed."

It wasn't that Katharine really wanted to wash the dishes before people had finished eating, but her constant, stressful anxiety expressed itself in dozens of ways. Perhaps there was also just a bit of passive-aggressive needling in the mother-daughter dance. At lunch one day, Katharine told Elisabeth that she would stay elsewhere while Tom and his wife, Lovelace, were visiting. "You'll have so much to talk about," Katharine said, "and I'll hate to miss it, but you all feel much less inhibited if I'm not around."

Perhaps Katharine had expected Elisabeth to respond, "Oh, no, no, Mother, please stay here, we always want you with us."

This did not happen.

"I said nothing," Elisabeth reported in her journal. "It was too true."

Elisabeth's preoccupation with her mother did not help her professional productivity. She reported to her journal: "2:15. Since 8 a.m. I have felt just on the "verge" of actually beginning to write again. Put the paper in the typewriter. Ran over my notes again.

"Blank.

"Well, write something.

"Blank.

"God help me!

"Mother is a hindrance to me psychologically," she concluded. "I simply cannot work well with her in the house."

And on it went.

"Don't you have a roaster like mine?" Elisabeth's mother burst out. "Do you not WANT ANY of the dishes dried? Did I do the wrong thing?" "You should teach Val to finish a job—she didn't clean the sink properly!"

Discussion proved fruitless, and only seemed to alienate them further, Elisabeth reflected. "My relationship to Mother is a new kind of experience and test of maturity. She feels belligerently defensive, it seems—throwing out little remarks calculated to get a rise, as Dad used so often to do. I am not sure what the best approach should be, but wait on God to guide in this situation as He has in so many radically different kinds of other situations."

Elisabeth coped by reminding herself of what her brother Tom had said about their mother, that "'The rational content has gone out of our relationship' and it is fruitless to try to operate as though it was still there."

Further, Elisabeth realized, "Mother has never allowed her children to be <u>persons</u>. They are mere projections of herself, and when they cease to project what she visualizes she feels threatened, she cannot cope. She has never acknowledged the validity of my experience. On what ground can we meet, then?"

In the margins of these 1960's frustrated journal jottings, there are addenda written in 1986 and 1997, as the older Elisabeth periodically reread her journals from earlier decades. "Conflicts with poor mother!" the '86 entry notes. "Forgive me!" Later, in a shakier hand, the seventy-year-old Elisabeth wrote: "Deep, heartfelt repentance, 9/30/97."

Any of us who has reread some of our younger journal-jottings with red-faced mortification and sorrow can relate.

Meanwhile, Elisabeth kept discovering writers who were new to her.

"Trying all week to write. Nothing. Read Hemingway's <u>The Sun Also Rises</u> and <u>A Moveable Feast</u>. So he is another one. I am hooked on him. And he is <u>dead.</u> All these people were living and writing and loving the world and living themselves while I was not living and not writing and not loving the world and not being myself in the jungle, and now that I know them and love them they are all dead—Dinesen and O'Connor and Hemingway and T. S. Eliot and who else?"

Hemingway had won the Nobel Prize for literature in 1954. To Elisabeth's surprise, his grandparents had attended Wheaton, and his grandfather was a close associate of the famous evangelist D. L. Moody. Hemingway had not retained much of that faith perspective, except in dividends of resentment. He had lived his large-scale life on the dusty battlefields of Italy and Spain, hunting on the African savannahs, cheering at bullfights, drinking in the cafes and bars and parties of Europe, Key West, and Cuba. He had weathered concussions, malaria, depression, injuries, electroshock therapy, addictions, affairs, four marriages, and two plane crashes. It all had come to an end one July day in 1961, while Elisabeth was still living in Ecuador. His early faith roots withered; Hemingway had decided the only thing one can control in this life is the time and means of one's own death. Accordingly, he took his favorite custom-made twelve-gauge Boss shotgun, propped it so he could trip the triggers, placed the cold barrel inside his mouth, and blew his brains out.

Yes, Elisabeth had discovered Hemingway after he was dead . . . but anyone familiar with his style can see the influence of his writing style in one of Elisabeth's journal entries soon after she had started reading his works.

"On Wednesday we took hotdogs and homemade rolls and Beaujolais and walked up to a high country cabin. Snow in the woods. Zippy tore off after rabbits real and imaginary, and the sun came through the fresh new green needles of the spruces and the brooks ran loudly over the boulders and it was lovely."

Around the same time, Elisabeth noted in her journal that her dear friend and fellow widow Marj Saint was now "engaged to Abe Van Der Puy." Another dear friend had also received a ring. Marilou McCully, also, was weighing whether to marry a particular suitor or not.

There was no one on Elisabeth Elliot's romantic horizon.

In the spring of 1966, Elisabeth received an invitation from the Latin American Mission to write a biography of a seasoned missionary named Robert Kenneth Strachan who had served as its leader for many years. Strachan had died in February 1965 at the age of fifty-four. Though not a household name today, at that time he was well-known among evangelicals; Elisabeth was familiar with the LAM as the sending agency for her younger brother Dave Howard, who had served with LAM first in Costa Rica and then in Colombia before going on staff with IV and eventually taking leadership roles in various evangelical organizations and outreaches. Ken Strachan had worked with IV, directing its triennial conferences in Urbana, Illinois, and later working with the Lausanne Committee on World Evangelism, Evangelism Explosion, International Director of the World Evangelical Fellowship, the David C. Cook Foundation, and eventually the president of the Latin American Mission. He somehow wrote nine books in the midst of all this, while also serving as a trustee at Wheaton College, the LAM, the American Leprosy Mission, and other Christian organizations.

Elisabeth did not jot much in her journal about the project except that she was happy to go to Costa Rica on an exploratory trip to go through Strachan's papers. "Excited about the trip, this time as a *writer*. What a freedom it gives me!"

Perhaps, after the excruciating angst of trying to write her novel, and then the exhausting, negative comments *No Graven Image* had received, the idea of writing a simple biography of a faithful missionary seemed like a relief. It was "an interesting and comparatively easy task," she wrote in her journal.

By the summer of '66, Elisabeth was in Costa Rica. She and Val stayed at San Jose's then-popular Hotel Europa while Elisabeth researched Kenneth Strachan's correspondence and interviewed missionaries who had worked with him.

Elisabeth found that missionaries and local Christians she talked with were "enthusiastic" about her novel, *No Graven Image*. They told her in Spanish, "Don't be afraid—go on and write the truth—don't stop, don't be discouraged. We understand and there are now 500 pastors from Latin America in the US who understand! We need leaders, people who will spread the truth."

Her study of Ken Strachan and his work had thus far, "only served to baffle me more—which may be another way of saying strengthen my faith, for it is the God of such anomaly and contradiction who promises us perfection and fulfillment in the End, it is He with whom we have to do. Lord—make me true to the Truth. This is my charge."

After the research in Costa Rica, Elisabeth and Val went on to Ecuador to visit the places that had once been home. In Shell, Elisabeth was devastated by the situation in Marge Saint's once-impeccably hospitable home. Elisabeth reported that the missionary couple now in residence "both have the Bible school look . . . Children (2) bedraggled, crooked teeth, wide stare, stained clothes. Rubber pants, potty chair, waste basket containing used Kotex in bathroom. No maids, so Mary is washing dishes. Breakfast: cool scrambled eggs, baking powder biscuits which were not properly browned, served without butter. Coffee was a cup of yellowish hot water with which we were offered a can of powdered coffee. I can't think what possessed me to subject myself to this again—worse, indeed, than ever before.

"Supper last night at [the home of another missionary couple]. She is fat, nervous, flighty as ever, frumpy. Meal poor. I enjoyed her company, however, and afterwards she played piano and he sang (tenor) beautifully." The couple told Elisabeth that Rachel Saint was currently in Quito, away from the Waodani settlement, and Elisabeth decided it would be a good time to go back and visit her old friends there.

"How very thankful I am to have been delivered from this 'death'" Elisabeth wrote in her journal. "It seems abhorrent and debasing to me now, although when I lived here I accepted it as the others do. Life—so unreal in a place like this, so ignored, so discounted, somehow. Have they the capacity to be grateful to the God who made them, for the beauty of the earth, for the greatness of the gift of life? I wonder. They are like ants, each rushing with his tiny burden."

Death was a severe word for Elisabeth to use regarding these poor missionaries' ways of thinking and their personal habits. But the time at Shandia echoed with more than this "death" she had once accepted. It reverberated with the post-traumatic stress of *physical* death. This was the place she had learned of the violent destruction of her husband and his friends.

"This house, with its sounds of rain and radio contacts, bring back so vividly those days and nights between Jan. 8–15 [1956] when [the] lines came to me over and over—'Rotting there in the rain.'"

Those words that drummed like relentless rain in Elisabeth's mind were from a grim poem she had read years earlier. Robert Service was a British-Canadian poet who had served as an ambulance driver during World War I. In his "The Blood-Red Fourragere," a squadron of troops comes upon a horrific tableau left by the enemy combatants they are pursuing. Their leader, a hardened colonel, weeps. His tears mix with the rain, and he orders his soldiers to look upon the scene to galvanize them for the battle ahead.

> *What was the blackest sight to me*
> *Of all that campaign?*
> *A naked woman tied to a tree*
> *With jagged holes where her breasts should be,*
> *Rotting there in the rain.*[1]

The poem had resonated in Elisabeth's mind back in 1956, when she thought of her husband and friends, their bodies left to the relentless jungle elements. She had harbored no illusions about the decay of their mortal remains . . . and now, the driving rain brought that post-traumatic stress back to her in a flood.

Even as she was haunted by such gruesome imagery, the compartmentalized Elisabeth went onward to visit Puyupungu, where she and Jim, vibrant and alive, had lived as newlyweds.

Atansio, the chief with a dozen children who had welcomed Jim so happily long ago, now looked "exactly as he did in 1953 when Jim and I came here. His wife Holy Water, though she has had a number of kids since then, seems to have no more wrinkles than [before.]"

Then they went on to Shandia, where Jim and Elisabeth lived when Jim left for his deadly trip to Waodani territory. Elisabeth's old colleague and occasional nemesis, the eccentric British missionary Wilfred Tidmarsh, was there as well. "Hair grayer, fur sticking out of his ears, speaking his own private sing-song variety of Quichua."

The home that Jim had built and Elisabeth had loved "looked sad, with weeds grown up, DDT all over house, furniture more moldy than before, rug and coffee table gone, etc. Dr. Tidmarsh served us a cup of tea, Antuca talked to me about various people's marriage problems and her own hopes of getting a husband. Venancio is as sweet and gracious as ever—I brought him a zippered jacket and he carefully laid it aside without unfolding and looking at it, as did Antuca the dress I brought her."

The house where Jim's closest buddy Ed McCully and his wife, Marilou, had lived was still standing as well. But Elisabeth could not help the feeling that each of the old places—formerly full of laughter and high hopes, once "places of contentment, now feel very saddening and unattractive," and "the feeling was strong in me that I no longer belong here."

A Mission Aviation Fellowship pilot named Bob Lehnhart flew Elisabeth and Val into Tewaeno, the clearing where they had lived among the Waodani. "Nearly all the Waodani were there. They remembered me (and Valerie) by name. I was reassured to see how little anything has changed there—houses pretty much the same, Rachel has moved into what used to be mine—Akawu (Dayuma's mother) dressed in a skirt pulled up under her arms, with one breast protruding through placket. Dayuma described in detail who had had diarrhea and what sort of noises he made. Everyone laughed and whooped at everything I said."

One of the old friends gave Val a fish net, another presented her with some tapir teeth. Elisabeth and Val distributed the gifts they had brought.

"The Waodani are sweet people," Elisabeth wrote in her journal, her tone fond but distant. "They talked at once of themselves, their children and illnesses and animals and hunting, who had died, who is pregnant, who is married to whom. Once more I was glad to be among them, and I was glad to see the Quichua in Shandia, but glad, too, that I have other work to do. And so I remember all the way, and give thanks. It is interesting to note how one can see that doors are closed behind one, and the only way is forward."

CHAPTER 12

The Way Forward?

"This I have resolved on, to wit, to <u>run</u> when I can,
to <u>go</u> when I cannot run, and to <u>creep</u> when I cannot go.
As to the main, I thank him that loves me, I'm fixed:
my way is before me, my mind is beyond the river that has
no bridge, though I am, as you see, but of a feeble mind."
—Mr. Feeble-Mind, *Pilgrim's Progress*

*E*lisabeth returned to New Hampshire, grateful for her ordered home and cozy life. "Fire in the fireplace, raw and cloudy outside, Zippy asleep on living room rug beside the chair where I sit . . . Val is a radiant, cheerful, enthusiastic eleven-year-old, full of joie de vivre and eagerness to be a lady . . . so beautiful, so sweet. Van is a dear, true friend. I am *grateful.* Hiked a little way today up Jericho Road trail and ate lunch: deviled ham sandwiches, cucumbers in sour cream, apples, cookies, hot tea and coffee."

She planned to write the Kenneth Strachan biography over the next few months, hoping to finish by February so it could be featured at a late summer booksellers' convention in '67. At the same time, she was considering another novel. She wondered if she should hire a literary agent. What about an income tax consultant? Though requests from churches had slowed dramatically, she was still receiving plenty of invitations from other entities. Various magazines wanted articles from her. A group in Canada was anxious to have her come and lecture. And here was an invitation from Tarkio College, a small but distinguished Presbyterian school in Missouri. Could she speak at a conference there next summer?

"Should I accept?" she wrote in her journal.

It is a strange thing to read a person's journals—which unfold in real time in the past—day by day, and yet to know information unavailable to the writer. As I look at Elisabeth's 1966 journal entry so many decades later, *I know* the extraordinary life change that will happen to her because of that visit to Tarkio College. She did not.

This strange foreknowledge, the dual then-and-now mindset, is the specialized purview of the biographer. Elisabeth felt it keenly as she dug through Ken Strachan's personal papers. In her journal, she called him RKS. "Two weeks to go through twenty-five years of a man's life. A catharsis experience. His fears and hopes and failures and love and disappointment and ambition and self-doubt and longing and loneliness and questioning and suffering and reaching out and drawing back and believing and disbelieving—no, it was thirty-five years that I covered by this afternoon, and I am exhausted and baffled and touched by it all.

"What shall I make of RKS? Strange man—was he real? Did he actually do the thing appointed? Can I understand him? Can I know and show the truth?" she wrote.

As she considered the puzzling pieces of Ken Strachan's life, she also had an unusual opportunity to try to articulate her own strange story.

A well-known *Life* magazine editor named Dick Meryman had contacted Elisabeth. He was interested in doing a long interview that profiled her writing life in the States and her evolving thoughts on faith.

Dick Meryman was a groundbreaker in long-form interviews. He developed this approach in 1962, when he interviewed Marilyn Monroe, one of the most famous—and troubled—actresses of her day. He gradually won the skittish Monroe's trust, and she allowed him to record their many hours of conversation.

The interview, Dick later said, was such a torrent of emotions, laughter, defenses, and accusations that he decided to weave it into a monologue, one that revealed her lonely insecurity, in her own expression.

Life published Dick's interview with Monroe in the issue dated August 3, 1962—two days before her death from an overdose of barbiturates.

By excising his questions and focusing on the interviewee's flow of thoughts, Dick created an intimate, trademark monologue. He was self-effacing, with insightful questions and palpable empathy. He went on to interview celebrities like Charlie Chaplin, Elizabeth Taylor, Billy Graham, Louis Armstrong, Dustin Hoffman, and Paul McCartney. He wrote a dozen books. He profiled unknown people going through harsh challenges—an unmarried mother choosing to place her child for adoption, the travails of alcoholic women, and his own anguish when he lost his first wife to cancer.

Now Dick was interested in profiling Elisabeth Elliot, the most different woman from Marilyn Monroe on the planet. He arrived at her home in the beginning of November with a large, bulky tape recorder, notepads, and plenty of questions for Elisabeth.

Dick may have coaxed many a story from Hollywood celebrities, but he would not have an easy time of it with Elisabeth.

"Dick Meryman—associate editor of Life—here for interviews. Every word I say may be used against me. Don't say anything? But I am being handed one of the world's most visible platforms. Speak the truth and let the chips fall . . . the truth? But Jesus said nobody who has an eye to his own reputation can speak the truth. Well, I am not free of that. I am afraid and . . . cautious and eager to please (everybody?)"

Dick recorded hours and hours of conversation with Elisabeth . . . all for an interview whose transcripts would so trouble Elisabeth that they would never be published.

After Dick's departure, the peripatetic Cornell Capa arrived. He would visit for five days in order to shoot candid photographs of Elisabeth that would accompany the magazine story. He came, as always, bearing gifts: a set of oil paints for Val, and innovative Flair felt-tip pens, which had just been invented, for Van and Elisabeth, and a big hamper full of wine. He was "his usual kind, humorous, gentle self and we all enjoyed him awfully much."[1]

Cornell had developed a strong friendship with Elisabeth in 1956, when *Life* magazine sent him to Ecuador to shoot photographs for the world-famous magazine story on the deaths of Jim Elliot, Nate Saint, Ed McCully, Pete Fleming, and Roger Youderian. Later Cornell had returned to Ecuador and profiled the work of Elisabeth and Rachel Saint's work among the Waodani.

A Hungarian Jew—born Kornél Friedmann—Cornell was in medical school in Paris in the 1930s when he began developing film for his older brother, Robert. Robert would become world-famous for his dramatic photos taken during the Spanish Civil War and the Allies' invasion of France on D-Day.

Cornell fell in love with film as well. He abandoned his medical studies. *Life* magazine hired him after World War II. As his brother's career as a war photographer was already well-established, Cornell determined that he would be "a photographer for peace."[2] Cornell's brilliant use of light, shadow, and poignant detail created photos that celebrated what he called "genuine human feeling"—the commonalities that draw people together across cultures and life experiences. His phrase "the concerned photographer," later the title of one of his books, captured his empathetic connection with his subjects.

Cornell's wife, Edie, whom he married in 1940, was an integral part of his work, curating and planning his photo exhibitions, as well as hosting a constant stream of fellow photojournalists and guests who dined at their table and slept on their sofas.

He had photographed John F. Kennedy's presidential campaign and first 100 days of office, Bolshoi ballerinas, political dissidents in Nicaragua, and Russian Orthodox priests in Soviet Russia. An agnostic, he was curious, intellectually honest, relentless, and dramatically different from the men Elisabeth knew in her church and ministry circles. He used his camera lens to capture fundamental human realities, without an agenda.

When Cornell first met Elisabeth Elliot and the other missionary widows in 1956, he was exposed to an evangelical subculture he had never known existed. He developed a great curiosity about the work of these people so compelled to carry a message of faith and redemption that they were willing to die for it.

Elisabeth, who had grown up in environments where depictions of life had to be airbrushed of any "wrong messages" in order to be presented in a religiously attractive way, loved Cornell's bluntness, good humor, and uncompromising eye. For Elisabeth, it was a unique relationship. There were not many men who could teach her much, but Cornell served as mentor, friend, confidante, and fellow explorer. He confronted the habitual patterns of thinking that she had grown up with. He drove her crazy. He taught her by example. Elisabeth wrote to her family about a woman who was helping Cornell with the layout for a book project, "She is an alcoholic, poor soul, divorced, brilliant, slaving away at the museum and doing jobs like this on the side. But I am always impressed with the way people of 'the world' simply accept one another without criticism, with openness and warmth and human love. Cornell was being held up because she was on the bottle and unable to come when she was supposed to—but he accepts it, and accepts her as a person, and appreciates the beauty of the work she can do."[3]

Cornell challenged Elisabeth to see, to truly *see*, the beauties in the ordinary people and settings around her. Though the camera was just a tool, he loved its power to "provoke discussion, awaken conscience, evoke sympathy, spotlight human misery and joy which otherwise would pass unseen, un-understood and unnoticed."[4]

Obviously Elisabeth knew that film images could be manipulated toward the "message" that the photographer might desire—like her fictional missionary Mr. Harvey in *No Graven Image*, who documented "what he already assumed; his preconceptions governed his selection of picture subjects. Propaganda."

Elisabeth struggled. What was *real*? "Capa sees Truth," she had written to her parents in 1961. "He attempts to capture it. The camera is the extension of his eye. What he freezes in that moment is a statement about life."[5]

Elisabeth also related with Cornell because he had endured suffering. His eldest brother Laszlo had died in his early twenties of rheumatic heart disease. His next brother, the larger-than-life Robert Capa, was blown to pieces by a land mine in Southeast Asia. And one of his closest mentors and friends, the photographer David "Chim" Seymour, was killed by gunfire covering unrest in the Suez.

Now, in the late fall of 1966, Cornell and Elisabeth stayed up late, no doubt sipping from the contents of his hamper full of wine, discussing her *Life* magazine interview issues. "Since he knows me . . . he can ask even more penetrating questions [than others] and demand much greater mental agility in reply. (A "severe mental scamper . . . !)" Elisabeth wrote to her family.

As a linguist with almost total recall when it came to oral information, Elisabeth had a knack for re-creating conversations in her journal. She did so regarding her fireside chats with Cornell, though many of his comments, as recorded, are perplexing.[6]

"Sweet as always, kind, generous, thoughtful. We talked 'til 1 a.m.," Elisabeth wrote in her journal.

"You climbed the mountain," Cornell told her. "What did you see? You cannot evade telling us. David and Goliath. You may be weak and alone, but you have come to this place and you must slay the giant.

". . . you have tried to say it one way [in *No Graven Image*], and you are going to try to say it another, but it won't work. They don't get it. They say there is something wrong with you, because it's either you or they, and they can't be wrong."

"Or," Elisabeth added, "they say, 'Poor Elisabeth. She seems so unhappy. Let's pray for her!'"

"You speak to the outside," Cornell continued, alluding to non-Christians who would see the *Life* magazine interview once it was completed—"to 10 million readers—and they have to listen. Dick is saying 'Tell us what you saw'—and you will have to take the risk."

"But," said Elisabeth, "I don't want to be a crusader or a campaigner."

"Well, you are."

"So should I write fiction or non-fiction?" she asked.

"Non-fiction," said Cornell. "Fiction is too roundabout. They simply don't get it. Tell it to them straight."

The conversation continued, with Elisabeth asking Cornell about his own faith, or lack thereof.

EE: "Do you think faith is contrary to reason, or might it be complimentary?"

CC: "It is contrary. It is <u>giving up</u>. The scientist who realizes there are things he cannot explain turns, at death, to the priest."

EE: "Why is it more reasonable to refuse to give up?"

CC: "The universe is great, I am small. Here I am ready to die. Centuries have passed, men have tried to explain without success. All right, so something is up there. 'O Lord, I fall on my knees.' At that point I must not. It is understandable that people do. We stop pitting ourselves against Him."

EE: "Are you saying you <u>will</u> do this?"

CC: "No."

"There are plenty of people," Cornell continued, who "know what's good for me. I say to them—'Well, kids, you have lots of evidence on your side. If it comes to doing what you want me to do—no, I'll take my chances.'"

He knew, of course, that Elisabeth's faith was deep. "Then there's you—and a million others—who are <u>not</u> satisfied with the trimmings. You are in the core. You know He is there because you know He is there. You know that it <u>seems</u> God was NOT THERE when you wanted Him, yet you say you know He was there.

"Where did the Universe come from?" he went on. "I don't know. I must accept some original force that created life. But . . . I am not going philosophically into the beginning of man. Church's rules affect my life—but I don't want that, I want to live a legally clear enough life.

"When I die [I'll] admit what I knew all along—'You are big and I am small and I hope I didn't insult You too much.' Then He will or He will not accept me.

"'Yes, I know I am nothing. Please accept me.' But I will not be on my knees, I will be on my <u>bed</u>. I have no fight in me at all.

"But let's come to you. You live in Him. You are daily guided . . . You have an entirely different situation. Then you feel you are closest to Him because you understand Him and vice versa. But you come repeatedly to the end of your rope. He led you there. What explanation is there? None, except that <u>He knows</u>. Repeat this 10 times.

"You are confronted. I did not claim to be led. I made my own mistakes. I cannot blame God for leaving me in the lurch because I did not invoke Him to start with. I have no confrontation. But <u>you have</u>. . . .

"There may well be an elite who have married God, who will be given a seat at His right hand. I can have no complaints. You may be rewarded. God has tortured you to see how deeply you love Him. You will come out a true one."

Elisabeth's scribbled journal notes of this exchange, written quickly with her new black Flair pen, conclude with Cornell's words: "If you have not broken before now, you will not. Whatever He dishes out you will take."

A few weeks after this strange conversation, and many others like it, Elisabeth spent three days in New York City.

"Dec. 15, 1966 1:35 a.m. Three days in NY have passed. I was hopeful. It did not happen. I am lonely.

"Today Cornell showed me the pictures he took in Franconia. I was demolished by them. Taken with huge, telephoto portrait lens which clearly states every line, wrinkle, and pore. I know, if I had never known it before, that I am a stern and sad-looking old woman. I . . . might as well be 59 to judge by these."

To add more pain to her awareness of aging, she and her brother Tom went to see *A Man and a Woman*, a movie "about a widow who falls in love, her hope, her sorrow, her loneliness, her love . . .

"If only I could cry . . ."

CHAPTER 13

The Biographer's Burden

"I have no knowledge, wisdom, insight, thought
Or understanding fit to justify Thee in Thy work,
O Perfect, Thou has brought me up to this and lo,
what Thou has wrought, I cannot call it good. But I
can cry, O Enemy, The Maker hath not done!
One day thou shalt behold, and from the sight wilt run."
—George MacDonald poem that comforted Elizabeth Strachan
on the death of her husband

*F*our days after Elisabeth jotted her raw loneliness in her journal, she typed an upbeat family letter to her siblings and mother. She mentioned the busy Manhattan trip, the movie with Tom, how she stayed up late into the cold night. But there was no angst, just a breezy report of events. Yes, she was just about to turn forty. There had been a flurry of meetings about magazine articles and books and interviews. She had contracted with an agent, Bob Lescher, to help her maximize her publishing opportunities. Returning home, she, Val, and Van had put up the Christmas tree, cleaned house, wrapped gifts, and Elisabeth had made her famous candied grapefruit rind.

All seemed well, and the new year began with a new page in Elisabeth's red journal. "1967. 'Yet Thou, O Lord, art in the midst of us, and we are called by Thy name; leave us not.' Jeremiah 14:9.

"Just now this prayer seems to me to say it all. No solutions, no answers, no way out—yet we know His presence in our midst, we know whose we are, we ask only that He stay with us."

Elisabeth passed these January days in her favorite sort of orderly routine. She would get up at 6 a.m., wake Val, and they would have breakfast together on two high stools in their kitchen, overlooking the snowy valley below. At 6:30 the dutiful Val would practice piano while Elisabeth wrote letters. The school bus would clamber away with Val on board at 7:30, and Elisabeth would work on her biography of Kenneth Strachan for two hours until coffee break and reading the morning's mail. Then she would work again until lunch at 11:30. After lunch Elisabeth and Van would go for a walk in the snow if the weather was good, or she'd read in her chair by the window for an hour or so. More work, then grocery shopping, banking, or other errands. Elisabeth cooked supper each evening, "prodded" Val with her homework and more piano practicing, then spent more time at her desk, then reading, and bed.

"A lovely kind of life!" Elisabeth concluded after meticulously listing this schedule in her journal.

Sometimes on the weekends there were movies as well. She saw *Khartoum*, with Charlton Heston and Sir Laurence Olivier. "A strange and gripping story of two men worshipping their God and feeling duty bound to destroy one another."

Elizabeth Taylor and Richard Burton starred in the film version of *Who's Afraid of Virginia Wolf?* "Great acting, a great tragedy," said Elisabeth. "Hatred, drunkenness, violence portrayed in all their ugliness. A Christian view."

And then there was Michael Caine in *Alfie*. "Another tragedy of a wholly selfish man, a playboy who grievously hurts many women, and ends up alone and empty, without peace of mind," wondering what life is really all about.

She worked steadfastly on the Strachan biography. His widow, Elizabeth, visited with Elisabeth before Christmas, and the two shared in-depth about their departed husbands. They also wrapped Christmas presents, shopped, and checked off items on their to-do lists. Now Elisabeth traveled to California to meet and interview the Strachan kids, who had idolized their dad but had been raised, day-in and day-out, by their heroic mom. They were "the most charming, articulate, lovable, polite kids I have seen for a long time," said Elisabeth. "I enjoyed every minute with them."[1]

As she wrote Ken Strachan's story, Elisabeth harvested everything she could—those interviews with Ken's family, his reams of correspondence, journal jottings, and ministry records. Elisabeth knew *about* Ken, of course, since her brother Dave had worked closely with him for years. But she was trying to get to the core of the man.

Like Elisabeth, he'd grown up in an uncompromisingly Christian home. He had known the gospel from the time he could remember. Like Elisabeth, he had been educated in boarding school and at Wheaton College. Like Elisabeth, he had carried on most of his courtship with his eventual spouse via letter. Like Elisabeth, he was subject to self-questioning; he also had a self-deprecating sense of humor.

"It is an awesome burden which the biographer takes up," Elisabeth wrote in the introduction to his story.

"I began—trying to *discover*, not to construct, the truth about this man. . . . Again and again I found myself tempted to ask what my readers would want this man to be, or what I wanted him to be, or what he himself thought he was—and I had to ignore all such questions in favor of the one relevant consideration: Is this true? . . . And of course this is the question that any writer, of any kind of literature, has to be asking all the time."[2]

The way Elisabeth wrote about Ken reveals some key insights for us about Elisabeth herself.

Ken Strachan was born in Argentina in 1910 to missionary parents. In 1918, Harry and Susan Strachan moved their three children to Costa Rica, where they led an outreach movement then called the Latin American Evangelism Campaign. Harry traveled a lot; at home he was usually a bit preoccupied, his desk swamped by piles of papers.

His wife was a force to be reckoned with. She and her husband complemented one another well. She was efficient, visionary, and committed. She told young Kenneth that she would rather see him "the humblest worker for God than the President of the United States out of God's will and service. What will the world and all its glory be worth when Jesus comes for His own?"[3]

Ken went on to Wheaton College, where he developed a lifelong disgust with superficiality in spiritual matters. He wrote to his mother about a church service in which a pastor had manipulated a student into what the man then touted as a "wonderful conversion."

"Mother, I'm convinced that it is because of such brainless, self-righteous fools that the churches of today are loaded with Christians who have not grasped Life Eternal. That kid was no more saved than the devil himself."[4]

After Wheaton, Ken went to seminary at the Evangelical Theological College in Texas. After an extensive correspondence courtship, he married a friend of his sister's, Elisabeth Walker.

Ken received his Master of Theology degree from Princeton Seminary in 1943; his father died in 1945, at which point Ken and his mother, Susan, became codirectors of the ministry, which by now had changed its name to Latin American Mission (LAM). Ken settled his family in Costa Rica and settled into an unsettled lifestyle of almost-constant travel, a pattern that would plague his wife for decades, and greatly diminish his time with his six children.

Ken became the General Director of LAM after the death of his mother in 1950. As Elisabeth would note, Ken saw that any evangelistic and discipleship work must be done through equipping of *national* leaders. "His understanding of the need for indigenous church principles was at least ten years in advance of average evangelical thinking." He repeatedly spoke of the need to establish indigenous churches, with national leaders, supported by the congregations themselves. In this he was hampered by attitudes among many Christians in the United States. "The cry has been for more missionaries and more support for missionaries. Promotionally speaking, no other appeal has been so effective in presenting the cause of missions to the home constituency. . . . But we may not be entirely right in the deduction which we unconsciously make that the chief medium of world evangelism is the American missionary."[5]

Ken coined the phrase "evangelism in depth," (EID) realizing that evangelism must be done by every national believer at a grassroots level, and he designed a massive training discipleship plan to make that possible. He longed for the ministry to become a service agency of and for the Latin American church at large, not a U.S.-led, traditional "missions" organization.[6] He started a file labeled "*Latinamericanization*," its long title not even fitting on the folder tab.

In that file, Elisabeth Elliot found this story.

After World War II, a distinguished gentleman named Colonel Lawrence Van der Post, a novelist and soldier, was asked why Indonesia had asked the Dutch to get out of their country. His questioner was a Dutch man, who sputtered, "We built up their country, brought in industry, lifted the people to a higher level of . . . living standards, and increased their span of living." Why in the world had the Indonesians wanted the Dutch to get out?

"Ah," said the Colonel. "It was because of the look in your eye. You did not look at the Indonesians with compassion, but condescension, not with sympathy but superiority, not admiration but arrogance, not pity but pride, not graciousness but greed, not to give but to get, and your true inner attitude came out through the look in your eye."

Elisabeth resonated with the focus on missionaries' "true inner attitude." She wrote that "Strachan was a man of vision." He was also a man with compassion. But, like many such leaders, he could be "inexplicably blind to needs much closer home." He was busy, busy, busy with the Lord's work. He loved his family deeply, and occasionally became aware of the pain his wife and kids felt. "People are always more important than things or accomplishments," he wrote to his son, "and the Lord Himself is more important than anything.

That's the end of the sermon, son. I love you, and we'll take up no offering."

At one point Elizabeth Strachan wrote to her husband, ""Dearest Ken, which would you rather have—no letter at all or a sad one . . . I am simply and completely fed up with being a widow and having a traveling husband. I won't go into details but last night I dreamed you had come home, was simply ecstatic, when just as you bent down to kiss me you vanished again, and I woke up with the emptiest of feelings." She went on to methodically explain to Ken the viable ministry he could be doing right at home in Costa Rica, rather than capitulating to his relentless drive to fly all over the continent.

Ken was a conflicted man. "He saw God's hand at work in a thousand ways," Elisabeth wrote. "[P]rovision of his own temporal needs, the comfort of the Scriptures in times of depression, the gift of a lovely wife and children, guidance in daily affairs, harmonious relationships among missionaries, souls saved through the various avenues of the work, an ever-expanding influence for the LAM in Latin America— these he gladly acknowledged as gifts from God."

But Ken still struggled with the depth of his own faith. He believed he should personally experience the "true Christian's" peace, joy, rest, and confidence. He wondered if he should resign as head of the ministry. "Was it honest for him to retain such a role when it did not 'feel real' to him?" There was no indication anywhere in Ken's writings, Elisabeth went on, that he found a satisfactory answer to that dilemma. She wondered, "Perhaps it was not necessary or even possible for Ken Strachan to 'feel real.'"[7]

After visiting the States to participate in Billy Graham's New York Crusade in Madison Square Garden in 1957, Ken returned home exhausted from years of travel, meetings, initiatives, promotion, publicity, and plans. He faced what Elisabeth called, "the most critical choice of his life." Would he do the thing he longed to do, stop traveling, learn to be quiet, give time to his family, live healthily and happily on the farm, and try to be a shepherd with his sheep, pursuing the slow, personal process of winning individuals by a life of love and holiness, or would he commit himself from henceforth to a program, to the immense griding of wheels which is a movement, and would require more of the things he really disliked: travel, responsibility, promotion, publicity, people?

To Elisabeth's sorrow, he chose "the machine."

Soon after, Ken made a staggering public claim; if he could get the funding, and of course with God's help, "I'll turn Latin America upside down and carry out an evangelistic movement which will transform and revitalize the evangelical church and its witness in every country, produce a new crop of Latin American leaders, make an impact upon the conscience of Latin Americans, develop a lay movement—such as has never happened in the history of Latin America or any other part of the world."[8]

Elisabeth noted that the Strachan family letter of February 1961, written by Elizabeth Strachan, included a telling paragraph. "It seems that so many of us suffer from at least partial blindness—blindness to all we could be enjoying of the Lord's presence and kindness and also blindness as to the needs and opportunities that surround us. Do we let busyness, activities, and material things crowd out that for which we were made—to know and love God? Do the opinions of other people make us forget that it is going to be before God Himself that we must someday give our account?"[9]

"No man sees the whole truth at once," Elisabeth concluded. She recounted Ken's awareness that he was in a "rat race," and that he was driven by what he called "pseudo-absolutes," artificial priorities and imperatives which were in fact not non-negotiables at all. She called him a "fearful, doubting, ambitious, hopeful, demanding visionary" in a letter to her family.[10]

In April 1961, something snapped. Ken was at a pastors' conference in Colombia and started behaving strangely. He was confused, uncharacteristically sharp, indecisive, and blank. He was dizzy and had terrible headaches. He flew to the United States and went through all kinds of medical and neurological tests. The diagnosis? He was suffering from tension.

By 1964 he and his family were living in Pasadena, California, and Ken was lecturing at Fuller Theological Seminary. He was ill and would soon be diagnosed with lymphoma. At Christmas time he was hospitalized, near death, unable to breathe. He miraculously recovered and was able to return home. He weighed 115 pounds. People all over the world prayed for him. Billy Graham came to visit, telling Ken that he, "envied me my experience, and knew that the Lord needed to teach him or bring him into closer fellowship through suffering."[11]

In the new year, Ken gained a few pounds. His outlook and his vigor improved. He began to talk about a trip to Costa Rica.

And then it started again. He began to choke. He was hospitalized, could hardly breathe, and suffered from itching, swelling, and pain. His wife said he looked like a "trapped animal." She agonized that she could not do anything to help him. At one point Elizabeth stepped into the hallway. "Oh, Lord!" she moaned. "The meanest man in Pasadena would put a stop to this if he could!"

But God did not put a stop to it. One dark morning Ken asked a friend to read from the Bible. He listened . . . and began to fade. The last words anyone heard him whisper were, "I feel trapped."

His heroic wife sat with him as he choked, gagged, struggled for breath, and sank into a coma. He died later that afternoon, February 23, 1965.

Believers around the world mourned. At his funeral service in Costa Rica, thousands of people crowded the *Templo Biblico*, which Ken's mother had built thirty-five years earlier. The congregation sang "Cara a Cara (Face to face with Christ)," full-throated, many in tears. The casket was carried for a mile and a half on the shoulders of a constantly rotating group of men. The crowd followed, their voices swelling in a glorious crescendo at the cemetery. Then the pallbearers carefully slid the casket into a stone tomb. It was closed and sealed.

After painting that scene, Elisabeth's writing in the last pages of Ken's biography resonate with her own hopes, convictions, and refusal to close out his story with some glorious coda.

"Ken had always prayed that the life of Jesus would be plainly seen in his own life, but he was not sure of the answer. Others believed they saw it in him. Who can say with any assurance? Can we ever for an instant contemplate a life as God sees it, without sentimentality? Or will we, the instant we see clearly, lacerate ourselves either for looking through rose-colored glasses, or for judging without charity? Sentimentality is not compassion, for it is blind and ignorant. Compassion both sees and acknowledges the truth and accepts it, and perhaps God alone is wholly compassionate.'

"And God alone can answer the question, 'Who was he?'"

"There is so much more that we do not know—some of it has been forgotten, some of it hidden, some of it lost—but we look at what we know. We grant that it is not a neat and satisfying picture—there are ironies, contradictions, inconsistencies, imponderables. The circumstances of his death alone, so far from crowning with glory a life of earnest endeavor to be a faithful servant, seemed like the last mock-cry."

Believers tend to expect a glorious end for the life of God's saints. Those who witnessed Ken's death did not see this. Elisabeth wrote that various observers tried to give hopeful "explanations," but "[t]hese were mere anodynes."[12]

If Elisabeth was committed to telling the truth, without sentimentality, without anodynes, that meant her book would have no tidy ending.

"Here, then, is as much of the truth as one biographer could discover about a man. Let the reader find as much of its meaning as he can."

Then she goes on. "Is it legitimate to ask whether the work for which this man is especially remembered is significant at all as the 'true' work of God in and through him? . . . Will Kenneth Strachan have been welcomed home with a 'Well done, good and faithful servant,' or will he simply have been welcomed home? The son who delights the father is not first commended for what he has done. He is loved, and Kenneth Strachan was sure of this one thing."

Ken's favorite hymn was the Billy Graham crusade classic, "Just as I am, without one plea/But that Thy blood was shed for me . . . Just as I am/Thou wilt receive/Wilt welcome, pardon, cleanse, relieve . . ."[13]

"This was his faith," Elisabeth concluded. "[N]ot that he would have earned a place, or built temples or won great victories, but that God had accepted him because He had once become a man, and had lived through the tortures of being a man, and died the death of a man, in order to bring the lonely race of men, from all their deaths of whatever kind, Home."[14]

Privately, Elisabeth wrote in her journal,

"The RKS first draft is nearly finished. I have looked in vain for the 'secret of power' or whatever it is that is supposed to inspire biography-readers. It simply isn't there. A weak, vacillating, ambitious, secularly minded man who earnestly wanted to 'serve the Lord,' who had the intelligence to see 'the tyranny of pseudo-absolutes in the lives of others and completely missed his own bondage to a program. 'What doth the Lord require of thee?' Somehow, Ken did not see that it was to do justice, to love mercy, and walk humbly with God. Does any of us see it? Does any of us do it?"

For her part, as she finished the book's first draft, Elisabeth jotted in her journal, "Having studied—and necessarily—judged his life, have I seen anything which ought to change me? At this moment, I am not sure that I have. I feel that I ought at least to pray—but do not know what to ask. I guess there is nothing more central than 'Lead me in paths of righteousness for Thy name's sake.'"

CHAPTER 14

The Unredeemable Elisabeth Elliot

*"These <u>men</u> who are leaders in missions simply
will not (or cannot, since the price is exorbitant)
<u>face facts</u>. Women, strangely enough, often see
through things which are opaque to men."*
—Elisabeth Elliot, 1967

Around the same time she finished the initial draft of the Ken Strachan manuscript, Elisabeth spoke at Wheaton College at a Christian Writers' Institute event. She titled her talk, "The Christian Writer's True Country," referring to the real world, seen through a Christian's eyes.

"Afterward one Mr. Yff, of [a missions organization] interrupted others to say to me, 'I want to tell you that you <u>baffle</u> me.' (Eyes steely cold, face livid with rage.) 'You did nothing but confuse people. Do you call yourself a <u>Christian</u>? Are you a <u>Christian</u> writer? I want to tell you that you ARE <u>NOT</u>! Never a word about Jesus or sin or our glorious salvation or anything. You ask who we think we are. I ask you—who do you think you are? Huh? Confusing people like that! Didn't you have a Christian husband? Didn't he die for Christ? Do you know Christ as your Savior? Are you washed in the blood of the Lamb? No you are not. I want to tell you that you are <u>totally LOST</u>!"

Stunned, Elisabeth responded, 'Do you think I am redeemable?'

'No! Not unless you are one of the called, and I don't think you are. You are going to have to answer to God for what you did here tonight—and maybe to your husband! I warn you in the NAME OF GOD!!!'"

"I was undone by it," Elisabeth wrote in her journal. "I cannot let it pass me unaffected. I am sure those to whom I spoke afterward wondered why I trembled."

An older lady approached her. "I can't tell you how the whole field of Christian writing has been illuminated and elevated by what you said this morning! I want to say thank you."

Of course, it is far easier to lecture about writing than to do it. In April Elisabeth had a rough session with Cornell Capa as he reviewed her manuscript about Ken Strachan. "[A] disturbing few hours, with such upheaval in my thinking. To him, the book is a case history of a screwed-up life. 'My Life in a Sausage Factory.' I have not brought to bear any significant judgment or meaning on the whole. Why ought the book to be written? The reason does not show. So—'it must all be done over.'"

She escaped from Cornell's critiques by reading more Hemingway, writing poetry, and playing with an idea of a story about the disciples falling asleep on Jesus. Spring crept up the mountains; she spent more time outdoors. "[L]ying in sunshine in open field, rabbit trails in the woods, buds beginning to redden, little rivulets running in all the hollows, old stone walls with ice between the rocks, utter stillness."

She roused herself from the woods in order to speak at the "last student missionary conference I shall ever attend (I think)" at Park Street Church in Boston. She noted that it had been badly organized, that she received "vague and ambiguous instructions on topics," was not told when she was speaking until the day before. "Found myself on a panel with Robert Brown of Bible Medical Missionary Fellowship (India) as moderator, and Howard Dowdell of SIM, Philip Grossman of SIL, and Virgil Newbrander of FEGC. Topic—the effectiveness of missionary work. None willing to define either 'effectiveness' or 'missionary work,' or to admit that it cannot be measured."

"Virgil Newbrander . . . was the only man there at the conference who seemed to me open courteous, humble, <u>sincerely</u> ready to listen," Elisabeth wrote later.

"It is a hard position to be in, and each time I find myself a target for criticism and misinterpretation I say 'why do I do it?' but each occasion has to be judged on its own merits, and I could say no to any one at any time. The Lord has, I do strongly believe, been my Shepherd up until now—He knows how to show me the path, I'll wager."

In spite of many criticisms, Elisabeth was not wanting for speaking invitations. One day's mail brought an invitation for her to speak at a Caribbean cruise sponsored by one of the then-popular Christian magazines, featuring various prominent leaders. The same day, Van, expecting a letter from her publisher, got nothing.

"The contrast was very painful for both of us, and I found her crying," Elisabeth wrote. "How does one, with <u>grace</u>, cope with success? It raises the deep question of <u>merit</u>, genuine and superficial; of justice—why should it be <u>me</u>; of accepting acclaim of any sort—what does one, in his inmost soul—<u>do</u> with it? And of course, to imagine for even an instant that Van begrudges it to me, or is jealous of me, or cannot rejoice with those who rejoice, is <u>very</u> hard for me.

"Van has been in the depth of despair of late, over her book, over the uncertainty of her future, over my thoughtlessness. I've spent endless hours (it seems) trying to help."

Elisabeth spent an entire day reading Van's draft manuscript. She cut and completely reorganized it, and "gave her an outline of what I thought it should be. She simply cannot <u>see</u> and <u>shape</u> it. Now, this morning, she asks what to do now."

Elisabeth had always deeply respected Van. When Van first arrived in Ecuador, her wisdom, insights, and understanding had been an incredible tide of relief for the lonely Elisabeth. Reflecting on this at the time, Elisabeth had noted that she had a deep need to "admire sincerely" anyone she let into her inner circle. Since Jim, there had been "very few whom I deeply esteem." But Van was one of them.

Now, though Elisabeth loved her dear friend, perhaps she was losing some of that admiration. Why couldn't Van just see how to restructure her book herself?

At the same time, Elisabeth was reshaping the Ken Strachan biography, now titled *Who Shall Ascend?* In addition to Cornell's input, she had critiques from her publisher, a normal part of the book-writing process. Part of the difficulty, she said, had to do with "uncovering and exposing the paradoxes" in her subject. She anticipated pushback from readers. "Probably a large part of the resistance which will be encountered will be from those who insist that the paradoxes are not paradoxes, that they do not exist. There will be many, of course, who simply will miss them, no matter how clearly they are set forth."

Like any biographer, she had found out things that were "disturbing" about her subject, and she had to somehow capture, with grace, these elements as well as his pleasing aspects. But two early readers of the manuscript encouraged her greatly. One editor wrote that the book was "tremendous," an "existential biography that is epic." Another reader wrote to Elisabeth that she thought she was a "genius (!)" and that "the biography may be my best-seller yet!" This was Elizabeth, Ken Strachan's widow.

By mid-May, Elisabeth, who would have been flabbergasted by the near-instantaneous electronic transfer of data that we enjoy today, had laborious retyped her hundreds of double-spaced pages one last time, lugged it to the post office, and mailed the heavy package to her publisher. She now turned her attention to a series of talks she was due to give in July, which were to focus on one of the most puzzling books in the Bible.

"Studying the Book of Job in prep for my Tarkio [College] talks in July. Discovered that he regarded God as his sole true witness and advocate. <u>That</u> is faith. His single enemy and implacable foe was the one who saw all, who knew all, and who alone judged impartially. Here, then, was Job's <u>refuge</u>.

"Job's friends sided with God. Maybe that's what was wrong. Maybe it is never necessary to be partial toward God. If there's one thing <u>He</u> doesn't need, it's support. <u>We</u> are the ones desperately in need of that. Perhaps this is why we usually get nowhere in our 'witnessing'—we're always defending God against His creatures."

CHAPTER 15

"I Am Hopelessly Vulnerable"

*"The forces are God's forces, and this creature
is God's creature and the promises are God's promises,
and in obedience, in recognition of his creaturehood,
this man has destiny and sonship."*
—Addison Leitch, *Interpreting Basic Theology*

The summer of 1967 would bring an unexpected and decisive moment in Elisabeth Elliot's life.

Elisabeth and Van drove to Florida to visit with Elisabeth's mother. They sunned and swam at the beach, and on the way back to New Hampshire stopped at St. Simon's Island, Georgia.

After they checked into their motel, they went exploring and decided to drop in on acclaimed author Eugenia Price, St. Simon's Island's most famous resident.

Eugenia Price was ten years older than Elisabeth, born in West Virginia in 1916. As a young woman, she was a self-proclaimed atheist. After college, she became a successful writer of radio dramas, then the head of her own production company in 1945. In 1949 she converted to become a follower of Jesus Christ, and began writing, directing, and producing "Unshackled," a popular radio series profiling lives dramatically transformed by faith. She published several inspirational books, and eventually turned her vast energies to meticulously researched historical fiction, mostly set in nineteenth-century Georgia.

As the *New York Times* said of her, "Her hoop-skirted heroines tended to be too unremittingly beautiful, her handsome heroes a shade too dashing and their problems a bit too easily solved for Ms. Price to have won serious literary acclaim. But then again, how many acclaimed authors sell more than 40 million books in 18 languages?"[1]

Charmed by St. Simon's when she first visited it in 1961, Eugenia had eventually bought property there. She built a pink mansion called "Dodge" after the real-life inspiration for one of her heroes—a clergyman buried in the local churchyard.

Eugenia had written to Elisabeth Elliot, inviting her to "drop by" any time. Perhaps that message had not gotten through to her friend and companion with whom she lived for decades, fellow writer Joyce Blackburn.

Elisabeth did not have Eugenia's phone number, so she and Van went searching for the landmark home. There it was, a five-acre, secluded plot set on a peninsula in the marsh, surrounded by trees cloaked with Spanish moss, enclosed by heavy double gates draped with shiny chains, and marked with "Private, Do Not Enter" signs. There was a house phone at the front gate. Elisabeth called. No answer.

By now storming the pink castle had become a challenge. Elisabeth and Van exchanged a look, passed around the gates, and made their way up the long driveway . . . and here came a "frigid woman with an icy glare. Joyce Blackburn. Perfectly <u>furious</u> at us for disregarding barriers, never inquired who we were, said Genie would see no one, and simply flayed us alive for 'climbing over' gates."

Elisabeth and Van apologized profusely, retreated, and Van called out to the indignant Joyce, "Just tell her Elisabeth Elliot called."

Joyce didn't register any positive reaction to this but did allow that perhaps she could go back to the house and check to see if Genie would see her. Not "them," as in Van as well, just Elisabeth.

"No, no," Elisabeth called down the driveway, still backing up. "We should go."

"Well," said Joyce. "Perhaps Genie could call you?"

"No," Elisabeth said. "We're staying at a hotel with no room phones. That's all right!"

"Well, perhaps Genie will see you."

"No, no, we must leave."

"Oh, but she will be so disappointed not to see you!"

After this confusing exchange, Elisabeth and Van found themselves heading up the long driveway after their reluctant guide and into the enormous house. Joyce called upstairs—"Genie! It's Elisabeth Elliot here to see you!" Soon, Eugenia Price appeared, wearing a "sloppy" blouse, blue jeans, and tennis shoes, all smiles, full of "Honeys," and "Sweeties," apparently unaware of the chilly reception the two had received.

As if by prearranged signal, Joyce whisked Van away for a tour of the house. Elisabeth and Genie sat down on two richly upholstered chairs. Eugenia lit a cigarette.

"Oh, this is a long-time prayer, now answered!" Genie said. "I have so wanted to talk with you!"

"She sat with feet apart, elbows on knees, smoking a cigarette in a holder . . . She wears a pixie haircut, is overweight, and had on no makeup."

They talked, as writers do, of their daily routines, how they produced manuscripts, what happened when they got stuck, and their experiences with publishers. They talked about Tom Howard's surprising new book, *Christ the Tiger,* which Eugenia had read in manuscript form. They talked about how big God is. Eugenia wanted to know how, really, Elisabeth had "come to terms" with her husband's eagerness to reach the Waodani and what had happened since. "Tour of the house followed," Elisabeth reported. "We had glasses of vodka and tonic in our hands as she showed me the deep gold guest room with expensive Korean grass paper on the walls (I pray for the dear people who wove that each time I come in here and somehow that redeems the whole thing)."

Much later that night, Elisabeth and Van finally got back to their modest room. And when they eventually reached home, an effusive Eugenia Price letter of apology was waiting in Elisabeth's mailbox, including invitations for Van and Elisabeth to please come for a week's visit, along with two plane tickets.

The next trip for Elisabeth was a visit for a few days with a friend named Margaret, a fellow writer who had a "little cottage on a rocky point" on a river.

"[We] talked of many things," Elisabeth wrote in her journal. "Margaret's church, Knox Pres., Toronto, her writing talents, health . . . Genie Price and Harold Ockenga." They went for walks and prayed together. "This morning we swam before breakfast, ate, read the Bible . . . sunbathed in the nude (she does it all the time, with all the female guests who have the courage), ate lunch in the nude, and I am now on her screen porch overlooking the river. A gorgeous day, for which I thank God . . ."

Elisabeth eventually put her clothes on and flew to Missouri, to the log cabin hideaway of friends she respected greatly, David and Dorothy Redding. Dave was a Presbyterian pastor and prolific writer who had been named by *Life* magazine as one of the top ten U.S. clergymen of the time, "one of the most eloquent younger voices in the U.S."[2] He had just taken on the role of Writer-in-Residence, Counselor and Preacher at Tarkio College. Tarkio was a small liberal arts school in Missouri that had been founded in 1883.

Elisabeth had accepted an invitation to speak at Tarkio's annual Institute for Basic Theology, a conference that drew serious-minded lay people for several days of intensive lectures and discussion. She had visited previously with the Reddings during a speaking engagement and held deep respect for Dave and Dorothy. Her visit at the Reddings' cabin gave her a few days of rest, preparation, and at least one provocative conversation before the conference started on the college campus.

Early one morning Elisabeth woke to find Mark Redding, age seven, standing at her door.

"Wanna see my hamster?" he asked.

Elisabeth leaned on one elbow, wishing for coffee.

"Of course," she responded.

"She doesn't mind if you pick her up," said Mark. "Doesn't squeak or anything. I'll go get her."

He came back cuddling an armful of mammal fur.

"What's her name?" asked Elisabeth.

"Phyllis."

"Where did you get that name?"

"Oh, I picked it out. She belongs to me and I thought it was a good name."

"What colors do hamsters come in?"

"Just brown and white, I think."

"No black ones?"

"No black ones. . . . But I think there are blue ones and yellow ones in Africa."

After sharing his hamster, little Mark watched intently as Elisabeth got up and combed and teased her long hair to put it into a French roll.

"You know what I think?" he asked, without waiting for an answer. "I think you need a haircut!"

Undeterred, Elisabeth got ready for her speech,

"I find that when I've accepted an invitation to speak, I think little about it at first," she jotted in her journal. "Then, as the time draws near, I begin to be terrified (more so for this institute than ever before because of the formidable erudition of the audience), and wonder whatever possessed me to accept. Then when it comes right up to the hour . . . I am greatly exuberated and tensed, very eager to get to the podium."

One of the members of that distinguished audience was a fifty-eight-year-old Tarkio professor of philosophy and religion named Addison Hardie Leitch. He was a tall, robust man with a quick laugh, strong features, and a classic pair of '60s-era black glasses. He held three honorary degrees and four earned ones, including a PhD from Cambridge University. He had served as dean of men and college pastor at Grove City College in Pennsylvania. He was a professor at and later president of Pittsburgh-Xenia Theological Seminary and would be offered the presidency of eight different academic institutions. He was a former athlete who'd once been considered by the Pittsburgh Pirates but chose to go to seminary instead, a thinker, a well-loved professor, an author of five theological books, and an editor, columnist, and occasional humor writer for *Christianity Today.*

Addison and his wife, Margaret, had been married since September 1936. They had four daughters, though one, born in 1943, had died at the age of two months. And now, in July of 1967, Margaret Leitch was courageously—and terminally—ill with cancer.

Elisabeth Elliot had met Addison Leitch (Add to his friends) the prior December at a gathering at Dave and Dorothy Redding's house. She did not write about the encounter in her journal at that time, but later noted, cryptically, that she had felt a tremendous magnetic attraction to the professor. It was mutual. And now here she was, seeing him repeatedly as she spoke each morning at his college's annual Institute of Basic Theology.

She jotted impressions and reactions in her journal.

"Great experience—liberal, well-dressed, intelligent, and to all appearances very <u>hungry</u> Presbyterians who sit on the edge of their chairs, take notes like mad, thumb through their Bibles and ask questions."

"Howard Jamiesen, prof at Pittsburgh-Xenia Seminary, came to tell me how delighted he was with my assessment of the Waodani situation. 'Who supported you in the field? How can you be so honest? I can see you are very hard to handle from a publicity standpoint. You just don't fit the image.'"

A "wild eyed old lady who had been to Ecuador for a visit: 'Your development is just incomparable! Oh, your logic and reasoning are superb. And you're so pretty to look at!'"

"Add Leitch: 'Warwick Deeping [the British novelist] said 'The most beautiful thing about a beautiful woman is courage.' That applies to you.'"

"Add Leitch asked me if we could get together to discuss his article on evolution from a philosophical journal. It is to be tomorrow at 9:30, and he added, 'If I feel the way I do now, I'll be outside waiting for you.'"

"It is certainly a happy feeling to be <u>sought</u>. No doubt a basic human need."

She met with Addison to discuss his piece on evolution as he had suggested (which certainly sounds like a bit of a premise).

"It's good to know you exist," he told her. "You're the discovery of 1967."

"I don't want to embarrass you, but I would like to say this—Jim Elliot must have been an awful lot of man, to have had a woman like you. But then I'm sure you're an even greater person now than when he was alive."

"If you could find the place I'd kiss you goodbye. And it wouldn't be a holy one, either."

Addison's words may sound creepy to a modern ear. But for whatever reason, back in the mists of 1967, Elisabeth was feeling swept in on a much deeper level.

She jotted a paraphrased line from a poem by Austrian poet Rainer Maria Rilke.

"How shall I guard my soul so that it be/ Touched not by thine?"

"I am hopelessly vulnerable," she continued. "Last night at a reception a lady asked if I wanted a refill on punch. 'Dr. Leitch suggested I get you one—he thought it would look better than if he got it.' O dear. And his wife Margaret dying with cancer—still up and around, bone-thin, cheerful, and energetic. Saw her <u>running</u> in the rain. Add told me yesterday he simply <u>did not know what</u> to do to cheer her. How could he?"

On the afternoon of July 28, Elisabeth wrote, "Add has just left my suite. Came for a visit from 2–3:30. We talked mostly about the Waodani. He asked how I had the courage, was I ever lonely, etc.

"Kissed me lightly two or three times upon leaving.

"'I <u>like</u> you. You're the best thing that's happened to me in a long time. Is there any way I can show my affection for you?'

"I told him he had just done it. What a lovely experience. What a strange one. But loveliness and strangeness are both welcome at times."

CHAPTER 16

The Writing Conference

"If our lives are truly 'hid with Christ
in God,' the astounding thing is that this hiddenness
is revealed in all that we do and say and write.
What we are is going to be visible in our art, no matter
how secular (on the surface) the subject may be."
—Madeleine l'Engle

*A*fter Elisabeth's emotionally complex time at Tarkio College, she pulled herself together. Elisabeth flew to Chicago, where she met up with a carload of travelers bound for the Bedford Center for Creative Study in Green Lake, Wisconsin. Elisabeth had been invited to teach and mentor a group of men and women who had signed up for a special writers' seminar amid the larger throng of Christian retreat attendees.

Such a cheery religious gathering was not exactly Elisabeth's cup of tea. Her journal entries from the week in Wisconsin veer between raw reflections on the state of her heart, and acerbic observations of her students and others whom she met at the conference.

She went on. "I slept, last night, for the first time in a week . . . fell asleep thinking over the Tarkio experience."

She woke and went to breakfast in an immense pink dining room (pink walls, pink Formica tables, pink waitresses). There was a lengthy blessing by a pink professor from a Christian college, and then, "the usual corny announcements over a loudspeaker. ('Teen-Tivities will be [led by] Dick So and So.'")

There was an art gallery on campus. Though most of the art seemed to Elisabeth to be "gaudy and shallow," she found some block prints that she liked a lot. Then she was accosted by, "a bearded young painter, whose oils-and-gesso things were on display. Engaged him in conversation and found him a pompous ass. He told us all about how serious he is, how very misunderstood artists are, how much he has known and suffered. Well—it may be all perfectly true, but one doesn't tell people in the first five minutes of acquaintance."

A person who impressed her far more was one, "middle-aged, hefty [black] lady swathed in white, diaphanous robes, named Rev. Sheila Earnestine Somebody. I'd like to hear her preach!"

For the most part, Elisabeth's students flummoxed her. She talked with a woman named Amy about her writing for a prominent evangelical publisher. "She admitted that she doesn't have much time to observe or to think," Elisabeth noted. "She has a one-track mind, she says, and [when she adds embellishments to her stories] she is only trying to make things 'interesting.' She does not read."

"Have you ever read a great book?" Elisabeth asked her.

"Oh, no," replied the woman. "They're too wordy."

Not to be daunted, Elisabeth met next with Bonnie, trying to work with her on the lack of clarity in her piece about her emotional problems in her marriage. She noted that in group discussion Bonnie was one of the most vocal and dogmatic, but perhaps, Elisabeth thought, this was simply because of "her own psychosis." Bonnie shared what Elisabeth called "an imprecatory prayer"—as in a curse or plea for God's judgment—she had written against her husband for his failure to assume spiritual leadership. Bonnie was funneling her boiling anger, feelings of futility, and sadness about her husband into her writing. This did not help her prose. Elisabeth reported, "She seems paranoiac, nearly in tears (of rage, perhaps) when I criticize her piece."

Mel, the organizer of the event, read the beginning of Flannery O'Connor's celebrated short story, A Good Man Is Hard to Find, to the group. He focused on the great writer's brilliant description of the grandmother character, who sadly enough, inadvertently causes the rest of her family's deaths in the dark story. Oh, sniffed one of the attendees. "Yes, the writing is good, but you certainly wouldn't find writing like that in one of our church publications!"

Next was a group critique of one of the members' short story about a Chicago firefighter. It was "appallingly bad," Elisabeth thought. One group member volunteered that the firefighter was not realistic, that he seemed to witness about Jesus with such ease and confidence, and it didn't make sense, that firefighters are generally "a tough bunch."

"Oh," the author responded, unwilling to adjust her story to make it psychologically believable. "But this firefighter isn't tough in that way, he's a remarkable fellow . . . highly unusual."

"The poor lady has no idea about anything," Elisabeth concluded.

Next, the group discussed someone's "story" about how to know the will of God. "A sermon," Elisabeth concluded. "Nothing more."

Next was a story by Dan, the college basketball player. Relief. "There, I believe, is a real writer on the way." The story was simply written. It sounded real, focusing on a boy's redemptive experience in giving of himself to help an old man. Bonnie, one of the attendees who was not satisfied unless every piece read like a gospel tract, suggested to Dan that he should have shown in his story that the boy was a Christian—because if readers could clearly see that the boy helped the man because of his relationship with Jesus, then Dan "would be really a 'Christian' writer."

"Oh, but you're limiting what constitutes Christian writing" ventured another group member.

"Yes," said Bonnie, her eyes flashing. "And I think it's high time we did limit it!"

"Well," another person said to the author, "you know, you could just have the boy look up at a picture of Christ that is on the wall and then let the old man win the checker game. Then it would be a Christian story."

Even as Elisabeth sighed over what she considered to be the shallow state of many who fancied themselves "Christian writers," her tart journal judgments did not mean she did not care about the participants. She was as hard on herself as she was on others, and certainly would have been the first to skewer herself in a few wicked and well-drawn lines, if she had thought about doing so. She cared about the men and women the writing conference had put in her path. By the end of the seminar, after many conversations, she wrote,

"Things have happened here this week, I believe. Poor Amy, Pentecostal, poker-faced, imprisoned soul, walked the woods for hours after her first talk with me, because I had questioned whether she really believed what she wrote.

"Today she said I had helped her greatly and had not discouraged her at all. She realized, she said, that her writing was superficial, and her characters like paper dolls. Who knows but what God may get through to her and she will make the break toward truth?"

After a long walk in the woods, Amy found Elisabeth in the dining hall, pulled her aside, and gave her a gift: a bright green leaf, filled with tender wild raspberries, each like a soft jewel, that she had carefully picked for her mentor. Elisabeth was so touched she did not know what to say.

Another prickly participant, the ever-combative Bonnie, went on a long walk with Elisabeth by the lake. Yes, she told Elisabeth, perhaps she had been conditioned to always say the "right" Christian thing. Perhaps she could not think outside of her religious boxes.

And then there was Melanie. She and Elisabeth sat out on the sunny dock one day from 10 a.m. until noon, talking about Melanie's short story, and then about how big God is. She had a glimmering, she told Elisabeth, of what it meant to write the truth. Not a sermon, but the reality of God's world and the human beings He has placed in it. She told Elisabeth that the week had expanded her thinking; she would never be the same.

Elisabeth felt the same way. Something in that little writing community, dysfunctional as it was, had touched her. She found herself in a heart-to-heart with Ted, one of the older male attendees, next. It was a long talk, she wrote in her journal, "about homosexuality (not an active [issue] with him) and the possibility of his getting married. The idea seemed hardly to have occurred to him. I talked a lot about the marvel of having one other being in the universe to whom you mean everything, the I/Thou relationship, one's own validity being attested to by another, etc. When I asked later what he had written that day, he said, 'I have written nothing, but thanks to Elisabeth Elliot I have begun a new chapter in my life.'"

Elisabeth was stunned. "To think that this poor little roly-poly bachelor of 40+ might suddenly find the world singing around him is exciting," she wrote.

Why? Because Elisabeth had found the world singing around her in the past ten days. "I am sure that my own—shall I call it love?—for Addison enabled me to speak as I did to Ted.

"I wasn't going to write this," she wrote, "but there is no good reason not to. It is the truth.

"It is impossible for me not to think about what it would be like if I were married to Add. I wish I could help thinking about it, for it violates something in me—I have a very great admiration and respect (perhaps actually this amounts to love in the I Corinthians 18 sense) for Margaret. A noble and selfless woman, dying inch by inch with cancer. The conflict arises is my mind when I think 'What if she knew my thoughts?' Heaven forbid.

"But then she is a very intelligent woman—very likely she knows my thoughts, not because I have given her reason to guess, but simply because she too is a woman.

"There is a great affinity of spirit between Add and me. This is inescapable. I knew, in Tarkio last December, that a spark had been ignited. As we talked in Reddings' living room something was alive. . . . Every word and look bore testimony to it last week. How can it be denied?

"He has suffered. I could not marry a man who has not. Margaret's cancer, his daughter, his seminary experience, and God knows what else, have brought him to his knees.

"He knows God. There is no pomposity about him, but a simple and direct honesty and humility.

"He thinks <u>clearly</u>. What a relief to talk to someone who <u>sees</u> and <u>understands</u> what he sees and articulates it clearly.

"He has a great sense of humor. Found that he reads <u>The New Yorker</u>, loves George Price and Charles Addams.

"He can be gentle, he is sensitive, discerning, gentlemanly, and has savoir-faire. He treats Margaret with tenderness and thoughtfulness.

"I could marry him, I think, if he should ask me. He would be a great father to Val—a <u>real man</u> who could dominate our home. He has three daughters of his own.

"He would take care of us—and how I long for that! Someone who makes the decisions and the plane reservations and, as K. Mansfield said, 'who goes to bed where you do.'

"He is a Ph.D. from Cambridge.

"He is also fatter than I would like, but he is <u>tall</u> and powerful. He is old (57 or 58) and probably would leave me again a widow. He cannot climb mountains, I suppose. I would surrender my separate identity, some of my 'image,' my independence (which I have come to cherish), my freedom to work without taking care of anyone, my status as a widow (and I cannot deny that I have now a certain attachment to that idea) and Jim's name (<u>this</u> would be painful).

"It is absurd thus to count one's chickens, as it were. But I lie awake nights as though the decision must be made at once! It is simply because I cannot help it. How could I help it? And if the thing in the end proves to be right, shall I look back and say, 'How silly of me to have been thinking of it then!'?

"And what about Van?"

Yes, what about Van? Increasingly dependent on Elisabeth, she was of course a dear friend—but one who perhaps wanted the Elisabeth Elliot household to stay just as it was.

And that was not to be.

CHAPTER 17

The Six-Day War

"This is the spot on the planet earth that the
Lord God looked upon and said, 'I will go there.'
And, in the flesh, as an ordinary Jew, He came."
—Elisabeth Elliot, Jerusalem, October 5, 1967

*I*f Elisabeth Elliot's heart was strangely warmed toward Addison Leitch in that pivotal summer of 1967, you wouldn't know it based on her journals after she returned home to New Hampshire. Surprisingly, she didn't write about the new developments in her heart. Instead, she focused on the stunning drama of international events that had begun with the Six-Day War in the Middle East.

It's hard for twenty-first-century readers to feel the significance of that war, not only in the history of Israel, but also its impact on conservative Christians in America. Many pastors tied the war directly into Old Testament prophecies about the End Times; many evangelicals credited Israel's victory to direct divine favor and intervention.

Ever since its establishment as a nation in 1948, Israel had been threatened on all sides by its Arab neighbors. Its War for Independence had concluded with a ceasefire that had left Jerusalem divided in two. The entire Old City, including the Temple Mount, the Western Wall, and other holy sites, was under the control of Jordan; Jews were not allowed to enter Jerusalem's walls or pray inside the city.

In the late 1940s and early 1950s, Egypt blockaded the Suez Canal and the Straits of Tiran to shipping destined for Israel. In 1956, a United Nations Emergency Force deployed to the Sinai Peninsula, and the straits were re-opened. But by the late spring of 1967, President Nasser of Egypt had again closed the waterways to Israeli vessels, evicted the U.N. peacekeepers, and mobilized troops along his border with Israel.

Egypt and Syria activated a mutual defense pact, and Syria massed troops on its 40-mile border with Israel. The Syrians occupied the high ground, including the Golan Heights, which they had been fortifying for eighteen years. Meanwhile, the nation of Jordan had deployed ten of its eleven brigades to defend its densely populated territory on the West Bank, as well as the Old City of Jerusalem, with the Temple Mount and other holy places that had long been denied to the Jews.

On the morning of June 5, 1967, small groups of Israeli jets took off from bases in their homeland. Their Air Force had amassed extensive reconnaissance of every air base in Egypt, Jordan and Syria. The pilots cleared their country's airspace and flew fifty feet over the Mediterranean Sea. They knew that their Egyptian counterparts were on alert at dawn, but now, at 7:45 in the morning, most senior Egyptian military and political leaders would be caught in Cairo's notorious traffic jams, and thus would be out of touch.

Still, Egyptian officers stationed at the radar station in northern Jordan did pick up the scrambling Israeli aircraft. They sent a red alert message to Cairo. The officer in the decoding room of the supreme command there tried to decipher the message using the usual code, but failed. The Jordanians evidently had changed their coding frequencies the day before, and neglected to inform the Egyptians.

Israeli pilots bombed more than 300 Egyptian fighter planes and rendered runways through the country unusable. In separate raids, their brother pilots took out two thirds of the Syrian air power, and most of the Royal Jordanian Air Force. Israeli ground troops took on the Egyptian army forces in the Sinai desert, the Syrians in the Golan Heights, and the Jordanians in the West Bank and East Jerusalem.

On June 11, a ceasefire was signed. Israeli had lost less than 1,000 fighters, while the Arab forces lost 20,000 troops. Israelis considered it a miracle of biblical proportions; their nation had crushed her enemies to the north, east, and south, and tripled her territory.

Now, for the first time in nineteen years, Jews could access the Western Wall, the ancient limestone segment of a retaining wall for the second Jewish Temple, which was constructed by Herod the Great about two decades before the birth of Christ.

Above it was the Temple Mount, a huge, rectangular plaza built for the Temple, its outbuildings, and its crowds of worshippers. This is the Temple that Jesus and His disciples knew. It was destroyed by the Romans in AD 70, with only the Western Wall section remaining. The Wall is considered holy to Jews and to Muslims because of its proximity to the Foundation Stone, revered as the place where God created the first man, Adam, and where the patriarch Abraham prepared to sacrifice his son, Isaac, until God stopped him. After the rise of the new religion of Islam in the seventh century, the Al-Aqsa Mosque was built on the site of the former Jewish Temple, while the Dome of the Rock, whose famous solid-gold dome still defines modern Jerusalem's skyline, was built in 691 to commemorate the site from which the prophet Mohammed ascended into Paradise.

For the Jews, the Western Wall segment was the place closest to the ancient Holy of Holies of their destroyed Temple. It was their sacred site of prayers, tears, and devotion to God. But they could not access it, and their sorrow over its loss designated the place as a place of weeping, or the Wailing Wall.

Now, with Jerusalem once again under Israeli sovereignty, Jews proclaimed that the Western Wall should be a place of general celebration rather than mourning. Three days after their victory, the Jewish army gave short notice, then bulldozed the Moroccan Quarter, a 770-year-old Muslim neighborhood of 135 flimsy homes and a warren of dark alleyways that blocked access to their Wall. This created an open plaza where Jews could now gather.

The Six-Day War was not the last word, by any means, in Israel's complicated history and the anguishing issues surrounding her borders for Israelis, Palestinians, Jews, Muslims, and Christians. But in 1967, many American Christians saw the war's conclusion as a dramatic fulfillment of biblical prophecy. For the nation of Israel to face—and crush—the much bigger armies of the Arab world was a modern-day David and Goliath story and a signal that human history was drawing to completion. Recapturing Jerusalem for the first time in 2,000 years seemed to be a direct fulfillment of Luke 21:24 (CSB, emphasis added), "Jerusalem will be trampled by the Gentiles *until the times of the Gentiles are fulfilled*."

Many pastors pointed to complex Old Testament prophecies they believed were fulfilled by the 1967 events. They exhorted their flocks with new urgency: the Bible was true, its interpretation of human history was real and relevant, Jesus was going to return soon, and evangelism was more imperative than ever in these "last days."

Elisabeth Elliot did not note anything about the Jews in her journal. But then her old friend Cornell Capa had a crazy idea . . . what if he and Elisabeth did a story for *Life* magazine and a book for Harper & Row about Jerusalem's first holy season since its holy sites had been liberated by the six-day war?

Elisabeth's agent, Bob Lescher, counseled her that a book about Jerusalem could be a great backdrop for writing about her own faith, though he had his doubts about her doing so in a book whose content would be dictated by photography.

Meanwhile, Elisabeth doubted that such an historic opportunity would actually come to fruition. She went on with her life, searching for an apartment in Manhattan. She had always loved visiting New York: why not live there? There was pushback at home. "Van does not seem able to rejoice with me. She feels her own insecurity and uncertainty more than ever when things seem to be going well for me." But, thought Elisabeth, "I want more than anything else to live in this exciting city, and I must find something." (She was looking for a two-bedroom apartment in the Upper East Side for $125 a month.)

A friend who had been serving as a missionary in Italy visited with Elisabeth. "[His] marriage is on the rocks, twenty-three-year-old fellow missionary (girl) in the picture. He has seven children. Is divorce permitted by God? What should he do? The girl has now got herself engaged anyway, to someone else. Ironic, that I, at this particular juncture, should be the one sought out for counsel. But it was a salutary exercise for me, grappling with the issue for somebody else."

Elisabeth did not get her New York apartment. What she did get was a cable from an exuberant Cornell Capa, who was in Tel Aviv. "JERUSALEM MARVELOUS, LIVING AND SCHOOL SITUATION FAVORABLE, CONSIDER BOOK WITHOUT PICTURES, CALL [MEL] ARNOLD."

Mel Arnold, Elisabeth's faithful editor, was in favor of the idea. He was willing to finance Elisabeth's trip and give her an advance for a book about Jerusalem. "It is a very good risk for Harper and for you," he told Elisabeth.

Later Elisabeth spoke with Cornell. "If you go to Jerusalem you'll be doing me a favor," he told her. "I think it will prove to be a favor to yourself as well. This has been what I've been calling my 'secret plan for Elisabeth Elliot'—I know you'll be terrifically stimulated by the experience. I know you'll do a good book, but you need time for quiet reflection and absorption, I want you to be liberated from the book pattern from the past, to learn your own flexibility as a writer."

The idea of being liberated from creative patterns of the past lured Elisabeth. Perhaps she also welcomed the distraction from her preoccupations with the as-yet-unattainable Addison Leitch. Within a few days Harper & Row issued a contract for the Jerusalem book, tentatively titled *Furnace of the Lord*. (This was based on part of Isaiah 31:9 (KJV): "The LORD, whose fire is in Zion, and his furnace in Jerusalem." Rather than taking Val with her to temporarily attend school in Israel, as she had first thought, Elisabeth decided that Val would be more comfortable staying with Van in her own home and among her own school friends. Before she left for Jerusalem, Elisabeth went to the opening of a New York photo exhibit that Cornell had organized. Her observations give a thumbnail sketch of '60s fashion. "What a show!" she wrote. "Not only the photographs (great) but the people. The exhibitionists, the mod types . . . and grande dames, the sophisticated and the hungry and the hopeful and the had-its. Woman in pseudo-Russian pink costume, pink tights and boots, black fur hat. Girl in 12-inch-long hip-hugger skirt with wide zipper down front. Another with crew-cut hair, black lace insert in dress with apparently nothing under it. Man in blue and red striped trousers and Christopher Robin haircut. Another with longer-than-shoulder length curls. Girl with what looked like maternity smock and no skirt at all. Woman in black flappy pajamas and silver slippers."

To Elisabeth's disappointment, Cornell let her know that he would not be going to Jerusalem with her.

On the morning of her departure for the Middle East, she woke at 4 a.m. "wondering what on earth I will <u>do</u> in Jerusalem. What a preposterous mission I am on, when you come to think of it."

"October 2, 1967. Aboard Al Italia #633, 10 p.m., headed for London, Rome, Tel Aviv. Strange unreality about the whole thing, in spite of small Italian children, grandmas, shouting and gesticulating, all in Italian."

The 19-hour journey had three layovers. First, in London, Elisabeth buzzed briefly around in a British bus with a "driver who looked like a Beatle." In Rome she toured as much as could be seen in four hours. In Athens she simply sat, exhausted, in the airport, listening to a large group of senior citizens "having a romp and discussing the best kind of shoe polish for travel." Finally, after the sixth meal of her trip, she landed in Tel Aviv, "so dead beat, so lonely for some familiar face, horrified at the task that awaits me."

In such condition she arrived at the American Colony Hotel in Jerusalem. It had originally been built in the late nineteenth century by an Ottoman *pasha* who lived there with his harem of four wives. Each had her own wing. Perhaps the fourth wife was too much, however; soon after that marriage, he died. The property was then sold in 1895 to a group of Messianic Christians led by one Horatio Spafford, the Christian who wrote the heartbreaking and poignant hymn "It Is Well with My Soul" after four of his children drowned at sea. The building was eventually sold to famed British actor Peter Ustinov's grandfather in the early 1900s and transformed into a hotel. Faithful to its history, it tended to draw all kinds of colorful guests.

Elisabeth felt marginally more hopeful the next morning. Drinking a demitasse of strong coffee at breakfast, she listened as a distinguished

British gentleman, also a hotel guest, chatted with an American tourist who would be visiting the Wailing Wall that day. "Please have a small wail for me, will you?" he asked. Elisabeth later discovered he was Malcolm Muggeridge.

Perhaps drawing some sort of energy from the distinguished writer, Elisabeth Elliot juggled her notebooks, her camera, and her mind, and set her face toward Jerusalem.

She was there for ten weeks, in an ancient city teeming with pilgrims, crowned with prophecy, filled with mystery. "This is the spot on the planet earth that the Lord God looked upon and said, 'I will go there.' And, in the flesh, as an ordinary Jew, He came."

CHAPTER 18

Jerusalem the Golden

*"Every happening, great and small, is a parable whereby
God speaks to us, and the art of life is to get the message."*
—Malcolm Muggeridge

*O*ver the next ten weeks, Elisabeth sipped innumerable cups of tea or
sweet coffee with everyone from the abbess of the Russian Orthodox
Church in Gethsemane to Sephardic Jews who had emigrated to Israel
from Spain. She visited with the Episcopal Bishop of Lebanon, Syria,
and Jordan, the president of the Arab Women's Union, and the mayor
of Jerusalem. She had a long, intimate discussion with a Scotch Irish
nun of the Sisters of Sion at their convent on the eastern end of the
Via Dolorosa. Her order was dedicated to the Jewish people, she told
Elisabeth, "But, oh! My heart bleeds for the Arab!"

An Arab man latched onto Elisabeth at the market. He smiled and
practiced his English and told her he had blue eyes because he was
descended from the Crusaders. Did she want a tour of the holy places?
"No," she told him. He continued. "You like a massage? I am masseur.
Especialist for ladies." She told him to leave her alone, he informed
her that she owed him money for his time, and they took their issue
to a bemused policeman, who encouraged them to go their separate
ways. Later Elisabeth saw the "masseur" escorting a well-to-do older
American woman around her hotel.

Elisabeth went to Yad Veshem, the museum commemorating those
who died in the Holocaust. She stared in horror at the remnants of
lives lost in the ashes of the death camps. She stood before the newly
liberated Western Wall in her assigned place with the women and
watched throngs of men swaying, weeping, and bowing in prayer. She
visited the shadowy Church of the Holy Sepulcher, shoved this way

and that by the crowds of frenzied pilgrims. She retreated to the peaceful quiet of the Garden Tomb. She went to Galilee with representatives from World Vision. She spoke at a Southern Baptist women's retreat meeting, improbably, in a Catholic convent. She went to a bar mitzvah with Jewish friends, then to the theater and a cocktail party. She went to Jericho, Masada, Absalom's Tomb, Bethlehem, Nazareth, and Ramallah. She flowed with a crowd of 100,000 people thronging the streets of the Old City for the first "Parading of the Scrolls" since Jews had taken control of Jerusalem. She went to a United Nations reception. She went up to the Temple Mount, toured the El Aqsa Mosque and the Islamic Museum. She visited small Arab villages that had been bombed and took tea with Jewish leaders. She was welcomed into poor, dim rooms without running water in the twisted passageways of the Old City, and the well-appointed homes of both Jews and Arabs.

It was a colorful, complicated, exciting, confusing, and lonely time for Elisabeth. She had grown up thinking of a bright, gilded Jerusalem, the centerpiece of God's ultimate plan. She had sung hymns about "Jerusalem the Golden, with milk and honey blest." She thought of the city as the locus for Jesus's trial, crucifixion, and resurrection, and the place that would ultimately be made new in its fullness in the book of Revelation. She knew of its conflicts, of its importance to Muslim tradition as well as Jewish history. But now, she was being told, it was a new Jerusalem already. "Prophecy is being fulfilled!" Christian friends told her. "Jerusalem is redeemed. It is a marvelous thing that is going on there."

Never one to jump on a dramatic bandwagon, Elisabeth wrote, "The Bible prophecies about the New Heaven and the New Earth had been obscure to me but intriguing, and if in fact the things . . . happening in Jerusalem signaled the beginning of the end—if the return of Christ was near—I should perhaps see them."[1]

Elisabeth went first to the Wailing Wall with the guide Cornell Capa had arranged for her, an Israeli man named Moshe. They followed a mob of people toward the open plaza, which was flooded with blinding sunlight. At the foot of the massive Wall she saw a mass of black-and-white clad men bobbing their heads back and forth, leaning their heads on the stones, rocking, and standing still with reverence. "From the mob rose a cacophony of voices—a shout, a wail, a roar, a song—it was all of these at once, it was perhaps none of them, for the men were . . . praying. The call of the muezzin from a mosque overlooking the plaza disturbed them not at all."

Elisabeth's Bible upbringing brought God's words to Solomon to mind. Solomon had built his temple on this site in the tenth century before Christ. God came to him at night and said, "Now my eyes will be open and my ears attentive to the prayers offered in this place. I have chosen and consecrated this temple so that my Name may be there forever. My eyes and my heart will always be there" (2 Chron. 7:15–16 NIV).

She mused on the Jews' deep love for this place, their outrage that it had been deprived from them for so long. She thought of the Arabs whose small houses had been destroyed to clear this plaza.

Moshe left her for another appointment, and Elisabeth walked back to her hotel alone. She pondered what she had seen. She had read the Bible all her life; she knew that Israel was chosen by God to be a people for Himself . . . "there was no surprise for me in Israel's victories. It was all in the cards, that is, in the Book. Everything I knew about what had happened in June fitted nicely my belief in miracles."

"To the Arab whose house is now an empty space it looks as though God is on Israel's side . . . I wanted to know whether Israel was on <u>God's</u> side." She thought about Old Testament mandates for justice. So complex; what were the answers to the problems in this parcel of earth? Isaiah wrote that, "the fire of the LORD is in Zion, and his furnace is in Jerusalem." Yes, Elisabeth wrote, and "whether or not all the fires kindled there have been His only He knows, but there have been many. Egyptians, Jebusites, Hebrews, Babylonians, Romans, Arabs, Turks, Britons, and Israelis have called the city their own."

A few days later Elisabeth went to St. George's Cathedral. The first hymn the congregation sang was "Jerusalem the Golden," and the Scripture for the day was from the Gospel of Luke: "Blessed be the Lord God of Israel for he hath visited and redeemed his people . . . that we should be saved from our enemies . . ."

The bishop who read those words was an Arab. The congregation was made up of Arabs and people from other countries.

Afterwards, Elisabeth could not remember what the sermon was about. She was thinking about "the Lord's people" and their "enemies," wondering who was which.

She thought about how she had made assumptions most of her life about such things, without truly investigating.

One Arab bishop commiserated with Elisabeth—how would she discern the "truth" about Jerusalem and write her book? "I am an Arab and a refugee. I speak what I believe to be 100 percent true. If you talk to a Jewish rabbi he will speak what he believes to be 100 percent true. If I were you, I would find myself on my knees asking for a revelation."

This was not particularly encouraging, as Elisabeth was already flummoxed at just how she would write her book.

She met an old man happily swinging a blue basket. He sat down on the grass in the shade, spread out a large handkerchief on the ground, and began to sing to himself. He laid out some bread and water. His song was a high, quavering Arab sort of tune that made Elisabeth conclude he was a Mizrahi, or Oriental Jew. He smiled and waved to her to join him on the grass. She smiled back and shook her head. He went on singing.

"Peace and war—and peace again. Sorrow and joy—and sorrow. This was Jerusalem."

One night Elisabeth went to the Western Wall for Simhat Torah, the happiest of Jewish Holy Days. There were wildly shouting groups of men parading huge parchment Torah scrolls. They danced in a circle, their arms around each other's shoulders, shouting and singing praises of the Book. Nearby oriental Jewish women keened in the piercing, Arab ululation of joy or sorrow, occasional shouting "aleluyah" as tears streamed down their dark cheeks. Children rode on their fathers' shoulders, laughing with the excitement of it all.

Elisabeth thought back to her own childhood. There certainly had not been much emphasis on plain human happiness. "Our gatherings were careful and quiet and controlled. The 'joy of the Lord' was to us a deep, serious thing not connected with celebrating in any way, let alone with dancing."

The celebration roared on. One handsome young Jew had an hourglass-shaped Arab drum he began beating with his fingertips. Young people began swirling in a new dance, "whirling and swinging in the cold night air, the stars above them . . . and no sound except the hard, strong rhythm of the drum and the soft thudding of their feet on the packed earth."

"I felt that a huge door had suddenly been flung open where I had not even known a door existed. Here was a revolution of joy. And it was Jewish joy, the wild, wholehearted welcome of a people for the written Word. This Word—Hebrew characters on parchment, lovingly copied, carefully preserved, beautifully displayed—had been the center of their dancing, the subject of their songs."

Later, she had tea with an Arab woman who wanted to live in peaceful coexistence with Jews. But during the Israeli bombing and shelling of the Six-Day War, in the midst of the terror and dust and hunger, she had laid on the floor with her children, covering their heads in terror. She told Elisabeth, "My Lebanese neighbor, also a Christian, lifted her head from the floor once and said to me, 'There is no God. If there is, He is a Jew.'"

One day Elisabeth hired a small boy to show her the way to the Dome of the Rock. She marveled at the "marvelous symmetry of the

Mosque surmounted by its softly shining golden dome . . . space and light and silence and beauty and peace." She crossed to the main entrance, which was guarded by two Israeli soldiers. She left her shoes by the door and entered. She was alone in the vast dome, except for one Arab man. Elisabeth watched as he silently bowed to the floor, stood, and knelt in silent prayer. "'There is no God but God, and Mohammed is his prophet,' he might be saying. 'There is no other name under heaven given among men whereby we must be saved,' I was thinking, and for me that name was not Mohammed but Jesus Christ."

Here she was, a Christian, in a Muslim temple. "But it was a temple erected to the glory of God—the one God—and as I watched the worshiper alone with Him I knew that I had better not exercise myself in matters too great for me."

Now the image she took away from the "golden city" of her childhood assumptions was infinitely more complex. But it was golden still.

Early one morning, Elisabeth walked on the Mount of Olives as the cocks began to crow. The olive trees on the terraced slopes grew softly green gold, the bells from a dozen churches pealed out the hour of six. Elisabeth thought of Peter's denial of Christ before the cocks of his day had crowed the morning of Jesus's death. He said he did not know Him. And then Jesus, bound, had turned and looked at him.

Elisabeth had met a Dutch priest at the nearby Church of Saint Peter in Gallicantu, originally established in AD 457 to commemorate Peter's miserable denial and his lifegiving repentance. The priest had told Elisabeth how much that moment in Scripture moved his soul. ". . . we are human, as Peter was, and apt to make mistakes. But there is that look, that hope. Could you take away with you from Jerusalem any better souvenir than to know that here Jesus had turned and looked upon you?"

Elisabeth thought now of the priest's simple words, and how they had struck her to the core. "We are judged by the phenomenon of Jerusalem. At every point we find ourselves. We meet a mirror at every corner. We sit in judgment on others, and we find ourselves judged." The Lord's judgment will be like a refiner's fire, but "[w]ho can say what transformations will come out of the fire?" For in the end, God's mercy is available to all.

Elisabeth looked over the valley. "As the sun climbed high enough to send its rays across the top of the mountain to the city of Jerusalem, I saw first a spot of deep pink in the silver of El Aqsa's dome, then the windows of the Armenian Quarter flamed all at once, and after this all the towers, minarets, domes, and cubes of the city were swept with gold."

After her ten weeks in Jerusalem's "furnace," Elisabeth headed home. She could not wait to see Val, to sleep in her own bed, to read and think and try to process all she had seen in the Middle East.

Perhaps her experiences in Israel had enhanced both her gratitude and her desire to build and cultivate relationships. Once Elisabeth got home to New Hampshire, she wrote in her journal, "I am grateful beyond words for all I have now in physical comforts in abundance, excellent health, peace in this country, and above all love and a new understanding and appreciation of it. I have not sufficiently appreciated and cultivated friendship, but it seems that in a sense life does indeed begin at 40, and I am filled with joy."

CHAPTER 19

1968

*"Before mass leaders seize the power to fit reality to
their lies, their propaganda is marked by its extreme
contempt for facts as such, for in their opinion fact depends
entirely on the power of man who can fabricate it."*
—Hannah Arendt

*M*ost histories of the twentieth century call 1968 a "turning point"
for the United States. It was surely a turning point in the life of
Elisabeth Elliot, but not because of the horrors of war, assassinations,
social unrest, and societal change that shook America.

In early 1968 there were more than half a million U.S. service
members in Vietnam. The draft called up 40,000 young men into military service each month, feeding them into a conflict that had begun
as an effort to stem the spread of communism in southeast Asia.

In January, North Vietnam's Tet Offensive—one of the most
famous and gruesome campaigns in modern military history—
exploded throughout South Vietnam with massacres, ambushes,
assassinations, and thousands of civilian casualties.

Seven American missionaries working at a leprosarium in Ban Me
Thuot, in Vietnam's Central Highlands, were killed by the Viet Cong
in that offensive. Several had been emboldened in their work among
an indigenous tribal people by the influence of Jim Elliot and the other
missionaries martyred in Ecuador in 1956. Now they gave their own
lives for the sake of the gospel and the care of the mountain tribe they
served.

Though the communists sustained enormous losses, the Tet
Offensive was a turning point in a terrible war. For the first time,
many who supported U.S. involvement in Vietnam now saw that this

was a war America would not win. Wounded American veterans threw away their war medals. Student protesters took over academic buildings on their campuses.

Meanwhile, it had been nearly five years since Dr. Martin Luther King's visionary "I Have a Dream" speech to a quarter of a million people in Washington, in which he called for an absolute end to racism and for civil and economic rights for African Americans.

In early April, Dr. King was assassinated, to the horror, despair, and upheaval of the nation. There were riots in city centers across America. Tanks rolled down U.S. streets. President Johnson signed the Civil Rights Act, which broadened earlier anti-discriminatory laws.

Americans ventured further into space than ever before, with *Apollo 8* orbiting the moon.

A cultural phenomenon known as the "Jesus Movement" swelled on the West Coast and spread east, as droves of hippies who had not found peace and truth in drugs, sex, rock and roll, or Eastern religions now embraced Jesus as their Savior.

Elisabeth Elliot noted some of these cultural tides in her journal and letters. She would comment on fashions like miniskirts and blue jeans—which gave her the willies—while continuing to wear what she'd been wearing for years. She might refer to what she considered the inanity of contemporary repetitious praise songs sung in Val's Christian youth group, but the Beatles, Rolling Stones, and rock and roll were not on her radar. She preferred timeless, classical music, and those who did not agree with her taste were just lowbrow.

Elisabeth was more affected by what she was *reading* than what was *happening* in the world around her. So, in the sixties, when she referred to the Vietnam War, for example, it was in the context of reading Mary McCarthy's book about it.

Elisabeth wrote to her family, "If any of you are not sure what to think about Vietnam, read Mary McCarthy's Vietnam."

A gifted writer and social commentator, McCarthy was best known for her *New York Times* bestseller *The Group*, the story of eight affluent Vassar grads in the 1930s, their sexual adventures, struggles with misogyny in the workplace, childrearing, and their place in male-dominated, mid-twentieth century America.

In early 1967 Mary McCarthy went to Vietnam. She was perhaps not the most objective of observers. As she wrote in her book, "I confess that when I went to Vietnam. . . . I was looking for material damaging to the American interest and that I found it, though often by accident or in the process of being briefed by an official.[1]

In her past, Elisabeth concluded and wrote to her family that McCarthy's book was "A clear-eyed report, by a modern-day prophetess, which shows things in a clear light—something you'll never get from the journalists or politicians, not in a million years. How do I know she's telling the truth? It rings true, and nearly every word she says applies equally to the Christian missionary program, which is unquestionably a product of 20th century Americanism. But 'who hath believed our report?'"[2]

Judging by her journal entries, Elisabeth would have been considered a pacifist if we wanted to categorize her. But for her, Vietnam was a case study in the need to reject, rather than unquestionably accept, the Establishment's version of Truth.

So McCarthy's opinions and conclusions about Vietnam reinforced Elisabeth's now well-entrenched distrust of the Evangelical Machine. If social critics accused the U.S. government of deflating numbers of U.S. troops killed in Vietnam, Elisabeth tied it to her own experience of U.S. mission agencies inflating the numbers of converts on the mission field. The Establishment manipulated facts for its own ends. It must be called out.

Around the same time, Elisabeth was reading *Eichmann in Jerusalem: A Report on the Banality of Evil* by Mary McCarthy's close friend, writer Hannah Arendt, which focused on Adolf Eichmann, one of the most notorious villains from World War II for his administration of the "Final Solution."

Reading Arendt's book, Elisabeth wondered, as millions have, how the German people had not seen what was happening in their nation under the Nazi agenda. Why did not the Jews resist? Why was the rest of the world silent? How could gross evil look so ordinary, so banal?

Elisabeth paired Arendt's question of societal indifference with William F. Buckley's book, *The Unmaking of a Mayor*—a snapshot of America's political atmosphere in the mid-1960s. To Elisabeth, both illustrated "the utter impossibility of persuading people of the truth. Truth is simply not of interest to the general public."[3]

Around the same time Elisabeth extolled the writing of novelist and cultural critic Susan Sontag. "Am reading Susan Sontag's *Against Interpretation* and to encounter such power of logic and flawless expression makes me ask what in heaven's name I think I can do as a writer! Why not pack in and leave the field to the experts? Then of course I can glance at the evangelical field and wince. Leave them? Without a voice or a vision?

"I do not want to be shut up to them, so I will keep trying as hard as I can to learn from people like Sontag and [Mary] McCarthy . . . and to write what I see. So help me, God!"

In addition to her roots in Scripture, Elisabeth was deeply affected by these secular writers she admired. As she grew older, she would not necessarily agree with their progressive conclusions. But in the late '60s, she felt that "worldly" writers, those she had grown up perceiving as skewed and dangerous, often observed things more honestly than Christian writers who could not seem to produce work that did not further a preconceived agenda, one that made God look good.

Thus fueled, Elisabeth sought to "speak truth" as she wrote her book about what she had seen in Jerusalem in the fall of 1967.

It would not go well for her.

The temperature in Franconia was not particularly Middle Eastern. It was -34 degrees outside, with two feet of snow cloaking Elisabeth's property. She stoked her fire and set her mind toward Jerusalem. She rolled dozens of 3 x 5 index cards into her manual typewriter with various topic titles like: "history," "religion," "mystique," "Israeli attitudes," "Arab attitudes," "definitions," and "problems of the new state." Her goal was to write five pages a day. Her manuscript was due to her publisher, Harper, at the end of April.

Elisabeth felt the constipation of mind that usually accompanied her writing. What made this writing blockage worse was the fact that the material was not compelling to her. She knew what she had seen in Israel; it was simply a matter of getting her words on paper. But, as she wrote in her journal, "The Jerusalem book does not always interest, let alone inspire, me."

She was far more voluble regarding her observations of blossoming teenager Valerie Elliot, who had turned thirteen in February.

"Val hit a new peak in absurdity in her efforts to conform. I had given her a little Tupperware container with a canned peach in it, with a spoon, in her lunch bag . . . When she came home, she explained she had been unable to eat her dessert, because no one—ever—had been known to bring a plastic container with fruit in it for his dessert. Oh, you could bring an apple or an orange or a piece of cake all right, but a peach? In juice? With a spoon? Mommie!!"

"Dear Val! She told me . . . she is going to change her life —i.e., study harder, practice more faithfully, be on time, be more careful, etc."

"Val spends an hour putting up her hair at night and rinses her mouth in the morning with Listerine . . . She announced last night that she no longer likes Ronnie, and that 'a lot of kids liked my new loafers.'"

Still, "She is at the age where the most important thing in life is conformity to her peers. Hair must be worn in the ugliest fashion possible, or 'all the kids will say, 'Oh Val Elliot thinks she's so great.' Clothes must be precisely the same cut, fit, style, color, etc. as everyone else's. Books can be carried only in the arms, lunches must be taken in paper bags, never in a lunch box, parka hoods never worn up, even if it's -50 degrees, gloves cannot be mittens . . . It is comforting only to remember that this is a <u>stage</u> (God help us all if it isn't!) and the less said, the better.

"'These ski pants are too baggy, Mommy.' (Baggy? They look as though she couldn't sit down in them, they're so tight.) 'Yes, <u>baggy</u>. <u>Look</u> at them. Can't you SEE that they're BAGGY?' Well. All this makes me remember . . . what it was like growing up. Oh dear, such agonies. Mothers NEVER understand! But each generation must suffer alone, and there's an end to it."[4]

"Oh, Mommy!" Val burst out at her mother. "You control my whole life, and I don't like it!"

Even as they had their misunderstandings, Elisabeth and Val were close. Val loved the sense of order, beauty, appreciation for music, art, and literature that her mother instilled in her. She thrived on Elisabeth's sense of adventure—after all, mother and daughter had lived in exotic jungle conditions that Val's classmates could only read about in books—and loved her mom's deep love of nature.

As spring unfolded, Elisabeth and Val climbed up to Bridal Veil Falls, a popular hiking trail not far from their home in Franconia. At a shelter, they cooked supper of freeze-dried meat and beans, bread and butter, tea, and dried fruit. They brushed their teeth in the racing, icy brook. They climbed into their sleeping bags and "slept with the perfume of spruce in our nostrils and the roar of the brook in our ears. It rained a little in the night, but we cooked breakfast just under the edge of the roof—buttermilk pancakes, coffee, brown sugar and butter." Then they packed up their stuff, hiked down to where Elisabeth had left her car, and made it home by 9 a.m., "in time to do our Saturday cleaning."[5] Of course.

Chores aside, Elisabeth was deeply affected by beauty, whether in nature, the fine arts, dance, or music.

"I suppose that the effect of beauty on one's soul is as important and as imperceptible as the effect of sunshine, but how deprived we would be if we had neither," she wrote in her journal. "Yesterday I lay on the sofa for 15 minutes in the afternoon sunshine which floods the living room and listened to that beautiful piano rendition of Adieu Madraz, by Don Shirley. I cannot describe what it does to me.

"Last night there was a huge full moon, illuminating the whole snow-filled outdoors. The shadows of the evergreens in front of the house lay pure and transparent across the glowing snow."

One cold, clear day, with ice and snow still patching the green woods, Elisabeth hiked alone to the Eliza Brook shelter, a wooden lean-to just off the Appalachian Trail outside of Franconia. Someone had scrawled on the wooden wall, "God was here." They were right about that, thought Elisabeth. She ate her lunch in the sun, sitting on the edge of the shelter floor. She built a fire to dry her shoes, and sat for two hours, relishing the quiet. Her faithful dog Zippy "scoured the woods, checking back every ten minutes or so to make sure I was where I belonged. He is such a nice companion—he just loves to go on such trips and seems to revel in the smells as he pushes his vacuum-cleaner nose along every inch of ground."[6]

What is missing from both Elisabeth's rich journal and her family letters in the first half of 1968 are any reflections, large or small, on one Addison Leitch. It is as if Elisabeth decided to rigorously omit Dr. Leitch from her paper trail until such time—should it ever come—that they could freely explore their attraction to one another.

CHAPTER 20

Things as They Are

*"But we will never try to allure anyone to think of coming
by painting coloured pictures, when the facts are in black
and white. What if black and white will never attract like
colours? We care not for it; our business is to tell the truth.
The work is not a pretty thing, to be looked at and admired.
It is a fight. And battlefields are not beautiful."*
—Amy Carmichael

One night the phone rang, and when Elisabeth picked it up, "a <u>man's</u>
voice asked to speak with Val." He was a kid from the local high
school, but it made Elisabeth realize, with a shock, that her daughter
was growing up.

"I find myself passionately longing for the smell and feel and look
and strength of a man. I want to be held, protected, cherished, loved.

"Well, who doesn't. But sometimes one asks for all this, even
though heaven is all that's promised."

Aside from the promise of heaven, Elisabeth consoled herself with
books and writing. She wrote to her family, "Was rereading Amy
Carmichael's biography today and was interested to find that she
had difficulties with her publishers because she told it too straight.
Couldn't she soften it a bit? Did she realize what she might do to the
cause? It hadn't occurred to her to ask what the public wanted. She
simply wanted to tell the truth. She was accused of painting 'only the
dark side.' Rather than change *Things as They Are* she left the [manu-
script] in a drawer until some visitors asked if they could take it to a
publisher in England who would be willing to do it without revision."[1]

Within a few weeks of her book's publication in 1903, Amy
Carmichael received letters from missionaries all over India, confirming

the truths shown in *Things as They Are*. But some readers back in England, accustomed to stories of victory and triumph, doubted its veracity. So the fourth edition of the book is prefaced affirming quotes from respected *male* missionaries. Amy's readership multiplied.

Amy didn't paint mission work as gloriously victorious. "Humdrum we have called the work, and humdrum it is. . . . dear friends, do not . . . expect to hear of us doing great things, as an everyday matter of course. Our aim is great—it is India for Christ! . . . [but] do not expect every true story to . . . end with some marvelous coincidence or miraculous conversion. Most days in real life end exactly as they began, as far as visible results are concerned. . . . I read a missionary story 'founded on fact' the other day, and the things that happened in that story on these lines were most remarkable. They do not happen here. Practical missionary life is an unexciting thing. It is not sparkling all over with incident. It is very prosaic at times."[2]

Elisabeth had felt the same way in the jungle among the Waodani.

And now, in her calling as a writer, Elisabeth had undertaken the same task as her hero . . . simply to tell what she had seen and heard in Jerusalem, to tell "things as they were" from her own perspective. "I am to bear witness to what I know, and this is as sacred a trust in the case of my observations in Jerusalem as among the [Waodani] (to them, and to the public about them)." She did not want preconceived notions, or emotions, to blur the issues.

Elisabeth wrote that whenever sentimentality comes into play, "it becomes nearly impossible to get at real issues. We have read books, seen films, and visited memorials which inform us of the sufferings of the Jews." The horrifying evidences of the Holocaust "disable us," she continued. To raise any serious question about the ethics of Zionism is to arouse cries of "anti-Semite!" or accusations of utter lack of human sympathy or sensibility. Few of us can face such charges.

"But the simple truth," Elisabeth went on, "is that to have undergone a holocaust . . . does not [turn a] person or a nation into saints. They are still human, and must be granted the responsibility of humans." Elisabeth went on to point out that God's charge to the Hebrews was the responsibilities of privilege—looking out for the welfare of the stranger within their gates, to do justice to the foreigner—and warned them that His promises were contingent upon their obedience.

On the most basic question of all, "who is a Jew?" Elisabeth could find no solid answers. Many of her interviewees simply shrugged: "Ask three Jews, get five opinions."

In a later *Christianity Today* article, Elisabeth summarized her search for answers.

"It is not, Israel officially proclaims, a *racial* question. There are Jews in every anthropologically-defined "race"—from the black Ethiopian to the Chinese orthodox Jew.

"It is not a *religious* question. Probably fewer than ten percent of Israelis are orthodox Jews, and many are not only not religious, but are militantly anti-God.

"To be Jewish is not a *linguistic* question. Over seventy languages are spoken in Israel, even though Hebrew is the official language and strong efforts are made to encourage everybody to learn it.

"It is not a *cultural* question. Some Jews, desperately casting about for a definition that would satisfy me, said that Jewishness is a "cultural consciousness." But what culture? Elisabeth had seen keening eastern Jewish women in Arab dress, Jews from New York's East Side, Russian Jews, and Israeli natives born on kibbitzes. There were clearly no common denominators in terms of rituals, speech, dress, or outlook.

"Is Jewishness then a *political* category?" Elisabeth continued. "Israel is a political state, but there are millions of Jews who are not Israelis. There are thousands of "Israelis" who are not Jews—every Arab now "assimilated" into the nation of Israel by conquest is officially an Israeli . . ." At the time the Israeli government defined Jews genetically, which to Elisabeth seemed a strange contradiction when they so vehemently deny that Jewishness has anything to do with race. But the determining question is, "'Who is your mother?' Anyone born of a Jewish mother is Jewish. The question as to what makes her Jewish has no answer. If your father is Jewish, if he is even a rabbi, it will not help you at all."[3]

"I have come to the conclusion that it remains for Israel; alone to execute justice for those who are its responsibility. If its highways must cut through the Arabs' desert, if it claims 'eminent domain,' it must justly compensate those who have been displaced, those whose empty houses and lands Israel is now determined to fill with its own immigrants.

"Quite apart from whether or not the people of modern Israel can lay claim to the title of 'chosen,' or whether the land promised to the ancient Israelites justly belongs to them, it is hard to see how 'redemption' can be spoken of at all without full regard for righteousness and justice."

She quoted from the Old Testament prophet Jeremiah: "Thus says the LORD of hosts, the God of Israel, Amend your ways . . . if you truly execute justice one with another, if you do not oppress the alien, the fatherless or the widow, or shed innocent blood to this place and if you do not go after other gods to your own hurt, then I will let you dwell in this place, in the land that I gave of old to your fathers for ever."[4]

Elisabeth was not unmindful of the immense complexities of the geo-political and cultural situation. She knew that her vision was narrow at best. She knew that only God Himself could see clearly and judge wholly. To change the metaphor Elisabeth wrote that Jerusalem and its people "is a box in which the pieces from a hundred puzzles have been mixed, and the task of sorting them out and putting them in their proper relationships to each other is one that only God would have the courage to undertake, for it is a task requiring both perfect wisdom and perfect love."

She finished writing *Furnace of the Lord* on April 20, 1968, at midnight.

She sent a copy of the manuscript to her dear, old friend, Cornell Capa.

He called her back in just a few days. He was livid. It was "a very unfair book. Heavily weighted against Israel. Mixed up, biased, and inaccurate."

Cornell further told Elisabeth the book needed a major overhaul, an interview with the Israeli ambassador in Washington, and a trip to New York. He was willing to come to Franconia for deep conversations with her. He was not, however, interested in anything Elisabeth had to say on the phone.

"I let him talk (not that I had much choice—and oddly enough, I had never asked for his opinion to begin with), thanked him, and sent off the [manuscript] with only slight changes yesterday."

"I keep pondering the phenomenon of Cornell. He has been of inestimable help in the writing of my other books. He has always (so far as I recall) won every argument with me except when he wanted to sleep with me.

"I take his criticisms seriously, and not to have managed to please him bothers me a great deal. I suppose the truth is that I love him, in a quiet, healthy and rather resigned sort of way. I appreciate what he is, and I can never disregard what he has done for me.

"But in this case it is hardly to be wondered at that he is upset by my book. What one is determines what he sees. He accused me of 'preselecting' my data. Nothing could be further from the truth. And what, pray, has nearly every other writer on Israel done? If the book is 'unfair' in his opinion, it is one man's opinion. I have put down what I saw."

Cornell wrote to Elisabeth, "I feel very badly about the final deadline having snuck upon us without a chance to talk. As always, I wish to be proud having taken some part in your doings. This has become an exception."[5]

In late May 1968 Elisabeth attended an evangelical THINK conference, which elicited her usual reactions to such gatherings. She wrote to her family on the list of male ministry and church leaders who deigned to grace the offensive site with their presence. They discussed such topics as church growth, mission financing, publicity, recruiting, financing, glossolalia, cultural adaptation, in terms of what to do about "polygamy, drum-beating, beer-drinking, the wearing of clothes . . ." Elisabeth noted that "I kept my mouth shut most of the time, but I did ask a few questions and offer[ed] a few illustrations."[6]

In her journal she ranted, "There are so many points at which I want to yell, 'Wait! Think what it is you're saying!' So many truths which I think I see clearly, which don't appear at all to these men. And they are disturbed by my presence (what might I write?) and my questions (why bring that up?) and I feel at the same time that I ought to shut up altogether and/or get up on a housetop and shout!

"These men are conscious of power. They move men in order to move nations in order to move God—to DO SOMETHING. Each has his road company, his show, his production."

By the beginning of June, Elisabeth had spent a month waiting for her publisher's final approval of *Furnace of the Lord*. Silence. She entertained herself with dark visions of having to do the entire book over from scratch.

On the night of June 4, 1968, Robert Kennedy won the California Democratic presidential primary. Just after midnight on the morning of June 5, he addressed supporters at the Ambassador Hotel in Los Angeles. Aides were escorting him through the hotel kitchen to an impromptu press conference.

Kennedy made his way through a narrow passageway. A seventeen-year-old busboy in a white jacket caught Senator Kennedy's eye. He'd served the senator a meal earlier that day. The senator recognized the teenager and stopped to shake his hand.

Suddenly, a dark-haired man with a gun stepped out and lunged toward Kennedy. He shot him three times and sprayed bullets into the crowd until he was tackled by the senator's aides and friends, five of whom were wounded.

One journalist snapped the photo that became the iconic image of the day: Senator Kennedy is splayed on his back, his legs at odd angles. The young busboy, Juan Romero, in his white service jacket, squats by Kennedy's side. His face is blurred with confusion as he cradles his hero's broken head. He's already ripped his rosary out of his pocket and placed it in Kennedy's open palm. Kennedy's eyes are open; he is still alive.

The shooter, a Palestinian radical named Sirhan Sirhan, would later say that he shot Robert Kennedy because the senator had supported Israel in the Arab-Israeli War of 1967.

"June 5. 8:00 a.m.," Elisabeth jotted in her journal. "TV is on, reporting on shooting of Bobby Kennedy. He's still in the operating room, six neurosurgeons working to remove bullet from brain."

Robert Kennedy survived that surgery, but his condition was grave. Twenty-six hours after the shooting, he died, his wife and other family members by his side. He was forty-two, one year older than Elisabeth.

For many young people, particularly in the wake of Martin Luther King's death, Kennedy had represented their last hope for social justice, racial tolerance, and an end to the war in Vietnam.

As after the assassination of John Kennedy, Elisabeth felt pain and deep empathy for Bobby Kennedy's widow. She understood the horror of the sudden, violent loss of a beloved and charismatic man. But in Elisabeth's journal, Kennedy's death is coupled with a far different kind of loss. Perhaps blinded by the overwhelming feeling that the human experience is far too full of deaths and losses, both large and small, Elisabeth coupled the death of Robert Kennedy with her publisher's rejection of her book manuscript.

"June 6. Well, I suppose there is some significance in this volume's ending with the death (this morning at 1:44 Pacific time) of Bobby Kennedy, and with my receipt of an utterly demolishing letter from Harper about *Furnace*.

"It's an old familiar song. 'You didn't see it right.' They give me complete freedom to go, look, listen, learn, and write what I see. Then they tell me, 'No, you should have told it this way.'"

A publishing executive had written the official letter, but Elisabeth felt "nearly positive that Cornell [was] behind it all—he must have contacted" the powers that be.

"I must see this thing very clearly. Am I being crucified for being a truthteller, or merely getting what I deserve for a poor job?"

"I am of course depressed, almost despairing. I have felt the axe. Who wants this? Why do I stick my neck out? Why not write nice things, popular, positive, 'helpful' things? O dear God—because I simply don't <u>see</u> things the 'right' way at the right time!

"Suppose the editors are right?

"Suppose, however, I am?

"Is Harper manipulating or enlightening me????

"So again I find myself in a wilderness of doubt," Elisabeth concluded. She had already felt like a beat-up oddball by the fact that *No Graven Image* offended church leaders to the point where her speaking engagements in such settings had dried up. She thought about her struggles with editors, publishers, and others on various books that she'd written, how she seemed to constantly be at odds with religious people at large.

"In the end God shall be wholly and absolutely God. (1 Cor. 15:28). What a prospect!"

CHAPTER 21

"I Simply Boggle"

"If only now I could recall that touch,
First touch of hand in hand—Did one but know!"
—Christina Rossetti

For some of us, it sounds tone deaf for Elisabeth to compare Robert Kennedy's death to her publisher's rejection of her book about Jerusalem. But we needn't give damning weight to what people include or don't include in their private journals. Most of us would cringe and shrivel at the thought of our personal jottings revealed against the immense backdrop of human history.

But what her remark does show us is the pain of her publisher's— and Cornell's—rejection of her work. It felt like death to her. And it felt like yet another case where she had come up against the religious establishment's "right way to tell the story," rather than the conclusions that she had drawn based on her own insights.

A few years later, Elisabeth would write a long piece for *Christianity Today* about what she thought happened with her book about Jerusalem. "Sentimentality is an idol. It has eyes but sees not. It stands in the place of truth. To raise any question at all nowadays about the ethics of Zionism or the nature of Israel (is it, for example, a racist state? Is there religious freedom there? Is their treatment of the Arab just?), to ask, 'Who is a Jew?' is to arouse cries of anti-Semitism. . . . To ask for sympathy or for even a moment's cool consideration of the Arab is to be branded at once as an opponent of Israel."[1]

When Elisabeth tried to get answers from Harper & Row about why the publisher was now rejecting her book, she got only one. "'You have treated a sensitive subject insensitively.' My observations, it turned out, were 'controversial,' not because I had taken sides but because I had not taken sides."

This treatment cut at the heart of what Elisabeth Elliot held dear in those fractious days of 1968: her freedom and ability to "speak truth" as she saw it. Again, as so many times in the past, she felt squelched by religious and commercial institutions that wanted her voice, but only if she parroted the party line.

Meanwhile, she "learned . . . of two instances in which it was claimed that Elisabeth Elliot has lost her faith." Then her friend Van was told that there was a rumor making its way through missionary communities in Africa, that Elisabeth was a Unitarian, that she had married again, and that her similarly heretical brother had "the same different ideas" that she had.

In the middle of that fractious summer, however, Elisabeth's pre-occupations suddenly shifted from rumors about her faith, concerns about *Furnace*, or anything else. She got the news that Addison Leitch's valiant wife, Margaret, had passed away on July 16. Elisabeth had closed a door in her mind to her feelings about Addison and any possibilities for their future together.

Now, however, the door stood open.

At the end of July, Elisabeth had been scheduled to speak at a writing workshop and conference at Judson College (now Judson University) in Elgin, Illinois, a short drive from Wheaton College. Addison Leitch met her there. Lunches, dinners. They went to see the film *Thoroughly Modern Millie* in Wheaton. They said goodbye on Thursday morning, August 2, and she boarded a TWA flight to New York.

Within a few days after that there were flurries of letters and phone calls. This was in a time before cell phones, when "long-distance" calls were a luxury for the frugal Elisabeth. For once in her life, she didn't think about saving money. She thought about Addison Leitch.

"I am incapacitated for work," she wrote. "I cannot sleep at night, have lost five pounds, am 'sick' with love. What a mysterious phenomenon."

Addison Leitch, like Elisabeth Elliot, was a gifted writer. His style is more fluid; he agonized less over his writing process and was more content to let it flow. His surviving letters show a winsome, witty, self-deprecating, and insightful man, a man with a certain comfort, but not pride, in his own skin.

Sadly, if his correspondence with Elisabeth Elliot still exists, it is not in a realm available to this biographer. Perhaps that's a relief—at one point elsewhere, Elisabeth wrote admiringly of Addison's "steaming" love letters to her, and such content may be more than any of us really want to peruse.

Elisabeth wrote, "To pray [that] God keep me from going [awry] with a thing that seems so miraculously of Him to begin with seems an odd course to take. How can He led me into temptation? Temptation to evil? If it's evil, why did He lead me there? If it's not evil it's not temptation that must be resisted. The Lord 'redeemeth thy life from destruction'—can I count on that?

"How like my first love experience this one is, with the risks and sacrifices and pitfalls and discipline involved. But oh God, what a thing, what an unutterable thing it is to be <u>recognized</u>. To know a perfect <u>response</u>, to be valued and missed and adored. I simply boggle. It can't be happening."

On August 14 she wrote in her journal, "Phone call came at about 9 a.m. yesterday. References to the big issue (working toward it), wanting to be face to face when time came to discuss it—not by letter.

"I was awake in the night, wondering, dreaming, doubting (e.g., where to live, what Val's reaction might be), remembering. One thing leaves <u>no</u> doubt in my mind—I love him.

"Another call just now . . . I think maybe we can open the door about Christmas time."

Elisabeth and Addison had decided to marry. Their "engagement," such as it was, would be secret until December. They planned to let their families know then, and would inform their wider sphere of friends, colleagues, and the public only after the ceremony had taken place.

Meanwhile, Elisabeth was like a love-struck girl on the inside, and her usual steely self on the outside. She thought endlessly about their time together in Wheaton.

"Two weeks ago today we were still together. Seems two years. Incredible what can happen to one's soul [in such a short amount of time]."

Elisabeth and her siblings and parents had circulated family letters for decades. They would type using an ancient invention called carbon paper. Sheets of tissue-thin paper were inserted between sheets of regular white paper. The carbon tissue would register the impact of the manual typewriter keys, making smudgy blue copies for the recipients. Personal computers, printers, and copying machines were far in the future for ordinary American consumers.

Given her giddy, life-altering love for Addison Leitch, Elisabeth rather duplicitously wrote to her family in the fall of '68, "I know I've not been terribly conscientious about writing family letters, but it seems sort of nugatory to sit down with eight carbons unless one has something to say, which I still haven't."[2]

She went on to write about how much Val was enjoying high school, and that she had a "boyfriend," which Elisabeth explained at this point meant "someone whose name she writes on book covers, and whom she looks for at football games. I guess he sort of looks for her, too, but that's as far as it goes."

Whenever Elisabeth traveled, she would bring Valerie a "small surprise." Val always looked forward to a scarf, or stationery, or whatever fun gift her mother had brought back for her. Late one night in the fall of 1968, Elisabeth returned home to Franconia, where Van, as always, had been with Val while Elisabeth was on the road. Val groggily heard her mother come home and went back to sleep. The next morning, Val bounced into her mother's bedroom. Uncharacteristically, Elisabeth was still in bed, sitting propped up against the pillow. "Do you have a small surprise for me?" asked Val.

"No," said Elisabeth. "I have a big surprise." Val looked around; she could see no bright box or bag in sight.

Elisabeth smiled. "I'm getting married." Val stared at her mom for a second, mouth open, shocked. Then she burst into tears.

Elisabeth jumped up to hug her daughter. "Why are you crying?" she asked.

Val shook her head, totally confused. "Well, it's not something to laugh about!" she said. She had no idea just *who* her mother was going to marry.

"You've met him," Elisabeth went on. "Do you remember the older man, the professor, who came to supper? You liked him. That's the man I'm going to marry."

Val calmed down. In her thirteen-year-old brain, it was hard to switch from her world of cute boys in the halls at school to her mother's dusty grown-up world of far-away travels and pipe-smoking professors. But over the past few years, she had seen her friends with their fathers and had thought how nice it would be to have a dad. She could not remember her own father; Jim was killed when Val was just ten months old.

"He's going to be your stepfather," Elisabeth went on, as if she was reading Val's mind. "But you don't have to call him 'Daddy.'"

Val's cheeks got pink. Wow. This *was* a big surprise.

"One last thing," said Elisabeth. "This is a secret. You cannot tell *anyone.*"

Few of us would trust a thirteen-year-old girl with such a secret, but as we've seen, Elisabeth was an unusual mother.

Val got her books, coat, and school stuff together, her mouth firmly shut as if the secret would pop right out if she wasn't careful. The long yellow school bus arrived. She climbed aboard and took a seat by her friend Jane. They settled in for the ride.

"So," said Jane, out of the blue, "Has your mom gotten married yet?"

Auuuggghhh! thought Val. *Why was God testing her resolve so soon? This was crazy.*

Still, she thought, *there was a way of escape. After all, her mom wasn't remarried. Yet.*

"Nope," she said. "Are you ready for the math quiz?"

Soon after that, Val got a letter in the mail.

October 1, 1968

Dear Val,

Your mother has told <u>me</u> that she has told <u>you</u> about <u>us</u>. So now you know the great news and I hope you sense how supremely happy we are. And we are both anxious to have you happy about it too.

On my last visit to your home I had something of an advantage over you because I was in on the secret. So I was studying you, I guess, a little more carefully than you were studying me. My, how I liked and enjoyed what I saw—your looks, your manners, the way you talked, and especially your good taste in clothes. You have style—in all kinds of ways!

So we'll be around each other now for what I hope will be a long, long time. I'm pretty bashful myself and I suspect you are too so I suppose we are both wondering how to treat each other. . . . One thing though: we both are living inside the wonderful love of your mother so I suppose that puts us in the same place to start off with, and the rest should be easy.

So sit loose. I am really very easy to get along with. I don't plan to storm the castle. But you can be very sure of this: my arms are wide open whenever you feel like walking into them, and I shall delight to hold you to my heart.

Affectionately, Addison Leitch

Within a month or so, the rest of Elisabeth's family knew the news.

Tom Howard was first, of course. He and Elisabeth had a special bond, and he lived in the same literary and academic circles as Addison Leitch. His letter to Addison captures both Tom's unique way of expressing himself and his deep understanding of his older sister.

"Well—I wish I could tell you how it makes me feel to know that once again [Elisabeth] will have the experience of romantic love—or already has it, rather, and will know the kind of blessing that is unique to married love. It's not really a mere 'once again,' though. It's unique and vast and thrilling and makes me want to dance with joy.

"You know better than I (I'll bet) what a passionate, sexual woman she is. Over the years how many times I've wanted to say to people who only knew her from her platform and public demeanor, 'Gadzooks man—you don't know that woman at all. She can <u>laugh</u> more joyously than anyone I know, and she can <u>cook</u>, and she can participate in an experience more fully than anyone I know—<u>any</u> experience—a glass of wine, a picnic, a woodland hike, a concert, the sight of another's candor or grief or courage or good will. . . . And she's a <u>woman</u>, man—she's a woman.'

"The irony of her having all these years apart from the love of a man has often assailed me . . . But now—Lord! I get carried away imagining the capacity for joy and love being brought from both sides to this rather breathtaking transaction."[3]

The "breathtaking transaction" would be sealed on January 1, 1969, at a small wedding in New York City.

In December Elisabeth wrote to her mother, "Thanks so very much for your letter, expressing your gladness for me. And it was nice of you to write to Add. . . . Yes, I agree that it is a good idea for him to call you Katharine. It's funny—he has a daughter named Katherine, and one named Elizabeth, and he calls me Elisabeth rather than any of my nicknames. I like this very much. . . . His wife's name was Margaret, and she too was never called by any nickname.[4]

Elisabeth went on to tell her mother about her honeymoon, a week at the Plaza Hotel in New York. "Neither of us has the slightest desire to go places and do things at this juncture. It is such an unbelievable resurrection for both of us, all we want is to be together in peace."

"Add is what I would call a very attractive man. He might pose for those 'men of distinction' [a 1950s advertising campaign featuring distinguished-looking male models], except that there isn't a weak line anywhere on him, and some of those men look vapid."[5]

Add was a "marvelous, loving, gentle, sensitive, thoughtful, powerful, intelligent man, and I am simply wildly and irretrievably in love with him! He is what Jim might have been with 32 years more of suffering and experience and learning. Add has suffered in many ways, and of course this is one of the things which first drew me to him. His wife had cancer for 11 years, he himself has been absolutely crucified by the Presbyterian Establishment for not toeing the party line, and he has had the heartache of having a child born with hydrocephalus and spina bifida. She lived for two months."[6]

Addison wrote to Elisabeth's mother.

"I am sure that you must wonder what kind of a character you are welcoming into the family and you certainly are good to give me such assurances with so little to work on. Elisabeth is in love and so somewhat untrustworthy in her estimate of me . . . So don't expect too much; I am just such a one as rejoices because he has come into the Howard orbit and especially within the love and grace of your wonderful daughter.

"My, what a family you have raised up—linguists, pioneers, writers, heroes. Elisabeth thinks Tom is a genius and I think Elisabeth is a genius. . . . Well, my claim to fame is that I love Elisabeth, truly, gladly, with my whole heart. . . . I shall certainly be looking forward to being with you.

"Most sincerely, Add"[7]

Elisabeth's next letter to her mother was more breathless. "Three weeks from today! I can hardly wait. In fact, I can hardly stand it. Can you imagine that, at 42? And to hear Add talk on the phone, or to read his masterpieces of love letters, it's worse at 60! 'I bleed,' he says."[8]

CHAPTER 22

Take Me!

*"ELISABETH ELLIOT WEDS OBSCURE
THEOLOGIAN"*
—fake newspaper headline created by Dick Kennedy,
Addison Leitch's best friend

On January 1, 1969, Elisabeth Howard Elliot married Addison Hardie Leitch in a small medieval-looking side-chapel of Manhattan's Brick Presbyterian Church. It was a very different ceremony than her 10-minute civil marriage to Jim Elliot in Quito in 1953.

Wearing a pink silk dress and carrying a single rose, Valerie Elliot served as maid of honor. Add's brother, Robert Leitch, was best man. The Reverend Richard K. Kennedy, the groom's best friend, conducted the ceremony along with the Brick Church's minister. Elisabeth was escorted down the aisle by her brother, Tom Howard. Tom wrote later, "I have never—repeat never—seen [Elisabeth] look so beautiful as she did for the wedding. Stunning is the word. . . . She had on a simple, straight light blue coat and dress ensemble of heavy silk . . . a blue bow on the back of her hair."[1] (Cornell Capa took photographs of the event . . . but sadly, these seem to have been lost or destroyed over the years.)

Dave Howard surprised everyone by showing up at the last minute from Wheaton. He met his new brother-in-law at the reception. "Add is a very impressive looking man," he wrote to the rest of the family, "and most amiable and easy to become acquainted with. I have been greatly impressed for years with his writings and am so happy for both of them."[2]

Addison, questioning his best friend Richard Kennedy before the ceremony, had asked if Dr. Kennedy would pronounce that he and Elisabeth were "husband and wife" or "man and wife."

"Husband," Dr. Kennedy replied.

"That's good," said Addison. "I don't need anyone to pronounce me a man."

Dick Kennedy had written Elisabeth before the wedding, speaking with love about his old friend. "I have never known Add to be so exuberantly enthusiastic about anything," he said. "He is a buoyant soul, as you know, but he has never been so eager or bouncy about anything as he is about [your marriage]. It is sheer delight to see him this way."

In addition, Dick had counseled Elisabeth that Add did not need to explain this marriage or its timing to anyone. Evidently referring to the amount of time between Margaret Leitch's death and Add's marriage to Elisabeth, he wrote, "The people who ask questions about it will not be his friends. The timing is certainly in God's hands along with everything else."[3]

Christianity Today reported on the wedding, "One of evangelicalism's few full-time women writers, Mrs. Leitch, 43, is well known for her missionary books, including *Through Gates of Splendor* and *Shadow of the Almighty*, her controversial novel *No Graven Image*, and her biography of Kenneth Strachan, *Who Shall Ascend?* Her seventh book [*Furnace of the Lord*, which had been picked up by Doubleday after its rejection by Harper & Row], is scheduled for spring."

"The Leitches first met in 1966 when a mutual friend invited her to speak at Tarkio College, where Leitch has been distinguished professor of theology and religion and assistant to the president. Later, he invited her to lecture on the Book of Job.

"Leitch, 60, whose wife of more than thirty years died last year after a long struggle with cancer, is presently on leave from Tarkio. The former president of Pittsburgh Xenia Theological Seminary has been a frequent contributor to *Christianity Today*, beginning with an article in its first issue and continuing as a columnist. For more than three years he was the anonymous scribe Eutychus II. In addition to teaching and lecturing, he has written five books and is working on a sixth."[4]

After a silver, crystal, flowers, cake, coffee, and punch reception at Tom Howard's home, the bride and groom retired to the Plaza Hotel. Elisabeth's journal reads, "My wedding day . . . [a man] willing to take unto himself a woman, and to come to her with all he is and has and say, 'I'm yours—take me!'"

The rest of the page is decisively cut out of the journal.

Once Elisabeth and Addison breathlessly arrived home to Franconia, "now we pray for guidance as to where Add will teach. Show us, Lord —You who are Wonderful Counselor."

They had already decided that they would prefer to be on the East Coast rather than the Midwest. According to his proud wife, Add had already received offers of the presidencies of eight colleges. He also turned down the presidency of Fuller Seminary and the editorship of *Christianity Today*. He loved students; he loved the dynamics of the classroom rather than the challenges of administration. Addison was adamant that his wife continue to grow and flourish in her writing life, and they both felt confident that God would open His doors for Addison on the East Coast.

"Happy in our marriage," Elisabeth wrote in her journal in February. "Add is wonderfully thoughtful and desirous of pleasing me. He understands me amazingly well."

Understandably, she was "finding it exceedingly hard to <u>work</u>. <u>Christian Herald</u> wants regular contributions. <u>Practical Anthropology</u> wants a review. I want to do a novel. I have a drawer full of stuff I keep 'MEANING' to work on. My reading falls sadly behind. Am on to Faulkner now (<u>As I Lay Dying</u>) and some of his short stories. God help me to produce—for His glory—or, as Faulkner puts it, to 'uplift men's hearts.'"

At the end of February, forty-five inches of snow fell on the top of Mt. Washington within twenty-four hours. In early March, the Leitch marriage encountered its first significant chill, a challenge in the form of a visitor named Hans Bürki.

Elisabeth had known Hans since her Wheaton College days. Associated with Inter-Varsity's (IV) ministry among college students in Europe, he came to the United States in the summer of 1947 to attend an IV conference. He then stayed at Wheaton, serving as a graduate assistant in the German department in the winter term of the 1947 academic year. He had been a friend of Jim's, and later wrote the preface for the German edition of Elisabeth's book *Through Gates of Splendor*. He was an academic and philosopher whose mind soared to sometimes inaccessible heights as he omnivorously explored the Scriptures, Freud, H. G. Wells, Oscar Wilde, secular historians, social scientists, avant-garde artists, and culture at large. In other words, his was a mind that appealed to Elisabeth Elliot.

Elisabeth had evidently corresponded with him in late 1967; he had invited her to visit him in Switzerland on her way home from Israel. After she had accepted his offer, he scribbled a strange note to her, which she received at the American Colony Hotel in Jerusalem.

". . . it is just before midnight . . . The letter is in the box. With affection and true love I shall welcome her. What does it mean—to her, to me? Something different? I would embrace her at the airport, kiss her as I do with some—some women who have my highest esteem.

But she is a widow—but she is the widow of my friend—and <u>she</u> is free . . .

"I would like to <u>be</u> with her, to show her something of my country, drive up into the mountains in solitude, snow, sun, a day and a winter night. This may be too much again. Show her, introduce her to some of my best friends, have fellowship. Introduce her to my <u>best</u> friend, my wife, the children. Shall I be able?

". . . What does it mean? . . . [Elisabeth] accepted my invitation and we shall meet. True love? May it be true, may it be love. May we be ready."[5]

Elisabeth didn't journal about her reactions to this letter. But she must have held it close. "What will it be to see Hans?" she wondered as she flew above the Mediterranean, away from the warm desert colors of light and shadow toward the pristine landscapes of the Alps.

After the visit, she wrote about it in her journal. "The time with Hans was truly a foretaste of paradise.

"He gave me his slow, sweet smile thru the glass doors of the airport as I waited for my baggage, then greeted me with both hands and a kiss. To his friend's widow's house for lunch... a wholesome meal, rich homemade soup; Prisca is a lovely woman, with an essential femininity, a directness and simplicity. After the three of us had had coffee in the living room Hans left us alone and we talked of widowhood, rearing children alone, the need of men to associate with the children.

"Then Hans took me on tour of Zurich . . . Castle on a hillside, black and white St. Bernard, a girl like Heidi, and we had hot tea with brown bread, country butter and raw chipped beef on a great round platter. Talked of Hans' life since I saw him nearly 20 years ago. Found in him all I had hoped for—a great warm humanity coupled with a deep spiritual perception and a hunger for God similar to Jim's hunger.

"Then to his home, where I met for the first time his wife Agatha, a Jewess, MD, very bold, straightforward, cordial, sexy (in tight gray sweater and skirt, bare legs and sandals), intelligent—in short, a formidable and friendly woman. And his children—black-haired, apple-cheeked, vibrant. His house teeming with creativity. Books, paintings, sculpture, building blocks, children's crayon drawings, magazine pictures, rock collection, ancient Hungarian furniture, etc.

"Next day touring around . . . castle on the point of a great rock, then to a little house in the woods, overlooking a valley, where he often goes to be alone and write or pray and think. We sat and talked; he spoke so freely of himself and his life, I felt glad and grateful to be thus allowed to know him. Supper at home—cheese fondue and tea by candlelight. . . .

"On the way to airport Saturday morning we stopped by woods, walked along a little road through fir trees where an old man was cutting boughs. Came out into the sunshine in a broad field of snow . . . so lovely. So very lovely.

"Recognition again of a great gift: a true friend. 'He that dwelleth in love dwelleth in God.'"

They said goodbye at the airport, and Elisabeth flew on toward London and home. His next letter to her overflowed with exultation at the "rare and precious knowing" that he had "truly . . . met a human face and heart. . . . I am full of gratitude knowing that no love can be without suffering."[6] He went on in subsequent letters, in between many philosophical effusions, to affirm their true friendship and his gratitude for it.

Now, two years after that visit in Switzerland, Elisabeth was newly married, and her esoteric and once-smitten friend Hans was traveling in the United States. He spent five days as a guest in her home with her new husband. Even someone as socially clueless as Elisabeth might have done well to think twice about this.

"Hans Burki was here from Sat. to Wed (yesterday). It was a severe test of the strength of our marriage. Add found himself jealous of Hans' position in my eyes." He perceived that Hans was "on Elisabeth's wavelength," and felt excluded.

Perhaps this caused him to engage Hans in academic discussions.

"Hans, although very able to argue theologically, did not want to argue or reply to Add's questions (many of which seemed to me wholly rhetorical). For one thing, Hans explained to me, he did not want to exclude me so that the two 'professors' could go at it.

"Add talked too much, did not give Hans a fair chance. Hans saw that I 'suffered' (he told me later) and therefore he suffered. Add also saw that I thought he talked too much. He took issue on logical [grounds] with statements Hans made on inward things e.g., 'We must be free to be ourselves.'"

In addition, said Hans, "We must not condemn ourselves for not <u>doing</u> more. To serve God is to <u>live</u> your life."

This evidently did not sit well with Add, who saw Hans as "a self-centered guest who thought nothing of asking for a second breakfast time, for music after the household had gone to bed, for condensed milk for his avocado."

Elisabeth noted that Hans wanted to speak of the soul, of our own immediate relationships to each other and to God.

"Add countered by quoting . . . his friends, (Whale, Gerstner, [etc.]) his theological idols, by telling stories ('When I was working in boys' camp;' 'When I was at the seminary;' or 'There used to be a fellow who . . .')."

Hans called these anecdotes "an artillery of externals."

Meanwhile, the hapless Elisabeth also came under scrutiny.

"I, in Add's opinion (and Hans') talked too little. Both wished I would enter in more to the conversation. Add cited the lunch he and I had with [friends] in Atlanta. 'Your attitude was 'the hell with it' and you made no effort whatsoever to show them what you are, to convince them that I had good reason to marry you.'"

One can only imagine the byzantine tensions between these three brilliant individuals at the Leitch residence. "I took Hans to the airport alone yesterday," Elisabeth wrote when the excruciating visit finally ended. "At lunch in the Hanover Inn he told me he had in fact fallen in love with me during my visit to Switzerland in 1967."

How Elisabeth might have been surprised by this is no small wonder. But Hans, to his credit, was coherent in his departing words to her.

"He exhorted me to believe in Add, to be patient in hope."

In her journal, she pondered Add's jealousy, and what that might reveal about his own sense of inadequacy and need to be affirmed. We can hope she might have also reflected on what seems to be an unrecognized need of her own to be adored, to be desired, to stir up desires and emotions in men. Maybe her innate view of herself as too tall, too gawky, too unattractive—thanks, in large part, to Jim Elliot's early summations of her face and figure—led her to enjoy stirring up romantic tensions when she could.

Or perhaps not.

"I pray for liberation for Add. For wisdom in knowing how to answer his cross-examinations.

". . . Evening. The above prayer is already being answered. He has 'begun a good work' in both of us. Surely He 'will perform it unto the Day of Jesus Christ.'

"Add told me this afternoon of the pain of trying to accept Hans and my reverence for him, while at the same time knowing things which seemed wholly inconsistent with the image. How would I take Add's having a woman visitor in Hans' position?

"So we talked, then we walked—up the road between the snow-fields in the late winter sunshine, and he told me afresh of his love, his longing to be what I want, his sorrow for past sins, his desire for openness and freedom between us. What a miracle!

"And tonight, a greater one. Upon completing Shadow and Gates he came in to ask if we could pray together. It was a wonderful seal to me of God's promise and blessing upon us, and of the reality of the man, AHL. He is a <u>true</u> man. Humble (imagine his willingness to learn from Jim, Hans, <u>me</u>!) and earnest and hungry. [He told me,] 'I never knew how small a man I was till I married you.'"

She concluded, "And oh, I love him terribly. Yesterday as I was dressing, he came to me, put his arms around me, and said, 'Whatever else you know, darling, whatever happens, remember there was once a guy who <u>adored</u> you!"

After Elisabeth dropped off Hans at the airport for his flight home to Europe and out of their lives, she remembered Add's words. She bent her head over the steering wheel and burst into tears.

CHAPTER 23

Domesticity and Complexity

*"The incarnation took all that properly belongs to our
humanity and delivered it back to us, redeemed. All of our
inclinations and appetites and capacities and yearnings are
purified and gathered up and glorified by Christ. He did
not come to thin out human life; He came to set it free. All
the dancing and feasting and processing and singing and
building and sculpting and baking and merrymaking that
belong to us, and that were stolen away into the service of
false gods, are returned to us in the gospel."*
—Thomas Howard

In March 1969, Addison moved forward on the professional front.
His two favorite options were a position at Dartmouth, or one at
Gordon Conwell Theological Seminary. Elisabeth noted in her journal
on March 20, "Add made his decision today to accept the Gordon
Divinity School offer. He had thought of calling Dartmouth, and
asked God to give him a sign. That Gordon would call before he called
Dartmouth. They did, about 9 a.m."

Under the leadership of Billy Graham, philanthropist J. Howard
Pew, and Elisabeth's sometime-nemesis Dr. Harold John Ockenga,
Gordon Conwell was the newly formed merger of several theological institutions in the northeast. Its vision was to "establish within a
strong evangelical framework, an independent, interdenominational
seminary whose constituents are united in the belief that the Bible is
the infallible, authoritative Word of God . . . consecrated to educating
men and women in all facets of gospel outreach."[1]

Addison would combine his seminary teaching with writing articles for Christian periodicals and books on theological topics. He also

would become one of the seminary's most popular professors. "He'd sit and have coffee with us and we'd talk about manly stuff. We'd all sneak into his classes, even if we weren't registered for them . . . He'd tell outrageous stories, and warn us about pastoring. He'd say, 'Never cry, whine, or call attention to yourself. When I hear a pastor complaining, it reminds me of a boxing match. A guy gets hit, and he goes over to the ref and cries that he got punched. The ref just shakes his head and yells, 'What did you expect?'"[2]

In this season of new marriage, the ever-present Van was living with the Leitches in Franconia, and there were constant guests. Add sometimes remonstrated with Elisabeth about her abrupt ways and lack of connection on social cues. Her journal notes, ruefully, "Tonight long discussion because I had not joined at all in dinner table conversation about the mission field and God's speaking to souls. Van and Add carried on a dialogue. Both had heard me on the subject before. I saw no reason to participate.

"On top of this, I left the table and started washing the dishes when they had finished talking. Then, I simply came on back to my desk and started working—without any explanation to Add of my 'plans for the evening.' Result: he feels completely excluded. I was rude to him, he said later. I am not being companionable. 'I can't understand it,' he repeated. I, for my part, cannot understand people's being affected so by my silence."

One area of adjustment that we need not worry about was their life of intimacy. Elisabeth mercifully eliminated much of the paper trail on this topic, but a few references sprinkled in her journal have survived. "It is a great thing to see a big, strong man sprawled, spent, on a bed. He is a real man who knows what to do and does it! How I thank God for him.

"You are pure delight to me, sweetheart. Fresh every morning!" he says.

"Yesterday afternoon—for the first time—in the sunshine! Soft moss, pine trees, blue sky, small clouds. Oh, ecstasy."

Perhaps outdoor ardor became a habit. In May she wrote, "My heart says, 'Could I love him more, better, than I do? Can he not believe that he fills my heart?' Yesterday—picnic in a sunny meadow. Afterwards, love. God—how beautiful it all was."

Addison, like Elisabeth, was a sensual person. This had caused him in the past to try to go too far with relationships with female students, and other behaviors that would never be tolerated today. There is no data to suggest that Elisabeth had crossed the same lines in her past relationships with men, but she understood, and forgave him.

Meanwhile, Elisabeth's mother visited. As always, Elisabeth noted the constant underlying domestic tension in her journal.

"Frying pan on stove.

"She puts in a teaspoon of bacon fat in (a huge pan).

"'Oh, Bets, you'd better do the eggs. I'll make toast.'

"I add a little more fat to the pan.

"'My goodness! Do you need all that? Well, there's another way we differ.'"

The Leitches were looking for a house not far from Gordon Seminary. Prices were astonishingly high, and nothing had the kind of feel or personality that they wanted.

As they drove along Bay Road in Hamilton, not far from the high school that Valerie would attend, they saw a cozy bungalow with brown cedar shingles, a curved drive and beautiful landscaping, nestled into mature trees. There was a "For Sale" sign in the front yard.

They viewed it the next day, and "were ready to sign papers in five minutes. We are simply overwhelmed with the perfection of the place for our wants and needs. Praise to Him who led us to it and gave us the money to buy it."

Meanwhile, Van was at loose ends. Before the move from Franconia to Hamilton, Elisabeth wrote in her journal, "Van is a real concern to me. Very depressed, unable to make any move at all toward finding a job or a place to live. Makes cutting little comments about how well things always go for me, cries in her room, where she often sits alone in the dark. Lord—do thou for her. Tonight Van tells me she is going to Hamilton tomorrow to look for a job. She says she has felt I am against her—in telling her flatly that she must leave, in not wanting her to 'wait on the Lord,' in not believing God with her for guidance.

"Add says, 'Why doesn't she move? Why doesn't she want to get out and earn a living? Why does she jeopardize her friendship with you?'

"She says, 'What kind of a friendship do we have if you didn't understand my position? Why were you against me—you, who had such long experience of waiting on the Lord for Jim, for going to the [Waodani], etc. I thought I was helping you here. I don't want to be in the way. I wouldn't dream of staying unless you asked me to.'

"And I say 'Woe is me! Only the Lord sees and judges rightly. She has told me what a misfit she is in society—how lonely, how adrift, and how much she wishes she could again be 14 years old and back on the farm. What am I to do to help her? I simply do not know anything other than what I do."

Van quickly apologized for her rants to Elisabeth, explaining that "her period had started that morning, several days late, and perhaps accounted for the 'chaos' of her mind."

Whether Van's moods were because of menstrual misery or not, Elisabeth went on that Van "still seems unable to take any drastic actions. Mrs. Neil came for supper last night and told Add, when he walked her home, that Van was totally dependent on me and ought to have the apron strings completely cut. Also that Van has no idea of what it costs to live.

"True—last year she made less than $600 but it does not seem ever to have occurred to her that I've been supporting her. She has never paid rent, and my car has been at her disposal at all times. (Even when she had her own, mine was used for nearly all errands, groceries, etc.) Now she keeps saying that she does not 'know how' to go about" making a change and becoming independent.

Elisabeth also worried about Van's volatile emotions and their effect on Val. She was thrilled that Val had accepted Addison whole-heartedly. She did not need a three-adult home setting. "Stepfather and mother are enough and right for her," Elisabeth wrote. "She has great ups and downs of emotion, and her work suffers accordingly. Van is surprisingly impatient and sarcastic toward her, and I some-times wish Val did not have to suffer this."

A close friend of Jim Elliot's during college, Van had known and loved Elisabeth through Jim's eyes, and then her own, for decades. As long ago as 1950 she had written to Elisabeth, who had sent her a photo, *"Your picture thrills me every time I look at it and I just wish for one more time to see you and talk with you. What will it be to be together forever? I am coming to know what the opposite of it means and the greatness of it makes me wait eagerly for the fulfillment of the eternal state. From your picture I believe that the grace of the altogether Lovely One has flooded your soul. Certainly its fragrance reaches to my heart even from that piece of paper."*[3]

Perhaps Van had hoped that after Jim's death, she and Elisabeth could be together always, raising Val, pursuing their work, enjoying their philosophical and spiritual oneness. When she and Elisabeth were living in Franconia before Addison entered the picture, she wrote to Elisabeth just after taking her to Boston for a flight to New York. "My sweet Bet, the house has been strangely still all day. A desperate kind of silence. Familiar things ceased to be familiar; it even seemed strange to be eating lunch alone. I listened to T. S. Eliot but heard nothing really. He seemed to be droning away in an empty tomb. The character of this place is gone, that's all there is to it. . . . My heart was landing at La Guardia."[4]

Van's love for, dependence on, and resentment of Elisabeth Elliot created a complex web of emotions. She was a faithful friend when Elisabeth needed her most, and in fact gave Elisabeth the freedom to travel widely for speaking engagements—as well as the ten-week trip to Israel—when Val was a child. She was an ally in Elisabeth's strong reactions against the platitudes and lack of intellectual honesty in some Christian and missionary circles. She was a hard worker, a strong housekeeper, and fell in well with Elisabeth's particular domestic ways.

But the fact was, Elisabeth in Addison Leitch had found the match she had never dreamed possible. So now, for dozens of reasons, it was time for Van to move on.

Elisabeth wondered what to do. "She does not put herself out to do for others. She does not go forward in any way at all. 'Paradise Lost'— she had it with us in Franconia. It's up to her now—is she prepared to meet change and growth? I think not."

After the Leitches moved to Hamilton, Van, now forty-five, moved into a dorm room at Gordon College. "She is at sea," Elisabeth wrote. "No job, no car, no idea how to go about getting either . . . Is she prepared to meet change and growth? I think not."

Van eventually became a residence hall director at Gordon College. She would later serve as a student advisor at Gordon's Career Development Office. Her obituary after her death in 2015 summarized, "Her work there was an encouragement to hundreds of students, who saw her as surrogate mother, teacher, mentor, counselor, and friend."[5]

For his part, it appears that Addison regarded Van, as he did many conflicts, with a certain degree of good will and equanimity. The situation stirred up nothing in him like the strange visit of philosopher Hans Bürki. He took Elisabeth to bed—or on a sunny hillside—with great fervor, cheered on her writing dreams, earnestly tried to help her become more socially aware, complimented her skills as a speaker, debater, chef, and hostess, and, with Elisabeth, opened their home to students, faculty, family, and friends. They became part of a local church. It was perhaps the most healthily social and community-grounded season of Elisabeth Elliot's life.

In June, Elisabeth, Add, and Valerie settled into their dream house on Bay Road, and began to establish new routines. Add was zealously determined to protect Elisabeth's writing time and encourage her creativity. "Elisabeth is hard at it," he wrote to a friend. "One way or another we seem to be getting her a little more time at her desk. I know that it takes some time for the care and feeding of a husband, but I still insist that that dumb dog that she and Val rescued from the

Animal Rescue League is more . . . trouble to her than I am. Still we keep up the battle: she must be released to write."[6]

"Add and I are so happy!" Elisabeth wrote in October. "Outrageously so, it seems to me at times. Today we sold the VW [her car] down in Beverly and then celebrated by having McDonald's hamburgers and 'frappes,' as they call milkshakes in New England."

By Thanksgiving, the turkey was in the oven, the table set for ten, with places for Elizabeth and Fred Bonkovsky (Add's daughter and son-in-law), Fred's parents, Val, Van, and other friends. Elisabeth congratulated herself that the turkey was not dry—always a peril, regardless of one's culinary expertise. The resident puppy, Muggeridge, stayed out of the kitchen. Elisabeth reveled in the sweetness of the day. The group played games after dinner, and then sang Tallis's Canon . . . "All praise to Thee, my God, this night . . ." as well other hymns.

The senior Bonkovskys loved the singing, wrote Elisabeth with uncharacteristic overflow, "and I loved them!"

After that happy Thanksgiving, in early January 1970, the hapless puppy Muggeridge was killed on busy Bay Road, right in front of the Leitch house. "He was a clueless little dog," Elisabeth wrote, "but I loved him, and his death made me cry."

Nevertheless, the Leitchs' first wedding anniversary was a joyous one. Recalling some of the emotionally difficult days from the year earlier, Elisabeth reflected that her uncharacteristic depression was because of the birth control she'd been taking since her marriage. "Having read some on the subject, [it] was the simple result of the Pill—it apparently produces [confusing] emotions in many women. Surely it had little to do with reality."

A week or so after Muggeridge's untimely demise, Val and Elisabeth "went to Haverhill . . . and bought us a tiny black purebred Scotty puppy! He weighs three and a half pounds, wears a bright blue collar and has shining black eyes, a shining shaggy little horse-blanket-like coat, and two very pointed ears. When his ears go back his tiny gay little tail wags, and when the ears go up the tail stops. His name is MacPhearce, an old and time-honored dog-name in the Leitch family, made up, I think, by my husband. He is box-shaped, with another box for a head."[7]

In March, Elisabeth and Valerie were confirmed as members of Christ Church of Hamilton and Wenham. Valerie, now fourteen, loved the youth group there. One evening she came home to inquire of Daddy about the topic of predestination. She felt he knew everything; he was "wise, funny, and smart." She sat down with him.

"Predestination," she said. "Can you tell me what it means?"

It was a question Addison had dealt with many times in the classroom, not so much with fourteen-year-olds.

He grinned and tamped his pipe.

"How much time do you have?" he asked.

Addison talked with Val about the mystery of it all, the enormity and grandeur of God. He talked about arriving in Heaven, passing through its entry gate because of the blood of Jesus Christ. The front of the gate, he told Val, is engraved with the words, "Whosoever will, let him come" (Revelation 22:17). As glad and grateful human beings pass through to glory, the back of the gate reads, "Chosen in Christ before the foundation of the world" (Ephesians 1:4).

The Gospel is open to everyone, freely. And God calls people to Himself.

"And both, of course, are 100 percent true," Addison told Val.

Content with the mystery, Val went off to do her homework. It was an enormous comfort to have a dad to come to with her questions, to rest in his love, to know his strong arms around her.

Elisabeth had wanted her younger sister, Ginny deVries, to come to New York for her miracle wedding to Addison. Add had offered to buy plane tickets for Ginny and her husband, Bud, to travel from the Philippines, where they served as missionaries. But it had not worked out. Now, in the summer of 1970, Elisabeth was excited to show off her wonderful new husband and revel in Ginny's exotic life in the tropics. Addison was no great fan of international travel, but, as always, he was enthusiastic to support his wife and to spend time with the deVries family.

Elisabeth and her five siblings grew up in a highly ordered home with clear rules and high expectations of Christian service. Devotions were held early in the morning and after dinner each evening. The Bible was read, classic hymns were sung—with all of the verses—and children were expected to pay attention and participate. A huge dictionary sat near the dinner table; conversation was expected with a high vocabulary level on theological topics and much more. They weren't stiff: the family loved word games, charades, and mimicry, with screaming fits of laughter at one another's wit.

Oldest brother Phil became a missionary to tribal groups in America's northwest territory. Elisabeth chose missions in Ecuador, and then her writing life. Dave served as a missionary in Latin America and served in leadership roles in a variety of Christian organizations. Ginny was a missionary to the Philippines. Tom was a brilliant writer, PhD, and professor, now on the faculty at Gordon College with Addison. And Jim became a full-time pastor and noted watercolor artist in Montana.

Addison wrote of his wife's family, "Elisabeth is a Howard . . . I get the feeling that all the Howards are geniuses and that all these Howard geniuses seek out the farthest island or the deepest jungle or the coldest north woods in which to operate. I feel very much on the second team when this crowd shows up. One week . . . four books were published by four different Howards in the course of that week! And one of the brothers [Jim] is an artist, to boot."[8]

Elisabeth deeply loved her sister, Ginny. Perhaps because of the seven years' age difference, there doesn't appear to have been competition between them, but more of a protective and proud stance from Elisabeth toward her younger sister. Ginny came up through the same home of origin, of course, and educational institutions that had shaped Elisabeth: the eccentric legalistic atmosphere of Hampden DuBose Academy and the evangelical bastion of Wheaton College. There Ginny met Bud deVries. They married and became missionaries to the Philippines under the auspices of a Baptist mission. Ginny was blessed with the same type of intellect and stunning linguistic abilities as Elisabeth as well as a strong sense of duty and purpose.

"Mom was fiercely loving and kind," says Ginny's son, Peter deVries, a noted violinist, concertmaster, conductor, and teacher who has performed and taught all over the world. "But she didn't rest and relax. She was very motivated with high expectations of self."

Again, the Howard family—Elisabeth, Ginny, and their male siblings—all carried that same high-calling drive. "It was 'exceptionalism,' not success in the world's eyes," says Peter. Ginny pushed herself to give more than her best, whatever the occasion, whomever the recipient. "From my earliest memories, I remember my parents' hospitality. My mom loved parties. She loved making people feel welcome."[9] Ginny and Bud, working through a Baptist mission, settled on Palawan in its capital, Puerto Princesa. Cuyonon was a largely unwritten language, and Ginny, along with two colleagues, set her formidable intellect and spirit to the task of creating a written version of it. Ginny then steered a translation project that would eventually culminate, in 1982, in the publication of the Cuyonon New Testament.

Ginny had a more naturally social personality than Elisabeth. Where Elisabeth sometimes obliviously projected diffidence, judgment, or rudeness, Ginny overflowed with a natural grace, kindness, and understanding. She had learned to defend her older sister when people complained about Elisabeth's odd ways. "What she lacks is not kindness," Ginny would say. "It's just that [Elisabeth] doesn't understand how her words might make the other person feel."

In June 1970 Elisabeth, Addison and Val flew to Manila. Ginny and Bud met them for two days of recuperation and time in the Philippines' capital before the group made their way to Palawan, a sliver of an island province situated in the southwest of the Phillipians, surrounded on the west by the South China Sea and on the east by the Sulu Sea. It was remote. Gorgeous. Teeming with exotic wildlife. Isolated.

"The beauty of this place is overwhelming," Elisabeth wrote. "Sirena Bay, backed by rugged mountains, floating clouds. Tropical abundance of flowers and trees . . . flowers all smelling like variations of gardenia and jasmine, pineapples, mangoes, bananas . . ."

Bud deVries, an incredibly handy sort, had built a beautiful home and an over forty-foot boat—without power tools. The deVries home was a magnet for guests. Missionaries and other visitors to the area seem to have assumed, "Oh, we'll just stay with the deVries!" One day twenty people showed up unexpectedly at the front gate . . . and Ginny and Bud welcomed them in. They stayed for three weeks. On another occasion, a Swedish couple who were sailing around the world capsized near the southern tip of Africa, where their mast was broken and they lost their dingy. They limped into the deVries harbor, and during their three month stay Bud fixed their mast and built them a new dingy. Ginny somehow seemed able to exercise hospitality without stress or apparent effort.

"Ginny's <u>beauty</u> and <u>loveliness</u> keeps me continually on the verge of tears," wrote Elisabeth. "She does all things so beautifully and so well, manages her home so . . . expertly, disciplines, trains, and loves her children so well . . . the house is a lovely, comfortable testimony to a staggering amount of hard work and imagination on the part of Bud and Ginny.

"Having lived in Shandia I have some idea of what each 'little' convenience represents—in vision, design, know-how, ordering of parts, repairs, etc.," Elisabeth wrote to her family. "The house is beautifully constructed with gleaming . . . floors, polished daily by a boy who skates on coconut hemispheres."[10]

Elisabeth continued to rave about Ginny and Bud's ingenuity and creative energy. "Last night Ginny had a dinner for 16, including us. Friends from town came in and we had a huge fat tuna fish" that Bud had just caught, rice, bananas, peanuts, rhubarb, and cashew pie with ice cream, all made from scratch.

"The kids are about the three most attractive kids of their age I've seen anywhere. All of them deeply suntanned and rosy-cheeked . . . blond and loaded with enthusiasm, humor, intelligence . . . beautiful manners, affectionate and sweet. . . . I can't get over . . . Peter's violin. Even Ginny's piano accompaniment amazed me. I had no idea she was so good.

"'Here we are,' I thought, 'at the end of nowhere, and here are these kids playing for all they're worth, accompanied by a mother who looked stunning in a black and white hostess gown, her hair in an elegant French twist, her makeup faultlessly done, earrings on.'"

Within a day or so Ginny told her sister that they were planning to have some friends over on Saturday evening. "How many?" asked Elisabeth.

"Two hundred and fifty," Ginny responded.

All the deVries, an incredibly competent, gifted, and enthusiastic clan, burst into action. They built an outside platform with a sound system, which would serve as a stage. They strung electric lights over the lawn and arranged borrowed benches, tables, and chairs for the crowd.

On the appointed evening, people began streaming through the front gate. There were women in long dresses with big, puffed sleeves and men in the *barong*, or traditional Filipino embroidered dress shirt. There were traditional dance performances, poetic recitations, and musical solos accompanied by Ginny on the piano, which her husband had rolled down from the house to the lawn. Eventually, as the lanterns twinkled in the night and the tropical rains started and stopped, the food—including an enormous suckling pig—was laid out on long wooden tables. The feasting went on for hours.

One fine day Valerie, Peter, and the other kids were swimming and skiing in the bay. A school of whale sharks—never seen in that area—appeared. Undaunted, the deVries chased several sharks in their boat. Val, learning to water-ski at the time, developed an immediate capacity for staying upright at high speed. She needn't have worried, her mother noted later. The sharks were huge, but basically toothless with filter pads that sifted their food from the water. They fed mostly on plankton rather than teenagers.

Peter deVries remembers the shark event. He also remembers how much he loved and respected his "Uncle Add."

"He was a remarkable human being," Peter says today. "A real athlete. He and Aunt Elisabeth were a perfect couple. He was warm, a big man with a big voice and a big presence . . . and he'd just die laughing at himself. He was so humble. He didn't need to be the center of attention."

Elisabeth's enjoyment of this colorful and glorious visit, however, was mitigated by Addison's worsening physical condition.

Add had suffered for years from something called a "benign hypertrophied prostate." It had been diagnosed while his wife Margaret was in the throes of her cancer, and he had put off having surgery. He was told that he would be fine unless it started acting up.

The trip to the Philippines set it off. He was having terrible bowel and bladder issues, exacerbated by the sweltering tropical heat and not being in his familiar, comfortable home setting. A local doctor diagnosed the problem as a urinary infection and prescribed pills. They did not help. "So we wait," Elisabeth wrote in her journal. "And we worry. (Add's father died of cancer of the prostate.) And we try to learn God's desires for us. O Lord have mercy upon us. Christ have mercy upon us."

After only six days with Ginny and family, Elisabeth, Valerie, and Add had to return to Manila. Elisabeth had thought some time in an air-conditioned hotel might help him. He got worse, with pain in his abdomen, swelling, and hardness.

"What to do? . . . It seems we are a million miles from nowhere. The last thing he can face now is the 12,000-mile trip home.

"Why does the Lord allow it? What are we to learn? What decisions are we to make?

"'Trust in the Lord with all thine heart and lean not unto thine own understanding.' 'Thou wilt keep him in perfect peace whose mind is stayed on Thee.'"

Elisabeth somehow got Add to the Makatu Medical Center in Manila. He was hospitalized for two days and drained of an enormous amount of retained urine. He was released with a catheter.

It became obstructed within a day or two. "Uncertainty, fear, indecision—how sore are such trials, aggravated a thousand times by being ill, and then by being in a foreign country. Lord—Thou hast been our <u>dwelling place</u>."

The Leitches got a plane for Tokyo and spent a miserable twenty-four hours there. "A strange day in our lives," Elisabeth wrote tersely. "Add in a state of fear and exhaustion last night—what if the catheter plugged up again and he found himself in the unbearable misery of last Friday?

"The feeling of helplessness—how can we get out of here?" They found a doctor to irrigate the plugged catheter. "Taxi ride in rain. Narrow streets, vertical signs, lanterns, umbrellas, gardens with dark, dripping shrubs and trees, moss-grown stones, lamps. People in clogs . . . Efficiency, busyness, speed, courtesy, bowing and smiling."

Elisabeth was able to get them on a flight from Tokyo to Seattle, then Portland. Add was "in agony and despair all the way," she wrote. "The memories of the past ten days hound his days and nights, and the vivid replay makes him quite sick."

The Elliots—Jim's extended family, who still lived in Portland—were a port in the storm. They took Addison directly from the airport to the hospital. He had nausea, fever, and pain. He stayed there for five days.

Meanwhile Elisabeth and Val lodged with Bob and Ruby Elliot, Jim's older brother and his wife. "I am surrounded by that matchless Elliot kindness," Elisabeth noted. "Thank you, Lord, for this." Happily, teenager Val "had a ball with her cousins." Eventually Add was stabilized enough to fly home to Massachusetts, where he would have surgery. Elisabeth called Van, who was taking care of their home and dog, to find out that the house had been robbed while Van was out one afternoon. The burglars took the Leitches' TV, radio, tape recorder, some cash, and many pieces of irreplaceable heirloom silver.

Elisabeth felt uneasy; strangers had violated her home. But the priority was her husband, and she and Add were able to schedule his needed surgery for soon after their safe return to Hamilton.

On the morning of July 20, before his surgery, Addison spoke with Elisabeth of how suffering "gets one's attention," no, "makes you pay attention," as Luther put it. He told her he had never understood prevenient grace until the Philippines trip—at each point God met us in some way. He opened his Bible, expecting to meditate on a psalm, but instead was drawn to Ezekiel's story of the dry bones made to live again.

"I should speak more often about this," he told Elisabeth.

Elisabeth went on to observe, with *her* own customary pessimism, that "a hospital is a terrible place because of the evidence on every hand of human weakness, devastation, mortality. 'Who shall deliver me from the body of this death?'

"The resurrection is the only valid ground of hope at all."

True. But Addison's "apprehension and dread had been great. Thoughts of his own father's death of cancer of the prostate, plus his own customary pessimism as regards himself have kept him on edge continually. His hands were clammy last night as I held them and we prayed together."

Within just a few hours, the surgeon called Elisabeth to report that the operation went well and that there was no sign of malignancy and no reason to expect post-op complications.

"Thank you, Lord, oh thank you!"

Add went through the usual post-surgery depression, discomfort, questions, and adjustments. He wrote to a friend in August, "Thank you for your card relative to the late indignities which I have suffered at the hands of many physicians. I know I am going to end up dead someday but I am sure there must be nicer ways of dying than by a professional jabbing you with needles and jamming you full of tubes. It seems so much nicer in the Old Testament when somebody is 'old and full of years and is gathered to his fathers.' To put the matter bluntly, I don't like hospitals."

In September his surgeon pronounced him in good health, and life began to return to its norms. By early October, Elisabeth was writing in her journal, "Golden fall days. Add is well—all systems go. Praise God."

CHAPTER 24

Reprieve

*"[C. S. Lewis wrote that] there is nothing
especially admirable in talking to oneself. Indeed,
it is arguable that himself is the only audience before
whom a man postures most and on whom he practices
the most elaborate deception.' . . . "No entries here
for a long time. Perhaps it is best not to practice
elaborate self-deception such as writing a journal!"*
—Elisabeth Elliot, December 30, 1970

At the end of 1970, Elisabeth took stock, and declared herself content.

"Add is well, our home is beautiful and comfortable, Val is lovely
(though still undisciplined in her study and practicing, still much
too self-centered), MacPhearce is cute, and I am a happy woman.
How well, how often, I acknowledge the precariousness of life and
how utterly we depend on God for all that we have. May we be true
disciples."

The true disciples sailed on.

There was a rogue wave, however, in the general domestic tran-
quility. Early in 1971, an item appeared in the Alumni Bulletin of
Muskingum College, Add's undergraduate alma mater. In the "births"
news section was the announcement of a son born to Addison and
Elisabeth Leitch, Isaac by name. Add and Elisabeth received congratulatory notes from strangers and acquaintances rejoicing over this bibli-
cally named son of their own age.

"I am hurt, infuriated, sickened, and humiliated," Elisabeth
wrote in her journal. "So I had better ponder the psalm, 'Fret not
thyself . . .'"

Addison fired off a letter to the *Alumni Bulletin*, letting the editors know that their error had caused the Leitches great embarrassment. He asked for a correction in the next edition, voicing his doubt that such a retraction would stem the misinformation that was now spreading with a life of its own.

Regarding his health, Add wrote thankfully to a friend after recovery from his surgery, "I am in wonderful shape. I am playing tennis two to three times a week, I get out for golf, and I don't think I have felt better in the last ten years of my life. We have a . . . very happy home and our work here at the seminary is going well. We are expecting 460 seminarians here in September, of which over a hundred will be Presbyterians."

Mourning changes he didn't see as healthy in the mainline denominations, Add noted that "the big wheels . . . have no notion in the upper levels of our church how people are really thinking. They talk to each other and they all read the same books and the church goes on in spite of them. To me one of the most significant things of recent years was that the National Council of Churches folded up its youth work in the same week in which *Life* magazine came forward with [its cover story on] the whole Jesus Movement, bubbling up in California. We have been so anxious to be so sophisticated with high school and college students and then suddenly we discover that they are interested in a religion which says 'Are you saved?'"[1]

"I guess I could write at length about our Presbyterian church but they seem to do things faster than we can cry about them. That last report on Sex left me incapable of doing anything but splutter. What next? The worst of it is you feel that no matter what is brought up, it will eventually get passed."[2]

Writing to a friend's wife after his death, he showed a sure sense of empathy as he spoke to her loneliness in her husband's loss.

"I recently married Elisabeth Elliot who had been a widow for twelve years and in the few years that we have been married she has shared something of the loneliness which is a part of this experience. In all my ministry I have never discovered any cure for being lonely. I went through the death of my first wife in her long struggle with cancer and the last three years of her life we hardly had any life together at all. So I know something of what you have been going through and what you face now. Be assured that our prayers are with you, that we have the deepest sympathy for the situation in which you find yourself, but be assured also that any filling of your heart of any replacement of the loss must come from our great friend and physician Jesus Christ. Only He can fill up where we are empty."[3]

In March 1971 Elisabeth reread her early 1969 journal, which had recorded some ups and downs in her new marriage. It was like reading something that someone else had written. The entries seemed "utterly unbelievable to me now. Utterly unbelievable. I cannot imagine a happier marriage. Add is an absolute marvel to me. Van is still my friend, my <u>dear</u> friend, but God had His own purposes to work out for us and I am full of thanksgiving. I cannot put into words the happiness we have here at 746 Bay Road! In another eight days Add and I will have been married as long as Jim and I were."

In April, Elisabeth's agent, Bob Lescher, abruptly dropped her as a client, saying he was "too busy." She felt hurt and confused. Her mood was not enhanced when she found herself speaking at small mother-daughter events with cheery titles like "Faithful, Fruitful Females of the Future."

In June Elisabeth spoke at a women's luncheon at Christ Church. It was the first time she'd ever spoken at a church where she was a member. "And as for some of these women, I suppose, the first time they had ever heard someone who actually took the Bible literally and personally . . . it leads me to hope that I may find some new doors opening for me (as, perhaps, the Lord's kind compensation for the rejection I've felt at Lescher's dropping me and the sense of failure in doing the novel."

She compared herself with writers who succeeded where she failed. She read *The House was Quiet and the World was Calm,* a book by Helen Bevington, a North Carolina poet and non-fiction writer. It fell into no particular category, but "simply tells of one segment of a woman's not very extraordinary experience as an English professor at Duke University. . . . and it comes out as an interesting book. Why can't I do that?"

Around this same time, she noted that "Add and I have been married 27½ months—Jim and I had only 27 months together." Soon after she had a strange and vivid dream that Jim Elliot returned. There he was, strong, real, alive. In the dream, she realized that she would have to choose. Which of these wonderful men did she want to be married to? She reasoned that the decision would rest on which of them would be more affected by her choosing the other. "Jim, I decided, could hardly care less." No matter, for she realized "that I really love Add more anyway!"

Addison Leitch, not Jim Elliot, was the "love of Elisabeth's life."

She thanked God for his "wonderful health," and turned her attention, like mothers everywhere, to her teenaged daughter. "Val is wearing the shortest skirts possible. Oh, these styles. Hair style is most depressing in girls—the long, lank look, no curl, no barrette, hanging over the eyes, constantly needing to be flipped back."

Excruciatingly, on June 4, 1971, "Death. Again the anguish, the sickness that this experience, in any form, brings. MacPhearce was killed this morning.

"Val was on her way to school. I was washing dishes, heard the screech of brakes, saw Val running back up the driveway with tears streaming down her face. The woman who had hit him stopped and was very kind, very upset, had her own little black dog in the car. . . .

"Of course I know I could have prevented it. Of course it had to happen, sooner or later. Of course no dog should be allowed loose on such a busy highway. But, oh, how I loved to see him run! He had such energy and spirit. He was so adorable and sweet, as well as being irascible and even vicious when his will was crossed. I somehow could not bring myself to keep him confined.

"Now the old question and strong feelings—how the sun shines on, just the same, the house is just as lovely and comfortable, cars go by as usual, everyone goes on about their business, 'but oh, the difference to me!'

"And of course I ponder the mystery of human feelings, the strange bond between a woman and a little black dog, the impossibility of my own surviving the loss of Jim, as I did, and why I should be devastated now. There is so much to be thankful for in my life.

"Tom—bless his kind and loving heart—came over just as we were burying MacPhearce. He had sat at the breakfast table, after my call, and bawled. Gallaudet [age three or so] told me, 'Papa was weeping.'"

Ten days later, Elisabeth and Add went out and bought a Shetland sheepdog named Tania, seven months old, graceful and beautiful. "I am learning to love her, but I am having a very hard time getting over MacPhearce's death. Sometimes I find myself feeling physically weak and sick, hardly able to contemplate the ordinary work of the day . . . He was a very stubborn and unmanageable dog, wild as a rabbit at times, but I adored him. *Sic transit.* (*Sic transit gloria mundi* is a Latin phrase that can be translated as, 'Thus passes the glory of the world.'"

The months to follow were like a movie montage of ordinary yet glorious domestic joys, the stuff that makes up most of the texture of our lives.

Elisabeth's brother Jim and his wife, Joyce, along with their four children—ages two months through seven years—visited for a week. "I am so thankful for this home—so comfortable and spacious and easy to entertain in.

"We painted the living room walls raspberry, leaving the woodwork white. It looks gorgeous," Elisabeth effused, loving the blue and rose Khirman carpets, flowered valances and slipcovers, Bokhara rug, and raspberry needlepoint chairs in the dining room. She reveled in the master bedroom with its white walls, mahogany furniture, fireplace, and rich red carpeting. "I love this house."

"I am not over the loss of MacP. yet."

There was a week-long visit to Trail West, the adult guest lodge run by Young Life, a ministry to teenagers. Elisabeth and Add went to Frontier Ranch, where a week-long camp overflowing with energetic teenagers was in full swing. Evidently the culturally connected and exuberant Young Life atmosphere of the day was just not Elisabeth's thing.

"Pandemonium. The kids were 'singing'—i.e., shrieking to the high-decibel beat of an electronically amplified guitar. The lyrics are tripe—e.g.

'When we walk in the light
We can trust each other
We can see ourselves'—10 TIMES!"

Elisabeth was similarly flummoxed by the cultural phenomenon of a big-stadium college football game that fall. "Harvard-Dartmouth game last Saturday. 50,000 people at $6 or more a head. Another big American enterprise." Addison and Elisabeth sat high in the stadium, surrounded by "middle-aged money and brains . . . Scotch and bourbon, Rolls-Royces, furs . . . marching bands . . . peppy girls with teeny-weeny skirts and bouncing bosoms, and a field full of strapping, strapped and padded and helmeted heroes, the Super Male."

Add, of course, was all in. For Elisabeth, it was a fascinating cultural phenomenon, but as foreign as a visit to Mars.

Valerie applied to Wheaton College, her parents' alma mater.

Then, on the last day of the year, Elisabeth wrote in her journal.

"December 31, 1971 . . . And now, I think I shall abandon this everlasting journal. Age forty-five surely is an over-ripe age to be recording oneself. I've had a very good life. Tomorrow Add and I will have been married for three glad years.

To do justly
To love mercy
To walk humbly with God—
Still my goals. And I am still as far as I ever was from reaching them."

It was a self-conscious coda, a farewell to self-reportage, and a rather artistic end of the personal written record of Elisabeth's Elliot's interior life.

Fade to sunset.

CHAPTER 25

"Is It Cancer?"

"Bees will not work except in darkness;
Thought will not work except in Silence;
Neither will Virtue work except in Secrecy."
—Thomas Carlyle

*B*y early March 1972, Elisabeth was back at the journaling business again, scribbling with a black pen in a dark green, leatherette, spiral bound Herald Square journal with eighty lined pages.

"I had decided when I finished my last journal, December 1971, that that was enough. It is a useless lot of drivel, most of it, and of no interest whatever to anyone but me. But it does, I discovered, do something for me—it marks progress of a sort. It numbers the trees in the forest, though I can't see the forest yet."

Val was accepted at Wheaton College for the fall '73 semester.

Her mother read G. K. Chesterton's *The Everlasting Man* and a biography of Phillip Brooks. She devoured Thomas Carlyle's *Sartor Resartus, Search for Science*, by Elizabeth O'Connor, and C. S. Lewis's *That Hideous Strength*.

Reading Carlyle, the Scottish nineteenth-century essayist, historian, and philosopher, Elisabeth had the time and margin to reflect on priorities and choices. As she considered an invitation to speak at a college in Kansas, she said no. "I need to focus my attention more. I am not called to the whole nation. Perhaps I should do less speaking and more meditating (and writing?)."

She found Carlyle, a "new-found friend. He has introduced me to other friends—[Samuel] Johnson, [Robert] Burns, [Martin] Luther—all humble, earnest, honest, peaceful men, eager for truth, grateful and good-humored." Whether all of these writers were peaceful and good-humored is a matter of opinion, but the point remains that Elisabeth mined their writings for enduring truths.

"Good seed, sown in my heart, is sown by the Son of Man. Thanks be to God for this."

Carlyle also gave her the blessing only an introvert could appreciate. She jotted his words in her journal, "In thy own mean perplexities, do thou thyself but hold thy tongue for one day; on the morrow, how much clearer are thy purposes and duties . . . Speech is too often not, as the Frenchman defined it, the art of concealing thought, but of quite stifling and suspending thought so that there is none to conceal."

She had written a short book on God's guidance; it was accepted by Word Publishing. She noted that she had sailed for Ecuador twenty years before. She worked on a new book she was calling *A Jungle Notebook,* about her first year on the mission field, with the Colorado Indians.

"Who am I?" Elisabeth wrote in her new journal. "An inane question, endlessly discussed. Carlyle says: 'A great soul, any sincere soul, knows not what he is . . . can, of all things, the least measure himself! What others take him for and what he guesses that he may be; these two items strangely act on one another, help to determine one another.'"

On April 7, she took the time to go through old files. She read book contracts from the past, old royalty statements. "I've had a certain amount of 'fame' and worldly wealth," she noted. "It's over now, and the temptation to try to recapture it comes. (Not that I suppose I really could recapture it, but I could certainly worry about trying. It is a thing I could stew about.) Rather ironic, since neither thing was of any special interest to me when they were within reach. This I take to be the action of grace. So now I prayer for grace to resist the abovementioned temptation. In Matt. 13:22 I see that 'delight in riches' chokes the word."

After Elisabeth spoke at an event in Maine, a woman bustled up to her, smiling. "Now what's your book again? *Splendor in the Grass?*" (For nonliterary types, this earnest fan was mixing up Elisabeth's book, *Through Gates of Splendor,* with the classic 1960s movie *Splendor in the Grass,* a story of teenaged love and angst starring Natalie Wood and Warren Beatty.)

After a dinner at a seminary couple's home with visitors from New Zealand and seminary president Harold Ockenga and his wife, Elisabeth wrote, "Add gets very depressed at the whole seminary scene. To stick it out or not? He wakes at night and mentally quits his job."

Tanya the Sheltie, no doubt knowing that she could not measure up to the late MacPhearce in Elisabeth's eyes, tried to redeem herself by having four puppies. Val was inducted to the National Honor Society. She graduated from high school. She applied for a modeling job. The Leitches went with Tom and Lovelace Howard to Blantyre Castle in Massachusetts, a majestic Tudor estate, for a couple of leisurely days of relaxation. "Too much food, too rich, too expensive," Elisabeth concluded. "It really is not my cup of tea."

In mid-July, Elisabeth found herself again speaking at Tarkio College's summer conference in Missouri, lodging in the very same room she had in 1967, when the sparks had first flown between herself and Addison.

"What hath God wrought!" she marveled, thinking of all that had transpired in that last five years. Worrying about her upcoming lectures, she noted, "Add is much loved here. I hope I don't disgrace him."

In mid-September, Elisabeth faced a challenge she had been both dreading and anticipating for years, as she and Val packed so she could take Val off to Wheaton College. Elisabeth had some of the same sensations she'd had years ago . . . packing for Hampden DuBose Academy as a young teenager, looking forward to all that her high school experience there would offer. Packing for Wheaton College in 1944, not knowing she would meet Jim Elliot there, nor that their short marriage would produce such a gift as Valerie. Packing to leave for Ecuador as an idealistic, unseasoned missionary. Pulling her few belongings together when she lived among the Waodani as a young widow with little Val in tow. Boxing up even fewer belongings when she and Val left the jungle . . . and then packing what little she had not given away when she left Ecuador to return to the United States and start a new life in New Hampshire. Then she thought of the most recent move, the happy transition of relocating from Franconia to Hamilton, energetically filling boxes and making glad plans with Addison.

Life. So many journeys, eyes on the horizon, not knowing what would come. "What is it?" she thought. "Not sorrow. It is an overwhelming realization of what people and places have meant to me." She felt gratitude, hope, longing, love . . . and some other emotion she couldn't quite name. Perhaps it was loss, that sweet-sharp sense that change, welcome as it may be, often brings a sense that though we are creatures of time, we long for eternity. We go through door after door; there are new rooms, new changes, and some are exciting. But there is still the pain of the rooms left behind, never to be lived in again.

Elisabeth wrote in her journal that Add had a strange dream. He was "going through door after door and reaching at last a door which would not open. When he turned to go back the way he had come, the door behind him would not open. Then, in the disconnected way of dreams, he was being wrapped and smothered in paper. He began to shout, 'Wake me up! Wake me up! And I was awakened by his groaning and repeating a muffled sentence, which, as I listened, became clearer and louder, finally intelligible: 'Wake me up! Please wake me up!' And of course I did."

By the end of September Elisabeth was back in her domestic routine, which always steadied her and made her sense of loss a bit less sharp. "The house is quiet. High school kids troop by on the street. Val is not among them. It is a week today since I said goodbye to her. No letter yet."

She went on to write out her prayer concerns for the day. Val topped the list. Elisabeth also prayed for her mother, for friends facing difficulties, for her own speaking engagement that night at Grace Chapel outside of Boston.

And then there was her concern for her husband's lip. Add had an ugly sore that had not gotten better; it would not go away.

"Please heal him," she asked of the Lord.

And then: "Is it cancer?"

CHAPTER 26

Selva Oscura

"Midway upon the journey of our life
I found myself within a forest dark,
For the straightforward pathway had been lost.
"Ah me! how hard a thing it is to say
What was this forest savage, rough, and stern,
Which in the very thought renews the fear."
—Dante Alighieri, *The Divine Comedy*

*I*t was cancer. This was not a bad dream from which Add could wake.

He would need surgery as soon as possible. Perhaps surgeons could get it all.

Add and Elisabeth drove slowly home from the hospital where they had met with his doctor. Add stared straight ahead. "'The curfew tolls the knell of parting day,'" he told his wife.

He slid down the slippery slope of dread. He felt like a burden to Elisabeth. He felt like an old man. He loved his life—his wife, teaching, planning the future, tennis, friends, feasting, reading, smoking, good conversation and debate. Was it all over?

Elisabeth wrote, "strange that I had written down this morning, on a piece of scratch paper:

How to deal with suffering of any kind:

1) Recognize it
2) Accept it
3) Offer it to God as a sacrifice
4) Offer yourself with it.

That night and the next morning, Addison bled when he urinated. Why?"

Elisabeth pled in her journal. "Oh, God, PLEASE . . ."

"C. S. Lewis wrote that grief is like fear. I have known grief. Now I know that fear is like that. Restlessness, loss of appetite, a sense of being in a wilderness . . . as I read the Gospels lately I am amazed at Jesus' ability to move steadily on, through all the events of a normal human life, toward that horrifying suffering which He knew awaited Him in Jerusalem. He did one thing, and <u>then He did another</u>, serenely, graciously, peacefully . . .

"Today I must do the usual things, the cooking and washing of dishes and straightening up. I must also write a column for <u>Christian Herald</u>.

"This takes a strict and narrow discipline of mind, so I will <u>have</u> to have divine help."

She cooked and cleaned. She wrote the article. Add's bleeding continued.

After his surgery, the cancer on the lip was considered "manageable." He also underwent a cystoscopy, during which a hollow tube with a lens is inserted into the urethra and advanced into the bladder. This would hopefully reveal why Addison continued to have blood in his urine.

The procedure showed prostatic carcinoma. Cancer of the prostate. The same disease that had killed his father. It was Add's worst fear confirmed.

Today, if it is caught early enough through PSA screening tests, and because of enhanced treatment options, most men diagnosed with prostate cancer do not die from it.[1]

But PSA screening tests did not exist in 1972. At the time of Addison's illness, prostatic acid phosphatase was the most common blood test for prostate cancer. Sadly, it was of no value for the *early* detection of the disease, as the serum acid phosphatase levels were elevated mainly in men who already had bone metastases.[2]

Receiving the news of a potentially terminal disease is like being given a ticket for a train you do not want to take. But you have to get on. You don't know how much you should have packed. You do know the end of the route, the terminus where the dark train is going. But you don't know if you might be allowed to get off at a station and get on the glad train that goes in the opposite direction, the train that will bring you back to the life you've previously known, or some approximation of it.

Happily, that happens to some people. Their loved one is healed, and they get to return to life as usual, or to a reprieve of some sort.

But for many, the cancer train just keeps going, sometimes excruciatingly slowly, sometimes at high speed. It passes through many dark tunnels. Sometimes you stop briefly at a station and kind people climb on board. They give you baskets of home-made food, fuzzy blankets for the journey, and hugs. A few give advice and opinions about just what you should do. Then they get off. The brave friends stay on the train with you, and ride it all the way to the end.

Elisabeth's account of her journey with Add on the cancer train is starkly honest, hopeful, despairing, and poignant. Perhaps more than any other writing she ever did, it captures her courage, her faith in God, and her vulnerability. For all of us who ponder the riddle of Elisabeth Elliot, it is this story, this season as the sun set on her marriage to this man she loved "more than Jim" Elliot, that reveals her core and gives us a key to understanding the unfathomable decisions she made afterwards that set the course for the rest of her long life.

Elisabeth called this new season the "wilderness of cancer," a wasteland of uncertainty and confusion.

"In the name of Jesus Christ, DELIVER US FROM FEAR," she wrote as she and Add digested the bad news of the new prostate cancer diagnosis and he lay in a hospital bed waiting for further analysis of additional cancer sites.

"'Fear not for I am with thee.' 'Be not dismayed, for I am thy God.' Nothing has changed those two facts."

Beyond the facts of faith, she found that little things comforted her back at home. A hot bath with her favorite scented oil. The inquisitive, comical face of her new little Scottie dog, MacDuff.

But Add lay alone, seven miles away, in a hospital bed, "angry, silent, beaten to the dust of humiliation," waiting for further word from his surgeon as to whether he also had cancer in the glands of the mouth.

He rallied for visitors. Two friends from church came to visit him in the hospital while Elisabeth was there, and within a few minutes Add was counseling and encouraging them. The four of them held hands and prayed. One of the men broke down and wept as he told the Lord of his love for Addison. The visit touched Add deeply.

Elisabeth prayed in Jesus's name for deliverance. Sometimes, for no apparent reason, she had a great sense of hope. The volatility of emotions. Her brother Tom noted that sometimes one's feelings had no relation to the data at hand.

On November 4, 1972 she could not sleep, her stomach in knots and her mind whirling. She felt it was the worst night she had had since 1956, when Jim was killed. The next day she wrote in her journal, "A downhill slide again today as the realization of what may be in store for us sinks in. Bleeding continues."

Add's letter to his three daughters from his marriage to Margaret was more upbeat.

"I decided to try again," he began in his teasing way, since they hadn't responded to earlier letters. "After all, Faulkner was turned down 43 times before his first book manuscript was accepted."[3]

He wrote lightly of the first snowfall, walking the dog, trying to get more exercise, thanked Fred and Elizabeth for a book on the Brooklyn Dodgers, and other newsy items, then went on to the elephant in his room.

"My health seems to be a big factor around here," he wrote. He described his lip surgery and then the indignity of having doctors also interested in his other end, where they "made the mistake of finding some cancer on the spot where [the surgeon] had taken the prostate out two and a half years ago. How many people do you know with two cancers—two different unconnected kinds of cancer . . . I have a hard time sorting out my worries."

He told Helen, Elizabeth, and Katherine that he would keep them posted on any further news. "Love to you all, Daddy."[4]

During this time Elisabeth received several phone calls a week, some at midnight, from Jandra, a friend in Oklahoma. They were cries for help; she was about to get a divorce, her teenaged children "hated" her and eventually left the house, certain she was going to take her own life. Another confided that she was in a polyamorous marriage and wanted Elisabeth's counsel.

Weary, Elisabeth sought solace, as always, in reading. She noted G. K. Chesterton's words from *Orthodoxy* in her journal: To the Christian, he wrote, joy is fundamental, grief superficial. "Praise should be the permanent pulsation of the soul."

So "joy is something gigantic, grief is something special and small," Elisabeth summarized. Ah, she thought. Let me remember that in my next grief.

Christmas 1972 came and went, with family visiting, church services, and festive gatherings at Tom Howard's home. Addison continued to have urinary bleeding issues. His prostate cancer turned out to be an inoperable mass. He would have eight weeks of the heaviest radiation therapy possible.

The new year would bring six to eight weeks of five-day-a-week trips to Boston, for intensive radiation at Massachusetts General Hospital.

Elisabeth called each treatment "three and a half minutes under the eye of a machine the size of a freight car, making the noise of three motorboats" in a DANGER—HIGH VOLTAGE subterranean vault studded with nuclear radiation warnings in the basement of Boston's famed Massachusetts General Hospital, as if they had stumbled into some doomsday scenario movie set.

When they emerged from the belly of the beast and made their way back to their peaceful hamlet, Elisabeth marveled at the white snow, the bare dogwood twigs against a cobalt blue sky, and the bounding joy of her black-fringed puppy MacDuff, running in the snow. "All these things, and we ourselves, and the action of the Betatron, held in the Hand that held the seven stars (Revelation 1) and is now laid on us again with love and with the words, Fear not."

"There is something marvelously sustaining about the knowledge that C. S. Lewis, his wife, Samuel Rutherford, Amy Carmichael, and countless hosts of others have suffered and feared and trusted and been carried through in the same Everlasting Arms that hold us."

Meanwhile Addison called himself, "the most hopeless of men."

"Should I write here?" she jotted in her journal. "Not that others may read this, but that I may have an accurate record of 'all the way[s] the Lord my God led me,' so that perhaps I may tell of it for the hope of others—this is a good enough reason for writing, I guess.

"This morning I am crying but I have physical energy to do the work I have to do."

"We cannot let cancer be our whole career these days," she thought. Add preached at a church in Boston. He taught a three-hour class, feeling shaky all the while. He spent his three-and-a-half minutes of radiation each weekday praying for a particular person, one for each day of the week. Elisabeth spoke to a church ladies' coffee. She consulted with Word Publishing about the company's handling of her book on guidance, which she felt had been edited "like a high-school term paper." She was pleased that her old publisher Harper, which had so hurtfully rejected *Furnace of the Lord,* came courting her about writing another book for them.

But life had changed. Add had pain. He was depressed. He sat in his chair, dozed, ignored his beloved books, and watched TV. He vomited on the red bedroom carpet. He bled when he urinated and had constant diarrhea. He groaned, sighed, and stared into the distance. Tortured every night by sleeplessness, he would not take sleeping pills. His "sins of the past torment him," Elisabeth wrote. "His theology torments him." He thought of the verse from Psalm 103: "As a father has compassion on his children, so the LORD has compassion on those who fear him."

"What does that mean?" he moaned. "I'm sick. I'm so sick! Can't you help me?"

God seemed so distant, and this was just the beginning of the journey. He thought of suicide. Elisabeth understood. "Who has not thought of it? Who, that is, who has suffered?"

"We have been on the Adele Davis diet and vitamin pills for three days," Elisabeth reported at the end of January. "There is remarkable improvement already. Add had no nausea at all. Less blood in his urine, less gastric distress, less sleeplessness."

Adele Davis was perhaps the most famous popular nutritionist of the mid-twentieth century, her books selling millions of copies. Her third book, *Let's Eat Right to Keep Fit*, written in 1954, became a popular handbook on nutrients considered essential to human health, and how to modify one's lifestyle to take in these vitamins, minerals, essential fatty acids, and proteins.

The book also railed against the typical American diet of the day, which was high in salt, refined sugars, pesticides, growth hormones, preservatives, other additives, and stripped of its essential nutrients by excessive processing. Davis decried America's seeming obsession with hamburgers, steaks, and other red meat. Davis said that since "genuinely wholesome food" was hard to obtain in 1970s-era supermarkets, she was a great advocate of vitamin supplements.

Though this perspective is common today, in 1973 it was all new to Elisabeth Elliot.

She was evangelistic about her nutritional epiphanies. "When I prayed, months ago, to be shown ways I could help Add . . . I certainty would not have imagined this answer." A friend brought more books, food, testimonials, and supplements. Another old friend, a medical doctor, urged her to make sure she and Add were both getting plenty of Vitamin C and E supplements.

Elisabeth started telling all her friends about the importance of nutrition.

"It makes sense to me that God does not need to work a 'miracle' if there are natural rules for us to obey. Cancer is, it seems to me, one of the inevitable results of our own and our society's sins against the laws of nutrition (as are all diseases.) Radiation massively destroys vitamins and cells in the body. A rigorous program of body-building nutrition is needed to replace these."

She got busy in the kitchen, and threw away evils like flour, sugar, chocolate chips, prepared foods, and a bag of marshmallows lurking on a pantry shelf. Add observed, "You're a true believer! Once you decide a thing is true, you act. And then you start being a missionary!"

Elisabeth had already lost three pounds. She'd also lost her craving for sweets. She had bounding energy. She woke at 6 a.m., eager to get up. She caused a rare rift with her brother Tom by treating her dog's torn claw with Vitamin C rather than taking MacDuff to the vet. She wrote in her journal that Tom and his wife "avoid the subject of doctors with me—my attitude—(although not one of total criticism) infuriates them."

There were occasional diversions from Add's illness. One cold day, a priceless letter arrived in the mailbox.

> *Dear Mrs. Elliot, I am Count Einar Olav Henrick*
> *Edvart from Norway. I have a B.A. (magna cum laude)*
> *in philosophy from Yale. (1942) I have a Th.D. I belong*
> *to 25 clubs in London. I have been promised a job*
> *teaching philosophy at Scarborogh College in Toronto.*
> *I want to marry you and be a father to your daughter*
> *Valerie. If you want, I am willing to be a missionary like*
> *your late husband. If you are interested, please write to*
> *me. Thank you. Sincerely, Count Einar . . .*

If Elisabeth responded to the Count, her letter, which would have been a great work of literature, has been sadly lost.

Two weeks into her vitamin supplement regimen, Elisabeth noted that "Add's spirits have unquestionably been higher." She could not help but believe that the diet and supplements were helping.

Finishing radiation treatments was also a factor. Add had marked the calendar hanging on the kitchen wall with big, black Xs as each treatment was finished, counting the days to completion.

Add wrote to a friend that they would have to delay some possible travel plans together. "The difficulty is that my health at this end of the line has thrown a lot of sand into the gears and I have no notion of what can be worked out."

"Just yesterday [February 22] I finished a course of 33 radiation treatments, and I must confess that they have driven me almost underground."[5]

On February 23, Add's doctor again told them that the mass in his prostate was too large to allow an operation. Add had had all the radiation he could take. The next option would be an orchiectomy, a surgical procedure to remove the testicles.

Meanwhile, Add's lip had not healed from surgery a few months earlier. It was swollen, red, and bumpy. He was sure it was more cancer.

"Oh, God!" Elisabeth cried. "We walk in an agony of fear, and read words like 'Rejoicing in hope!' We <u>cry</u> in prayer, two agreeing on earth [regarding] <u>healing</u> and we hear no reply, only faint hopes that at least we will be given your grace to endure, but grace is not what we ask for. Lord, have pity, have mercy, is our plea."

"Help Thou our unbelief!"

On February 27, away at school, Valerie turned eighteen. Elisabeth and Add discovered that his lip would need more surgery. Immediately.

And now there was a blow to Elisabeth's supplement hopes. She asked Add's surgeon about Vitamin E on the lip area after the operation to reduce scarring. By no means, the surgeon told her. There was an outside chance that Vitamin E may promote the growth of genital tumors.

"Blind alleys," Elisabeth moaned. "Now what do we do?" She quoted King Jehoshaphat's prayer from 2 Chronicles 20:12. "We know not what to do, but our eyes are on you."

"I know you have both sympathy and empathy," Add wrote to friends while he was enduring the after-effects of radiation. "What has really rocked me, however, is that now with just one week after my radiation, they have discovered that my lip is acting up again, so I have to go in for surgery again tomorrow. Since it was operated on only three or four months ago, I am not too full of assurance that this second operation will be any more final than the first one. . . . If all is well, I will be a very happy man and if all is not well, then the options which are in front of me are very narrow ones indeed."[6]

The next day, on the way to the operating room, a nurse said to Addison, "Dr. Leitch, you're so tall!" to which he replied, "Yes, but they're about to cut me down to size."

Afterwards, Elisabeth peered at his sleeping form in the hospital bed. "They didn't take his face off," she thought. Thank God. But it looked like he was missing quite a chunk. The bandage was huge.

Surgeons had to remove some of the muscle of the mouth. Pathology reports would be back in a few days to let them know if they should go back to carve out more.

Add came home from the hospital with the shape of his mouth changed, "extremely depressed and discouraged."

Unsurprisingly, Elisabeth woke the next morning "terribly depressed" as well. A student at the seminary dropped off a lush, flowering African violet. The violet, she told Elisabeth, had not bloomed for three years. The student said she had actually prayed for the violet to bloom, and now it had bloomed for Addison Leitch. "I will pray for Dr. Leitch," she told Elisabeth.

"May her prayers be as effective for him as for the flower," Elisabeth thought. The gift encouraged her greatly, as did other calls from her doctor friend telling her she believed that Addison would get better, to hope for healing, to continue using Vitamins E and C.

"Thank God," wrote Elisabeth. "I believe Add will be healed."

CHAPTER 27

"Oh! If Only . . ."

"The fiat God asks of us when we suffer is not the fiat of insensibility, but of suffering. When our heart is torn and continues to be so, we must give it to Him as it is. Later, when peace returns, we will give it to Him at peace. What He wants is for us to give ourselves as we are."
—*They Speak by Silences*, by an unnamed Carthusian

*I*f Elisabeth believed that Add would be healed, she was willing to consider anything that might help achieve that end. She noted in her journal that a dear friend was flying to Montreal to procure some "'underground' Laetrile, as neither Canada nor U.S. permits its use."

Laetrile was popular in the 1970s, though controversial. It's derived from amygdalin, the bitter substance found in fruit pits like apricots, raw nuts, lima beans, and clover. When ingested, it converts into hydrogen cyanide. The idea was that the cyanide would go after cancer cells, deprive them of oxygen, and kill them. However, because it was never demonstrably shown to be effective, and because of serious side effects that mirrored effects of cyanide poisoning—such as death—the Food and Drug Administration never approved its use in the United States.

One evening Add and Elisabeth watched an interview with Corrie ten Boom on Kathryn Kuhlman's television show. Kuhlman was a controversial evangelist and faith healer; her TV show ran from 1966 to 1975. Kuhlman interviewed guests who were both famous and unknown, asking them about their spiritual experiences. Viewers felt like they were listening in on a real conversation rather than watching a show.

Corrie ten Boom was a household name in Christendom at the time. Because of her faith in Jesus, during World War II Corrie and her family had hidden Jews from the Nazis in their home in Amsterdam. They were found out and taken to Ravensbruck, a Nazi concentration camp. Corrie's father and sister died there.

Corrie lived. She spent the rest of her life preaching about God's miraculous capacity to both sustain His people and to empower forgiveness. Her first book about her prison experience, *The Hiding Place,* sold millions of copies, was made into a film, and has inspired Christians ever since.

Corrie told Kathryn Kuhlman about her time in solitary confinement, alone with no sense of the passage of time. But then she was no longer alone.

"Into my solitary cell came a small, busy black ant. I had almost put my foot where he was one morning . . . when I realized the honor being done me. I crouched down and admired the marvelous design of legs and body. I apologized for my size and promised I would not so thoughtlessly stride about again."[1]

As more time went by in solitary, she hoped for another visit from her small friend. He did not come out. He and his fellow ants were "staying safely hidden. And suddenly I realized that this too was a message, a last wordless communication among neighbors. For I, too, had a hiding place when things were bad. Jesus was this place, the Rock cleft for me."

Add stared at the amiable, gray-haired Dutch saint on his television screen, her hair in her customary bun, her square shoes solidly planted on the stage.

"That's only out-faking yourself," he said to Elisabeth, "like setting your watch ahead so you won't be late."

Elisabeth blinked a few times. At the time, questioning Corrie ten Boom, renowned believer and Holocaust hero, was like questioning evangelical icon Billy Graham, or maybe the apostle Paul.

She reminded Add of the Scripture, "Fear thou not, for I am with thee, be not dismayed, for I am thy God."

"That stuff's not worth a nickel to me now," Add said.

It was all so grossly sad and discouraging. Elisabeth saw her husband's startling cynicism as the power of the Enemy of our souls to "take advantage of physical weakness and undermine the spirit. Nothing looks worthwhile or hopeful to someone in that grip."

Their friend returned from Canada with Laetrile pills and an armload of supplements and instructions, throwing Elisabeth into "a welter of confusion" about the "outrageous dietary restrictions: no meat, no dairy products. How is one to thread his own way through the intricacies of chemical balance and physiology?"

Elisabeth decided that Add ought to continue to eat meat and dairy foods since, she wrote—in spite of nutrition guru Adele Davis' animosity for beef—"they are so nutritious."

Add started the Laetrile. He had ups and downs; when he was doing better, Elisabeth's hopes soared. He wrote to former seminary students,

"I have not been teaching this last term in Gordon-Conwell because of cancer . . . a combination of two operations and some long radiation treatments unman me for any further work. I think I am picking up some now and if all goes well, I will be able to pick up at the end session or certainly resume in the fall.

"And if all does not go well, my story will be the story of all those people you have heard of who have had cancer. It is a very vicious disease, and I am far from being out of the woods yet, although I am feeling much better than I did for a while. There are days when I am very much down and back to where I was, but in general I am out ahead.

"No matter how hard I try or how much I think, there are no solutions having to do with what I can do or say or try. The problem of just waiting it out is the sort of thing I am not used to and maybe that's the lesson I have to learn, to rest in the Lord instead of trying to work everything out myself.

"Elisabeth is a tower of strength, as you know, and she has been more than that, not only in herself, but for me."[2]

Elisabeth's dear old friend Katherine Morgan came to visit. Katherine had lost her husband when she was a missionary in Colombia with four daughters. As a young widow, she decisively carried on a vibrant and fruitful ministry in Colombia that lasted for decades. There were few—if any—women Elisabeth admired more.

Katherine firmly believed that Add would be healed. She effused about what she had witnessed in terms of the movement of God's Spirit in the Roman Catholic Church. "The Wind is blowing," Elisabeth wrote. "What a woman she is! A whole person, sane, well-balanced, profoundly spiritual, intelligent, humorous, compassionate, loving. Thanks, Lord, for sending her."

Add had pain in his kidneys. "It's kidney cancer," he moaned. He continued to lose weight. He had pain in his nose. "It's nasal cancer." He had a sore throat. Back pain. He was now off dairy, as several friends had told the Leitches he shouldn't be on it while taking Laetrile. Another friend recommended an incredible cancer clinic in Florida. Add called, only to discover that it had gone out of business.

Everyone must make their own choices as to what paths they will follow and protocols they will engage in, homeopathic and otherwise, in their cancer journey. As Elisabeth sought the best options for Addison, it was confusing.

"We find ourselves in *selva oscura*," she wrote, referring to a reference in Dante's *Inferno*, the sense of being in a dark and shadowed wood, a season in which one loses one's way.

She called a doctor at the National Cancer Institute outside D.C. He told her there was no need to eliminate dairy, and that "Laetrile was about as effective as any orthodox cancer treatment, i.e. about 15 percent chance of actual cure."

The doctor was a respected, prize-winning biochemist. Many years later, the *Los Angeles Times* wrote that he was officially reprimanded by the National Cancer Institute in 1973 for his "outspoken support of the controversial cancer treatment Laetrile." He considered the compound "in front right now as a treatment for cancer" and urged that it be tested on humans who gave their consent.

This rankled officials at the institute, who "issued [him] an official reprimand, saying he had the right to exercise his freedom of speech as a private citizen, but he did not represent the government agency."[3]

Val came home for spring break in March, then returned to school. Her grades were slipping; Elisabeth and Add both exhorted her to shape up.

The days dragged. Add no longer trusted himself to try to teach any classes; he might well collapse. He was weary. Weak. Still losing weight. Throwing up. The smell of Elisabeth's bath oil at night sickened him. "By next week I'll be too weak to carry out the trash cans," he told Elisabeth. "I'm traveling the same route Margaret did—weaker and sicker every day. I think the cancer's really getting to me now. I think it's in the liver."

It was hard for Elisabeth not to note his complaints. "Every day, three or four times a day, I hear 'God, am I sick.' 'I'm really a sick kitten,' etc. This morning Add said (very seriously) how impressed he was with how seldom he speaks of his sickness."

In mid-April Elisabeth and Add were able to have dinner at Boston's Algonquian Club with Tom, Lovelace, Elisabeth's mother, Van, two other friends, and Add's daughter Elizabeth Bonkovsky, who was visiting.

Easter. Trumpets and tympany at church. Add felt terrible all day, "sick and hopeless, and resentful of God's not hearing his prayers."

After this, the next line in Elisabeth's journal cites that Add's doctor "declared him, 'to all practical purposes, <u>cured</u>.'" Add's lip was healing well, and no mention is made of the prostate mass.

"Thank God!" Elisabeth wrote. "Was it

1. A miracle
2. The radiation
3. Adele Davis
4. Laetrile ???

Or was it all four?"

Add had terrible pains in his head and was sure he now had brain cancer. He taught a class. He and Elisabeth attended the seminary's senior banquet.

This may not have helped Add's uncharacteristically dismal point of view. "All your prayers and fasting have done me no good," he told Elisabeth.

Her spirits soared though, as Add's appetite improved, and his headaches lessened. His spirits were more like his real personality. Elisabeth dared to have hope.

"Lord, have mercy on us. Let there be no more dashing of hope, O God of health and hope!"

One morning Elisabeth stroked his arm to wake him up. "Viewing the remains?" he asked.

The doctor recommended radiation for Add's lip. "Another plunge into that long, dark tunnel," Elisabeth wrote. "O Lord, save us and help us."

The next day they were told that the lip cancer was spreading aggressively, with gland involvement under the chin, biopsies needed, perhaps surgery to remove parts of the jaw.

Even during this time, Add would still teach classes when he was able; he was still asked to fill the pulpit of pastors who were away. Each time, he spoke what he knew to be true, not what he was experiencing in his *selva oscura*.

DOCTOR'S NOTES: Addison Leitch UNIT #181-51-85

The problem here, which is now a quite difficult one and the prognosis of which is quite grave, was discussed at length with his wife who is quite upset, and I believe justifiably so.

The fulminating character of both his lip and prostatic carcinomas would lead one to believe that we are dealing here with a situation of lack of whatever it takes on the part of the patient to resist florid tumor growth.

> *Ordinarily both lip and prostatic carcinomas are both*
> *indolent lesions and proceed leisurely, if not treated, for*
> *many months; whereas here we are dealing with quite*
> *fulminating disease in both instances.*

—M. D. S., M.D.[4]

They returned to Mass General for more radiation.

Add gagged on pills, suffered excruciating headaches, refused to attend at least one "healing meeting" that Elisabeth suggested. He was too tired to shave. What difference did it make, anyway? Students came to visit him, and he "talked entirely about his troubles," she wrote sadly, then explained, "I only put all this stuff down so that when he gets better we will remember how bad it was!"

Add often apologized to Elisabeth, telling her how sorry he was for what he was doing to her, how this time was an "awful waste" for her. He told her he expected to be bedridden all of July and August and could only hope for "an early demise." His brother Robert visited, alarmed by Add's depression.

Val came home from college for the summer.

On June 7 Elisabeth got word that her troubled friend and phone-pal in Oklahoma, Jandra, had committed suicide.

Add's two best friends, Frank Lawrence and Dick Kennedy, came to visit. They cheered him immensely.

But briefly. The next day Add left the breakfast table to vomit. He came back, then spilled egg on his shirt. It was hard for him to eat because of the scarring around his mouth. He shook his head and mopped furiously at his shirt, enraged at his own weakness. He told Elisabeth he thought of suicide every day.

The days went by, agonizingly slowly.

"Each day is a little worse," wrote Elisabeth.

"I pray for courage and understanding and heroism," Add told her angrily. "God doesn't hear me. Nothing works. Nothing works. Your prayers don't work. Your diets don't work. Your child psychology doesn't work. Can't you do anything for me? Can't anybody help me? Suicide would be a thousand times better. Don't you think we'd both be better off if I were dead?"

The doctor told Elisabeth that he would be "very pessimistic" regarding Add's prognosis.

Still, Elisabeth never gave up. She rallied constantly, holding onto shreds. If his appetite improved for a day or so, she saw a trend. If his headaches weren't as bad as they had been, maybe they were on their way out.

Add's greatest misery was his own inability to live well while he was dying. "I love you, darling," he whispered to Elisabeth one evening "Stick with me. Maybe I'll make it."

It got worse. He kept collapsing, and Elisabeth did not have the strength to get him up. At one point he crawled on his hands and knees, gasping and moaning, across their red bedroom carpet. "Can't somebody help me?" he cried. "God, take your hand off me, please have pity!"

"I am witnessing the total emotional and physical collapse and dissolution of the man I love," Elisabeth wrote in her journal. "I still have no doubt at all that God could heal him—indeed might heal him, but I pray that it be soon, or that God take him quickly."

X-rays showed widespread metastases in Add's skull, spine, and pelvis. And if Add's calcium levels in his bloodstream did not decrease, he could die at any time.

"The face of death is, as always, overwhelming. I can't let him go. 'Not now, Lord,' I find myself saying, as if any other time I might be willing. I want the best God has, I tell Him, but then in the depths of my head I want only one thing: Add. It's Add I want, Add I need, Add I can't bear to live without.

"Oh—if <u>only</u> . . ."

CHAPTER 28

Thy Will Be Done

"Thy will be done, though it be my undoing!"
—Elisabeth Elliot

Visitors came and went. On one busy Sunday in June 1973, Tom, Lovelace, Ginny, Katharine Howard, Miriam, Roger and Annette Nicole, and Bill Bronson all stopped by. Addison rallied, joked, asked questions and told stories with a brave shadow of his former ebullience.

After they'd all left, Addison wept. "The thought of how much he mattered to so many people just overwhelmed him." He and Elisabeth talked of the enormity of God's forgiveness. They marveled at the absolute surprise, joy, and "wonder" of their marriage. They updated their wills, and Add told Elisabeth what hymns and speakers he wanted at his funeral.

Addison's siblings, in-laws, and daughter Elizabeth also came around this time.

On June 15 he was admitted to Cable Memorial Hospital in Ipswich, Massachusetts, about five miles from home.

"Life is stranger—it has been strange indeed for seven months, but now, with this sentence of death actually upon him, I go on eating and drinking and talking to people, trying in my quiet moments to peer into the future. I can imagine widowhood, and [I can also imagine] a trip to Cambridge together with Add well and strong again."

The next day she wondered what death would be like when it came. "Cancer is a <u>great</u> and terrible <u>wilderness</u>. Lord God of Abraham, lead us through it. God of Moses, go with us, please."

She saw that her journal freshly started on January 1 of that year was about half full. She looked at the blank pages ahead. What would they hold?

6-18-73 Addison Leitch   UNIT #181-51-85

Our concern that this man was an example of one who does not have what it takes to contain malignant disease apparently has now been borne out. During the past week or 10 days, he has grown increasingly depressed, somewhat obtunded and wracked with pain. The bony metastases apparently are quite fulminating in character for metastatic [studies]carried out here a month ago showed only questionable bony lesions . . . Widespread bony metastases from lip are quite unusual . . . In any event, further radiotherapy to the lip would seem to be overridden by the urgency of the systemic metastases. . . . Plan is as follows: Dr. P to admit him to the hospital for appropriate chemotherapy and management of his abnormal blood chemistries. . . . If he responds to appropriate chemotherapy, then we can resume treatment of the lip in about 2 to 3 weeks; knowing of course that ultimately this is futile . . . Problem discussed with patient, and particularly his wife, who quite understands where we are.

—M.D. S., M.D.

Elisabeth had five bottles of pills, "powerful poisons" to help him sleep, decrease anxiety, relieve pain, and "combat cancer." The doctor was not allowing her to give him any vitamins. "I am out of it now—useless, and waiting on the pleasure of the doctors, waiting on Add, waiting for the God who hides Himself."

Addison Leitch UNIT#181-51-85

Patient was seen with Dr. R. having in mind the question of additional radical surgery. This, of course, can be done, but it would mean essentially sacrificing the lip, intervening skin of the anterior chin and mandibulectomy in order to remove the fixed node with supraomohyoid neck dissection. . . . The patient . . . and his wife as well, will not accept deforming surgery.

A few days later, at a friend's suggestion, she tried to give him vitamins. "He gagged on them—not having gagged on <u>any</u>" of the prescription drugs. "<u>How</u> does one help a person in such a bind?"

She now bathed, shaved, and dressed her husband, as he was too weak to do so.

Elisabeth thought of her hero C. S. Lewis's experience of a remission in his wife Joy's terrible cancer. She was "apparently dying, with nurses around the clock, and then a month or so later was apparently well."

> "Dear Lord—You can do that for Add. Please do it."
> "If on our daily course our mind
> Be set to hallow all we find
> New treasures still, of countless price
> God will provide for sacrifice.
> (John Keble—Episc. Hymnal #155)

"Add was perhaps given to me, as a treasure of countless price, that I might offer him back to God."

"What happiness Add and I have known!"

CONSULTATION RECORD, 6-16-73 #39935

Should the tumor be an anaplastic carcinoma of the prostate, diagnosis is grave as this usually is not a responsive tumor.

—J. R. P., MD

"It is a strange thing to have Death at your elbow, so consciously, at every moment." She made spaghetti for dinner, Add's favorite. As she put the leftovers in the freezer, she wondered, "Will Add eat this, or will he die before I get them out again?"

On July 15, Elisabeth woke with glorious hymns echoing in her mind. She quoted one to Add.

> "'Lord by the stripes that wounded thee,
> From death's dread sting they servants free
> That we may live and sing to thee
> Alleluia!'"

"Got any hymns for pain?" Add responded. He spoke of verses that refer to God torturing unbelievers in Revelation. "Are we supposed to love a God who tortures people? Is that why we are to love Him? He scares me to death. Not much hope in Revelation. I never know which crowd I'm in."

The doctors wanted Add to walk as much as he could. Every wobbly step was painful. He did not want to move.

Elisabeth tried to get him to do a few laps around the house.

He leaned heavily on her, gasping and groaning.

"You're heartless," he said. "Absolutely <u>heartless</u>. I simply cannot. I cannot get through to you. I hurt. I'm tortured with every step. But do you care? 'Come on,' you say. 'It'll do you good.'"

Elisabeth was torn. If she left him alone, his muscles would atrophy. But she could not give up. "He is a sick man. I am well, I love him—I <u>must</u> keep on, hoping, urging, trying to help. If only I knew how to do it without irritating him every minute."

"The spiritual darkness in which Add is engulfed is perhaps the worst aspect of this disease. He doubts the kindness and care of God, doubts his own salvation, fears death because he fears what happens next will be worse than this suffering. Lord, loose his bonds."

"God doesn't want an honest man," said Add. "Only a man who will whistle in the dark."

Meanwhile one of his doctors told Elisabeth that he thought Add's shaking and collapsing episodes were nervous reactions, and that "much of the back pain is muscular (needs exercise!). But he will not walk—says pain is excruciating."

On July 25 he was admitted to Cable Hospital in Ipswich.

"My loving Father. Loving Father! Where are You?" cried Addison. "I'm supposed to become as a little child. I have. I'm helpless. I can only hope against hope that somehow I will die like a man.

"You will know," he told Elisabeth, "on the Judgment Day, that you have been the instrument of my salvation."

"Oh, no!" she responded, her theology offended.

"Yes," Addison responded. "Perhaps it won't be seemly then to wink, but when it's announced I'll wink at you."

The next day, Elisabeth read Romans 8 out loud to Add in his hospital room. "I want that at my funeral," he said. Elisabeth leaned over the bed. "You are a lovely woman," he told her. "A glorious woman."

Oh, God, Elisabeth thought. She thought of Mary saying to Jesus, after her brother Lazarus had died, oh, Lord, if you had been here, he wouldn't have died. And then Mary had said, "And I know that, even now, God will give you whatever you ask of Him."

"Add lies here now, Lord, desperately ill," Elisabeth prayed. "Sinking. Beyond the reach of medicine. But EVEN NOW . . ."

"You—there were so many things I wanted to do with you," Add whispered to Elisabeth. He choked with tears. "The brightest thing in my life—and I've lost it."

They made funeral plans. "We are forced to think of the unthinkable." Death. It seemed so arbitrary, Elisabeth thought. She remembered C. S. Lewis's image, after his wife died, of some sort of capricious cosmic sorting:

"'You, madam to the right. You, sir, to the left.'"

"That is how it is," Elisabeth thought. "Summarily dismissed. Finished. Dispatched."

Add's daughter Helen arrived to visit and say goodbye to her father, who was still in the hospital. He was thrilled to see her. She stayed a few days, helped Elisabeth clean the house, and went to a friend's house for dinner with her. Both father and daughter wept when they parted.

"I keep wanting to plan things—plan going to heaven, what I'll do the first day."

Elisabeth received a letter from a missionary friend, reporting that he had heard Add was not expected to live and that Elisabeth was unable to accept it. "O God," she moaned, "must we have a whole new circuit of rumors?"

Pain. Agonies of discomfort over inability to have a bowel movement, the need for enemas. Oh, these grave indignities and humiliation for such a man.

Add's daughter, Katherine, had recently delivered a baby. Now she had an appendectomy and gynecological surgery. His other daughter Elizabeth went to Katherine's home to care for her newborn son. They could not visit.

One afternoon, after a variety of visitors, Elisabeth asked Add if she could lower his bed a little so he could rest.

"I don't want to do <u>anything</u>," he said.

"But you don't have to," Elisabeth responded. "I'll put the bed down, just to change your position."

"Oh, Sweetheart," he said. "Leave me alone. You can outthink me, out argue me, outdo me in anything. I can't meet challenges anymore. Every person who's been in this afternoon, I've had to <u>react</u> to. I'm exhausted."

For her part, Elisabeth felt like she wanted to "use every minute, talk, ask questions learn from him, harvest his wonderful mind of whatever these nine long, long months have taught him.

"But silence and peace are what he needs."

On August 7, Elisabeth wrote in her journal, "COULD TODAY BE THE TURNING POINT?"

Addison was calmer, had less pain, more strength to stand and walk. Two friends both felt he was going to be healed. At college, Valerie was fasting from lunch each day until Add was healed.

"Something surely remains to happen before healing comes," thought Elisabeth, "but I believe it will come."

"But faith is sorely tested every day," she wrote in her journal. "Yesterday Add was miserable. . . . His spirits were sunken and almost bitter, asking again how God can look on His suffering children so coolly, not lifting a finger to help. I am dumb when he goes on like this—he has done it for nearly 10 months now. I have no replies left. I am, as he points out, <u>well</u>."

The next day he was in a state of near-euphoria—painless, eager to get up to eat lunch with Elisabeth. By the afternoon the tide shifted completely.

Elisabeth's uncle recommended that she persuade him to go to a doctor in Mexico for Laetrile treatment. (The doctor would later be widely condemned in the medical community for his false claims about Laetrile's healing properties for cancer patients.)

Add was exhausted. He didn't want to talk, didn't want Elisabeth to cover him up, didn't want lunch. She asked a question about a letter he had received. "Don't cross-examine me!" he rasped.

"I know these are nothing but the ravings of a sick man," Elisabeth wrote in her journal, "and it is foolish to take them personally, but I am a person!"

Friends came and encouraged Elisabeth by saying that Add was putting up a tremendous fight.

He was able to walk, with a walker, and sat in a chair for a half hour. He spoke of having to develop a will to live—before this it hadn't been strong because he felt life would be a very poor business as only "half a man, good for nothing but raking leaves."

"Now the healing process may have begun," wrote Elisabeth.

The next day was Addison's worst day of pain yet.

CHAPTER 29

Does the Road Run
Uphill All the Way?

*"I am grateful, too, to Lewis for having the courage to yell,
to doubt, to kick at God with angry violence. This is a part
of healthy grief not often encouraged. It is helpful indeed that
C. S. Lewis, who has been such a successful apologist for
Christianity, should have the courage to admit doubt about
what he has so superbly proclaimed. It gives us permission to
admit our own doubts, our own angers and anguishes, and to
know that they are part of the soul's growth."*
—Madeleine L'Engle, foreword to Lewis, *A Grief Observed*

Add came home from the hospital for the last time on August 22, 1973. Elisabeth felt horribly anxious about how to care for him when he could not move, how to endure his pain and crying, and how to best care for his bodily functions.

Today many of us who have been in Elisabeth's situation have relied on hospice care, with its compassionate expertise in dealing with those who need palliative, rather than curative, care. Hospice nurses, social workers, chaplains, and nursing assistants take the burden off family members in everything from pain management to funeral planning to bathing and physical help to empathetic counsel. But hospice care was not introduced to the United States until 1974.

And who knows if Elisabeth Elliot, strong and independent as she was, would have availed herself of such help and relief.

Elisabeth jotted her frustrations, fears, and sadness in her journal.

"August 26. Greater weakness than ever before. More yelling and disgust with me." She read to him out loud from Martin Luther's "marvelous sermon on Abraham and Isaac."

He stopped her before she was done.

"Enough of that! Very cheerful reading! Do I <u>hurt</u>! Would you plump up the pillows and turn on the TV?"

"August 27. O Lord—why don't You just <u>heal</u> him?"

"September 2. Steadily downhill. I am always torn between two things: do I insist that he move (e.g., to the commode, or to turn on his side in bed, or allow me to [elevate] the head of the bed, or do I allow him to grow weaker by not moving at all (which means having [bowel movements] in bed, no bedpan, since he cannot raise hips)."

"The power of evil—death, desolation, dissolution—is tremendous."

"September 4. Dave Howard [Elisabeth's brother] and his son came. Stephen had been given the gift of healing while in Colombia, and has just now spent three days fasting and praying in the woods of New York, preparing to visit his Uncle Add. He laid hands on Add, prayed, and told him he believes he'll be healed."

Add put out a fleece—that the purple marks on the backs of his hands would have begun to fade by this morning.

Nothing happened.

"He hasn't been out of bed to walk for five days. He grew weaker each day."

Addison's sister, Margaret Leitch, arrived on September 5. A nurse, she was a great help to Elisabeth.

But still, Elisabeth's grief was private, excruciating, specific. "Thy will be done, though it be my undoing!"

"September 8. The doctor visited. A horror of great darkness looms in front of me. I try to prepare myself for Add's death, try to accept it, while at the same time praying earnestly . . . for a miracle."

Elisabeth thought again of C. S. Lewis's wife, who had a few weeks to live, then recovered and lived another two years in remission. She pled with God for the same for Add.

"September 9. Tonight after the going to bed ritual—urinal, clean-up of stool, back wash and application of silicone ointment, pills, face wash, I prayed with him as I always do, then we went over some of our most exciting and happy times until the Nembutal had him almost asleep. I went to bed, at peace once more after a very sad day and lots of tears. I do not think God means to heal him now. I hope I am wrong, and I still pray for it."

On September 10 Mair Walters, their close friend who was a doctor, came and found Add's pulse very weak. She told Elisabeth that he had made up his mind to die, and not to try to make him eat or move.

"How does one die?" Add asked Elisabeth. He felt sure that he would run the gamut of all the stories he had ever heard about death. Would he go out screaming or choking? Would his pain increase? What time of day do people die, anyway? Since the lump on his lip continued to grow, would God let him live long enough to have to have his jaw removed?

Friends came, in and out all day. They held Add's hands, told him of their love, and wept. Some said goodbye.

"I am, as before, wondrously sustained," wrote Elisabeth. "Peace. Anticipation of joy for Add, quietness and confidence from God for myself. How is this? I do not know. One thing I know, that whereas I was terrified and stricken, I am calm."

On September 11, Elisabeth thought about how grateful she was that Add was not in the hospital, but home, in his own study, with his Michelangelo pictures over the bed, his Cambridge diploma framed on the wall, and the garden outside the window. The comfort of the familiar . . . yet these were strange days. It was as though an unknown visitor was about to appear. You try to prepare for him, but you have no idea how to do so. You imagine the moment you'll hear his knock on the door.

"I don't want anybody to come in," Add whispered. "Don't touch me. Let me alone. Let me die."

The nurse returned, baffled that Add's pulse was strong, his blood pressure normal. He ate and drank a little. Elisabeth wondered about remission. "I simply cannot face life," said Add, exhausted. "I can't die but I can't live.

"I'm so frightened and lonely and I don't know what to do," he told Elisabeth. There were no options but to accept or reject what God was doing. Elisabeth spoke to him of the Old Testament account of God leading Israel into Marah—where the Tree made the waters sweet.

"In my wildest imaginings I can't picture healing," he said.

"No, nor I," said Elisabeth. "But we pray, 'Help Thou mine unbelief.'"

"Something is happening in Add," she wrote in her journal. "Some subtle change and softening."

"You have brought me peace, darling, when you talk to me like this. And when you pray for me. Please keep on." She read him all of 1 Peter, Romans 8:14–28, and 2 Corinthians 1:9–11, which says, "Indeed, we felt we had received the sentence of death. But this happened that we might not rely on ourselves but on God, who raises the dead. He has delivered us from such a deadly peril, and he will deliver us again. On him we have set our hope that he will continue to deliver us . . ." (NIV).

"That was wonderful," said Add.

Tom Howard felt that Add was being gradually divested of all that had shaped his personality and experience. "Little by little his responsibilities were stripped away, his powers dissolved, his helplessness more obvious, and, finding himself unable to do anything for anybody, including himself, he could not come to terms with the fact that there was, at last, absolutely nothing to do. Just lie in the Arms," Tom told him. "The everlasting Arms."[1]

"But I don't know how," Add said. "I try to let go and let God, but I don't know how."

September 13 was a night of wild dreams. Add asked Elisabeth, over and over, if his blood calcium level was rising. He knew that if it reached a certain level, coma and death would follow. He wanted to know if there was any way to *make* it rise.

Val was getting ready to return to Wheaton College. Gordon Conwell was gearing up for a new academic year as well. Elisabeth had sought out a student as a lodger, someone who could help her with the physical chores that Add could no longer do. "Walter Shepard, seminary student, will be moving in to board on Monday," Elisabeth wrote in her journal. "Thank God for this provision."

Elisabeth read Add the gospel account of the servant of a faith-filled Roman centurion, whom Jesus healed when he was "at the point of death."

"I'm so frightened," said Add.

"O Lord," Elisabeth prayed. "Deliver him, dear Lord, from <u>all his fears</u>."

At 2:30 in the morning, Add woke without pain. He told Elisabeth of his dreams. He was at a country fair with his daughter Katherine and her husband, Tom. Wild animals roamed the grounds. There were snuckleberries.

"*Snuckleberries?*" asked Elisabeth.

"Shhh," Addison said. "Don't mention it, darling. You'll make me sick. I've been fighting snuckleberries all night!"

He went on. "My head feels square, doesn't it? If I were <u>you</u>, I'd look after <u>me</u>."

The next day, September 14, his head still felt square. He felt "close to the edge." He wanted Elisabeth to hold him. "What am I supposed to <u>do</u>?" Elisabeth read Scripture, Amy Carmichael poems,

Psalms, parts of *Pilgrim's Progress*, and some of the classic hymns they both loved.

> "And when my task on earth is done
> When by Thy grace the victory's won
> E'en death's cold wave I will not flee
> Since God through Jordan leadeth me."[2]

On September 15, as Elisabeth bathed Add's poor, thin body, he talked about Christianity and suffering. "Do they have to go together? My kind has ignored all that. My life has been easy."

"Perhaps it seems easy as you look back," said Elisabeth, "because you were simply using what had been put into your hand."

"But what about all this doing-the-will-of-God sort of thing?" he responded.

"That's what it means—doing what has been given you to do, using your gifts."

Elisabeth washed his purple-blotched hands. Words from British poet Christina Rossetti came to mind. "Does the road wind uphill all the way?"

She rolled him to his side. He had lost so much mass that he weighed about the same as Elisabeth, and it was easier than it had been for her to physically manage him. She bathed his reddened, bony spine with its pressure sores, quoting the story of the Prodigal Son.

After Add was cleaned up, a friend came to visit. He reminded Add, a former athlete, of how the football coach claps his quarterback on the back. That's how Add would be welcomed into the Kingdom, the game completed.

On Sunday, September 16 Val left for the fall semester at Wheaton. Add's nights were hideous, filled with swirling currents of disorientation, nightmares, dark tides of swirling fear. When Tom Howard came to visit, Add asked him if he'd do him a favor and bring him a gun.

On the morning of September 17, Add was weak, confused, and sleepy. Elisabeth filled a basin with warm water. She elevated the head of the bed slightly and sat by her husband. She took Add's thin hands and tenderly dipped them in the water, soaped them, rinsed them, and dried them. She cleaned and trimmed his fingernails. She wasn't sure just why she needed to do this, but it was important.

Elisabeth's memory brimmed with King James Version Bible texts she had known since her childhood. Her mind now went to Jesus and the woman who had washed His feet, dried them with her hair, and anointed Him with perfume.

"Against the day of my burying hath she done this," Jesus had said.

Tom Howard stopped by the house at about noon before he headed over to Gordon College to teach his 1 p.m. lecture. He found Elisabeth siting in her upholstered rocking chair next to the head of Add's bed. He seemed to be sleeping. Tom and Elisabeth talked for a while, and Tom asked about Add's breathing. It seemed so shallow and rapid, and Tom was trying to figure out if Add looked worse—or not—than he had a week earlier when they had all thought he was going to die.

Tom went on to his lecture.

As Elisabeth sat with Add, his respiration became more of a rattle. At about 2 p.m. he tried to cough up some phlegm, then his eyes rolled back, and his head fell to one side. Elisabeth couldn't find a pulse. She shouted for Add's sister Margaret, who came running and could not find it either. They called the doctor.

Elisabeth also called Lovelace Howard to see if she could get hold of Tom.

After his lecture, Tom was talking with one of his colleagues, a history professor who had asked about Addison. They were coming through the entrance to the administration building, and the receptionist came running out of her office.

"Dr. Howard!" she called. "Your wife is on the phone. Your brother-in-law needs you!"

Tom sprinted across campus to his car, jumped in, and drove as fast as he could to the Leitch home. He ran in the front door.

In the ninety minutes since Tom had last seen him, Add "seemed to have crossed whatever that frontier is that lies between one's being gravely, terminally ill, and the business of dying. This was death now. Life was over. No more marking time."[3]

More cars screeched to a halt in front of the Leitch home as other family and friends arrived. Add hovered in and out of consciousness, breathing shallowly, speaking a few indecipherable words. He asked Elisabeth to pray the Lord's prayer. He asked Tom and Elisabeth if they were sure he was going. How did they know? Why were all these people here?

Their rector and friend, Jim Hampson, read the Psalm 23. Elisabeth quoted from Add's favorite hymns. His loved ones held his hand. He seemed to hear most of the time as they talked to him.

"Is everything all right?" asked Elisabeth.

"Great," he responded. Van put a hot water bottle at his feet. "That feels marvelous." He seemed to believe he had committed suicide. Why all these parade of people here? What had become of his plan?

"Let 'er go," he said.

He said something about Jesus Christ, of being raised up. He seemed, at last, at peace. Rector Jim Hampson asked him if he was trusting in Jesus Christ for his salvation.

"Yes."

At 11:30 p.m., Elisabeth asked the others to leave her alone with him. At 11:45, though she saw no change, she felt her husband would die before midnight. She prayed to God to take him.

His breathing slowed. And then, at 11:55, he slid away to freedom.

CHAPTER 30

A Paper Streamer

"Grand, Almighty God, as the darkness and hardness
of our flesh is so great that it is needful for us to be in
various ways afflicted—grant that we patiently bear thy
chastisement, and under deep sorrow flee to Thy mercy
displayed to us in Christ, so that we depend not on the
earthly blessings of this perishable life, but relying on Thy
word go forward in the course of our calling, until at length
we be gathered to that blessed rest which is laid up for us in
heaven, through Christ our Lord. Amen."
—prayer with which John Calvin concludes
his exposition of Habakkuk, carefully noted in
Elisabeth Elliot's journal October 3, 1973

The day after Add's death, Elisabeth wrote in her journal, not for the
first or last time, the fourteenth-century mystic Julian of Norwich's
words, "All shall be well and all shall be well and all manner of things
shall be well."

Elisabeth went on, "The whole sequence of the last 11 months
looks to me now utterly unendurable and nightmarish. Oh, the suffering that dear man underwent. What an exquisite torture of mind, soul,
and body. I do not know how we got through any of it. How ironic
that Add was <u>able</u> to live through one phase in order to experience
another and worse one, and another. . . . <u>Hideous</u>. Entirely hideous.
Lord have mercy. Christ have mercy."

Still, she was grateful that Add had died soon after he fell into
a coma. Dr. Mair Walters, who had been such an encouragement
through the long, horrible months, had told Elisabeth that she had
seen people in Add's condition go on breathing for a week or so.

Elisabeth filled out paperwork, made phone calls, put plans in motion that she and Add had made together what seemed like a long time ago. On Tuesday, the day after his death, there were viewing hours at the funeral home. Though she had never liked that practice, Elisabeth now found it comforting to "see Add dressed, groomed, peaceful. . . . There is something to be said for looking death in the face once more in the detached environment of the funeral home— as opposed to the deathbed itself—accepting it finally, and turning away."

The next morning, there was a gathering at Gordon Seminary before Add's late afternoon funeral service. The Dean of Students opened the microphone to anyone who wanted to reflect on Dr. Leitch.

"It was wonderful," said Tom Howard. "Student after student, and faculty members too, spoke of his humor, of his incisive mind, of his magnanimity, of his stature, and of his friendliness."[1]

The family returned home to Elisabeth's house for the final journey. A long line of cars followed the black hearse. Addison's coffin was covered with a white and gold pall from Christ Church. The service was simple, with the elements Addison had chosen with Elisabeth back in June. Armand Nicoli spoke, and Add's best friend Dick Kennedy brought tears and laughter in his words about Add. The organ swelled with Add's favorite hymns. Then the coffin was carried out to the hearse, and there, "across from the chapel, on the knoll in front of the library, stood the whole student body, those who had not been able to get into the chapel—absolutely silent, watching their great teacher and dear friend being taken away."[2]

The solemn procession arrived at Hamilton Cemetery, established in 1713. Sunshine filtered through the soaring, old trees. The moss-covered gravestones marked the lives of those who had fought in the Revolutionary War and lived their lives in the rocky New England soil ever since. Led by their rector, Jim Hampson, in the Office for the Burial of the Dead, Elisabeth, her family, and Addison's loved ones commended his remains to the earth, confident of the resurrection of the dead.

I am the resurrection and the life, saith the Lord; he that believeth in me, though he were dead, yet shall he live; and whosoever liveth and believeth in me shall never die. I know that my Redeemer liveth, and that he shall stand at the latter day upon the earth; and though this body be destroyed, yet shall I see God; whom I shall see for myself and mine eyes shall behold, and not as a stranger. For none of us liveth to himself, and no man dieth to himself. For if we live, we live unto the Lord; and if we die, we die unto the Lord. Whether

we live, therefore, or die, we are the Lord's. Blessed are the
dead who die in the Lord; even so saith the Spirit, for they
rest from their labors.[3]

The days went by. Elisabeth waded through paperwork, filling out forms about "the decedent," who was "gone now, not to return, and the mind cannot apprehend it. His strong step, cheerful voice, large masculinity are in every room. I threw away combs, toothbrushes, cancelled checks . . . [and] old letters."

"I am a social misfit again."

A friend had invited her to a concert, telling her to "Bring a friend."

Elisabeth repeated his words in her mind. *"Bring a friend"? What friend? Add was my friend.*

She and Tom went to a movie. Tom could not comprehend that Add was actually gone. "I have found my imagination utterly rejecting the whole thing. A thousand times a day I am jolted to my senses and realize that for a few minutes or moments I have been blithely and semi-consciously assuming that it was all an unfortunate [misunderstanding] and I can ring him up for some tennis, or whatever.

"[Elisabeth] and I went to a movie last night, and I sat there thinking,

'Dear Christ, this is a grotesque farce—me squiring her out here, when this was Add's and her favorite pastime. Where is the man who has sat next to her in theatres for four years?

This is a beggarly stand-in, for heaven's sake.'"[4]

But, as all who have been bereaved know, life somehow goes on. You do the next thing. By October 5 Elisabeth was on a plane to Colorado Springs, where she honored a previously committed speaking engagement at a conference for Mennonite women. Then she spent three days visiting Val at Wheaton.

Back home, Add's absence was unfathomable.

"Today was a bad one. The idea of dressing in a long dress to go out to dinner at [a friend's home] seems a horrible charade. I don't want to go out or go to bed without Add. As long as I am at the desk or reading, I am all right for those are things I always did without him."

She thought of all the "lasts." The last time Add wore a tie, the last time they slept together, the last time he wore his glasses or his watch. She remembered how anxious he had been about the passing moments, asking her repeatedly what time it was, feeling so distressed that it was always <u>earlier</u> than he thought. He longed to die.

"To me," Elisabeth wrote, "in the face of his death, I was overcome with the pathos of mortality. The sense of a steadily widening gulf between us. Last November [when the cancer was diagnosed], the ship's whistle blew and slowly, imperceptibly, she began to pull away. I held a paper streamer, which broke on September 17.

"But what a <u>gift</u> he was to me! O God, what a gift! Thanks, Lord, Father of Mercies. And now in this strange land where I live, how shall I sing the Lord's song? How? 'By My grace,' I hear You say. So, by your grace, I sing."

For Elisabeth, mundane routine was the best support for her soul, the unlikely mechanism by which she could "sing" of God's grace. "I can function with almost my customary efficiency and concentration so long as I operate by habit—the sameness, ordinariness and necessity are comfortable for me. It is in the interruption of routine, especially in social life, that I find myself beginning to disintegrate and turn inward. This is hazardous, and I have to take the reins firmly and say <u>giddyap</u>."

She kicked her inner horse toward the holidays. On Thanksgiving she remembered the apprehension of the year before, when she and Add were living with the dark cloud of cancer's possibilities, but carrying on as if all was normal. She reflected on the tenth anniversary of C. S. Lewis's death; he had died just before his sixty-fifth birthday, as had Add. She read Clyde Kilby's beautiful new book, *Images of [Lewis's] World*. If Lewis had had a "normal" life, Elisabeth reflected, with the bustle of a wife and children during his adult years, the rest of us would not have had the great gifts of his books.

"I supposed the reason that the huge joys of the flesh seem so all-important when one has been bereaved is that we <u>were</u> 'one flesh.' So what am I now? I am quite literally lost, i.e., I can't find the way. Fragmented. Disoriented. My body, my face in the mirror, my clothes, my perfume all are divested of meaning. It was all his. He's gone, he doesn't need any of me any more than he needs his own clothes, some of which hang in the closet."

She felt so alone.

"The Great Shepherd of the Sheep brings His flock, slowly and carefully as they are ready for it, to the dark valleys and ravines. One of these valleys is where the sheep finds himself apparently cut off from the rest of the flock. Loneliness, perhaps ostracism because of misunderstanding, perhaps another isolation. And he must then learn that the Shepherd is all he needs."

Here, in the core of her hideous loss, Elisabeth looked back again to the fundamental losses of her life. It was not hard—they were always, it seems, present in her mind, part of that which shaped her experience and her understanding of the mystery of faith in an inscrutable God. Now Add's death would seem to be the crowning loss.

"My Macario experience: all that had been so wonderfully given in answer to prayer was withdrawn suddenly and brutally."

Macario was Elisabeth's language informant and irreplaceable interpreter during her early days in Ecuador. She was trying to translate the New Testament into Tsafiki, the unwritten, difficult language of the Tsáchila people. Macario was a godsend for which she thanked the Lord every day.

Then he was shot in the head. She had stared at his body and railed at the cruel sovereignty of God . . . "the sight of those spilled brains, the only brains in the world that contained the languages" she needed. Was she an absolute fool for even attempting to carry out what she believed was God's will?

After Elisabeth picked herself up and painstakingly, agonizingly recreated her language notes, cards, indices, and explanations, she'd carefully stored them in a hard-sided suitcase for safekeeping. The suitcase was stolen.

Around the same time period, Elisabeth's fiancé Jim Elliot had nearly died when an enormous flood washed over the Shandia mission station. Jim and the other missionaries feverishly moved as much of the buildings' contents, supplies, and materials as they could to higher ground. The waters churned, rose, surged, and the entire mission station was washed away into the raging river. All their earnest, painstaking work for God, lost. Why?

This, she wrote now, was a demand from God for unconditional trust.

Then Jim, passionately committed to bringing the great news of the gospel to the Waodani, was brutally speared and hacked to death. Slaughtered at age twenty-eight. Why?

This, she said, made the meaning of the Cross actual, rather than theoretical.

Then, improbably, Elisabeth's dream to reach the Waodani came true. She lived among them . . . and had to leave because of an elemental inability to get along, not with the tribal people, but her fellow American missionary, Rachel Saint.

In this, she surrendered her goals and reputation.

Then, much later, she'd poured herself into writing *No Graven Image*. Though her fiction was set in a different location, it was the best rendition she could do of the real story she'd lived in the jungle, and the absolute mystery of God's sovereign, sometimes agonizing ways. And Christian people had hated it. Bookstores had refused to carry it.

This, she said, was the destruction of her "spiritual self-hood."

And now. God had surprisingly gifted her with her spiritual, intellectual, emotional, and physical soulmate. Then He had ripped Add away. Slowly. Cruelly. How much more might the Almighty rip from her hands?

It wasn't just the loss of her beloved, but "another death to who I am. Another '[kernel] of wheat' (what I was when I was his wife—my body his flesh, my mind the answer to his, my personality molded and changed and nourished by his, my self-image the image I understood him to see) falling into the ground to die—and now, if it is, what fruit is it to bring forth?"

She went on to plumb the "hope" that she had had when Add was first diagnosed, and to analyze its place in the whole mystery of hopes dashed and losses endured. It had been hope in a particular outcome . . . an outcome that God did not choose to grant.

"How to describe the hope on which we fed a year ago? Our souls are narrow, our vision limited, and we could not bear to think that the happy promises would only be fulfilled on the far side of death. The hope that they mean NOW was the hope we could cling to and operate on. But the day-by-day going forward in the strength of this (false) hope was what brought us to the place of final surrender and acceptance. We hadn't the grace to surrender at the beginning—it was not time. It was time to hope and to go on in faith."

By Christmas time, and Elisabeth's forty-seventh birthday, she and Val were in Ginny and Bud deVries' new home in Grand Rapids.

"As I think of my widowhood," Elisabeth wrote, "I see it as a displacement, of course. But a Christian is only 'displaced' in relation to human society and as he experiences loss in his immediate situation. He is still a member of Christ's body, irreplaceable in the total prayer of the Church. I pray for wholeness and continuance in the great movement of the church toward God, for the humble and grateful acceptance of the obligation laid upon me specifically by this 'displacement'—which is really a reassignment.

"Marriage is normally the first opportunity to know ourselves, our weakness, and our capacities. Day by day, in the business of loving and living with another who is a part of ourselves and yet opposite, we discover much that has heretofore been hidden from our own eyes. It is a fire, a purging fire, and we should recognize and accept its action.

On Christmas Eve, Peter deVries and a Finnish exchange student who lived with the deVries' family played violin and cello, with Ginny accompanying them on the piano. "So heavenly I found myself crying as I listened. What music—what gifts of God to lighten our darkness."

Fulfilling another commitment made long before her life turned inside out, Elisabeth spoke at Urbana, the 10th annual InterVarsity

Christian Fellowship student missions conference. Begun in 1946 and held every three years, it was a five-day celebration with plenary speakers and dozens of seminars on various aspects of missionary service, culminating in a midnight worship service on New Year's Eve 1973. Students and speakers attended from all over the world. Elisabeth Elliot was the first woman to give a plenary speech at Urbana, whose main-stage platform previously had been confined to men.

Elisabeth gloried at the music and singing of 16,000 souls in the Convention Hall. Tears stung her eyes at the great choruses of "And Can It Be," and the convention hymn, "Lord of the Universe." She thought how Add would have loved being there.

The discussion groups Elisabeth led in the afternoons were packed. She was asked about single women on the missions field, "fulfillment in marriage," language work, writing, *No Graven Image*, and the hot topic of the day, women's liberation. She noted that "One militant women's libber gave me a note afterwards telling she 'happens to know that Dr. Mollenkott [Elisabeth's old friend] has bitter feelings toward me.'"

Sigh.

There were believers from around the globe, testimonies of God's improbable grace in Asia, Africa, Europe, and even the United States. John Stott, who won Elisabeth's heart when he said, "Freedom is submission to truth."

She described the scene as Philip Teng of CMA Hong Kong spoke. "People swing their legs over railings, bounce their feet up and down, cough, . . . , put on coats and take them off, and when it is on such a grand scale (16,000) it is a continuous flutter."

An earnest male student approached Elisabeth one afternoon and told her how he had heard that she and Jim Elliot, who he evidently thought of as spiritual superheroes, would memorize an entire chapter of Scripture in preparation for every single date. Elisabeth let him know that that was not quite the case.

"The entire Urbana experience was indescribable and unbelievable. Final communion service from 10:30 to midnight on December 31 was as close to anything I can imagine heaven's being like. Everyone shouting with a loud voice, WORTHY IS THE LAMB!"

The entire congregation, thousands upon thousands of formerly noisy students, were absolutely silent for forty-five minutes as the bread and wine were served and the new year—1974—dawned.

"It seemed to me," Elisabeth wrote, "that God had timed this thing 'just for me'—I was immensely helped, healed, heartened, and inspired to give myself and all I have for the world, especially for the world of students if God wills."

Elisabeth's green leatherette Herald Square journal was almost full as the sun set on 1973.

Elisabeth used its last two pages to list, first, the notable deaths of 1973:

Addison Leitch . . . brilliance, creativity, bravery

Pablo Picasso, the renowned abstract painter

Lyndon Johnson, former president of the United States

Edward G. Robinson, one of the top-rated stars in Hollywood's "Golden Age"

Noel Coward, British playwright, actor, and composer

David Ben Gurion, first Prime Minister of the State of Israel

"It was the year of Watergate, of POWs coming home, of Le Duc Tho and Henry Kissinger's agreements in Paris, of Princess Anne's wedding to Mark Phillips, of the fuel shortage and Arab terrorists hijacking a jet in Rome."

It was one of the few times, really, that she consciously set her journal writings in their historical context.

"I look at the new blank calendar for 1974, remembering the big black Xs on our 1973 kitchen calendar for January and February, each marking a radiation treatment in Boston, each a symbol—'Now that one's over, finally all 33 treatments will be finished and we can begin to look for improvement.'

"And there were those hideous nights when Add could not sleep. And the continued sense of balancing on a knife-edge of sanity and faith, an abyss of madness and despair yawning on either side.

"Once again, peace. 'O God, You have always been our home . . .'

"And once again I commit my life into those strong hands, praying the prayer of Betty Scott Stam, 'Work out Thy whole will in my life, at any cost, now and forever.'"

CHAPTER 31

Men in the House

"Life must go on, I forget just why."
—Edna St. Vincent Millay

I now have two lodgers," Elisabeth had noted in her green journal five days after her husband died. "Walter Shepard and Lars Gren."

Both Walt and Lars were students at Gordon-Conwell. They were both tall. They both had Southern manners and charm. But any similarities ended there. It would be difficult to find two more different human beings. One would marry Valerie. And the other would marry Elisabeth.

In 1973, Walt Shepard was a long-haired piece of work with a colorful past. He'd grown up in what is now the Democratic Republic of the Congo. His parents were brave, godly missionaries. Walt loved his friends and his freedom in Africa. When he was ten, he heard on the radio—Voice of America—about the death of Jim Elliot and his missionary colleagues in far-away Ecuador.

The Shepard family returned to their home in New Orleans in 1960. Walt was sixteen, a sophomore in high school. He'd grown up playing soccer with his African friends; now, in the American South, football was king, and soccer was for wimps and foreigners. His buddies in Africa had all been black. Now he heard people with dark skin called horrible names. "The word got out that my parents had been missionaries to Africans," Walt says today. "I got beat up a lot."

He graduated from high school, played football in college for a while, then messed up his knees. He graduated from Belmont and planned to be an interpreter for the United Nations in the Congo. He changed his mind and worked construction, then worked in management with Pan American Airlines in New York for two years, making decent money and living the high life with friends on Long Island, drinking a lot of Schlitz beer and eating a lot of spaghetti and Ragu.

He decided to head toward home. He stopped in Nashville and met up with college friends who were starting a nightclub there with an African safari theme. They wanted Walt to manage it.

It sounded good. The club booked the big bands of the day and made tons of money. The police looked the other way when some of the club's under-the-radar activities got their attention. The assistant manager insisted on a gun at the front door. The volatile atmosphere started to make Walt nervous.

One night Walt was working the bar, moving fast, angry with one of the wait staff. He felt a pair of eyes on him. He knew it could not be the cops.

It was worse. His dad.

Walt had been living on vodka and grapefruit juice; he had enormous, dark bags under his eyes that were visible even in the low light of the bar. His dad just looked at him.

"How are you doing, Son?" Walter Shepard Sr. asked. "Your mom and I are kind of worried about you."

Walt's dad left soon after that, but his nonconfrontational words broke something inside of Walt. He had known, but not really admitted, that things were worse at his place of business than just the nightclub scene. He started asking questions and discovered that there was a secret business partner who was part of some dark dealings that made him very uncomfortable.

Never one to be shy about making decisive moves, one night Walt just quit pouring drinks, closed the cash registers, stopped the music, and told everybody to go home. "We're closed," he yelled.

The next morning, there were some violent repercussions from his decision. It would be prudent for Walt to move on. He went home to Louisiana. He thought about Jesus. He read Christian books. He wanted the faith of his parents, but he wanted the dark side too. He was popular with women—partially because he asked great questions and sincerely cared about people—but he felt like a phony. He got engaged. His fiancée knew his conflict within but hoped for the best. They visited his parents' home, and one Sunday when they were sitting in their church, she jumped up and bolted out of the service.

When Walt found her, she was weeping. "I saw your parents holding hands in church," she said. "I don't want what they have. I can't share you with someone else."

"Who are you talking about?" Walt sputtered. "There's no one else."

"I'm talking about *God*!" she whispered.

Her jealousy floored Walt. Here he was, trying to inch back toward life and faith, and she wanted nothing of it.

They broke it off. One evening Walt had been drinking heavily. In the middle of the night he decided he would go see his lost love. Even in his altered condition, he knew it was a poor decision.

Why are you doing this? he thought as he sped down the highway to meet her. *You're just going to royally mess up her life.* And down deep, he knew she wasn't what he yearned for, anyway. His speedometer kept inching up, faster and faster—140 miles per hour. 3:42 a.m.

A car had stopped in the road shoulder in front of him to switch drivers, both of whom were not in the vehicle. Walt plowed straight into it. He went through his windshield, ending up somewhere on the engine. His sports car burst into flames. A hotel manager saw the fire and called 911; troopers were there almost immediately. They could not approach the vehicle because of the blaze.

Standing there, helpless until firefighters arrived, the troopers saw two unknown men walk straight into the flames, pull an unconscious Walt out of the fire, one lifting his shoulders, the other holding his legs. The ambulance arrived, and the paramedics rushed to lift Walt onto the gurney. They loaded him into the ambulance, and blared away to the hospital.

The troopers looked for the two guys who had pulled Walt from the fire. They needed their testimony as witnesses so they could charge Walt with reckless driving. If he lived.

The two men were nowhere to be found.

On arrival at the hospital, Walt had to be resuscitated. When he came to, eventually he became aware that his ear was on his shoulder, connected by a tiny flap of skin, he was bleeding everywhere, and his leg was broken in four places.

"You ought to do something about that leg," a nurse whispered. "He won't need it where he's going," the doctor replied.

But Walt lived. He eventually got out of intensive care. He told the nurses not to let any pastors or chaplains in. He was angry, bitter, hopeless.

His parents came. His dad brought Walt his Bible, the one they had given him when he was ten years old, the one that he'd kept under the seat of his sports car like a good luck charm. It was covered with dried blood.

That night something broke inside of Walt.

"Oh, God!" he moaned. "If you can forgive a guy like me, don't just forgive me, give me a new life, because I can't do this one anymore."

He slept. It was his first deep, untroubled slumber in years.

The next morning his usual, hearty African American nurse bustled in, humming hymns, arranging the blinds . . . and then she stopped to take a second look at Walt.

"Oh, my Lord!" she yelled, running out of the room. "He's got it! He's got the Holy Ghost!"

Many months later, Walt could hobble on crutches. He read and reread Luke 15, rehearsing the speech of the prodigal son. He made an appointment with his dad's assistant to see his father at his office. He took the bus to the stop nearest the office.

Since he was expected, he shuffled straight in, awkward on his crutches. His dad jumped up from his desk. He had no idea that his "next appointment" was in fact his son. "It's you!" he cried.

They went down the hall to a private meeting room.

"Dad!" Walt sobbed. "I've lived a terrible lie. I've done everything I can to deny everything you've stood for. Please forgive me!" His dad cried too. "Has God forgiven you, Son?" Walt's dad replied. "Then I forgive you."

Next, Walt took the bus to his parents' home. He tottered up the front walk and to the screen door. Through it he could hear the telephone ringing. His mother answered it, then came to the door to find her son.

"Oh!" she said, smiling big. "The phone's for you, Walt!"

Walt came into the house and picked up the old-fashioned black telephone receiver. "Hello?" he said, tentatively. Then he heard his father's voice. "Welcome home, Son!"

Buoyed by the mighty tide of forgiveness and the love of the Father, Walt continued to heal, physically and spiritually. He was able to start working construction. He carried a Bible in his bib overalls. He started reaching out with the gospel to high school kids, street people, and hippies. He decided to go to a new seminary run by 1970s "end times" author Hal Lindsey. It was in California; Walt could just see beach ministry in his future.

Walt's dad and Billy Graham were great friends. When Dr. Graham heard about Walt's seminary plans, he gave him another option.

"Son," he told Walt. "I serve on the board of a seminary called Gordon-Conwell in Massachusetts . . ."

Next thing twenty-seven-year-old Walt knew in the late summer and fall of 1972, he was enrolling in Gordon-Conwell Seminary and showing up at classes smelling of manure since he was working mucking stables for the polo ponies at the tony Myopia Hunt Club. While he looked for a permanent place to live, he was sleeping on a friend's too-short couch.

During Addison Leitch's long illness in 1973, Elisabeth needed help with the house and chores. She became aware of the long-haired homeless seminary student from New Orleans. She called him, in her businesslike way, and told him about her situation. She also gave fair warning: "I am a meticulous housekeeper. Does that pose any problems for you?"

Desperate to get off the short sofa, Walt immediately lied.

"Oh, no, Ma'am," he said. "I love to clean and set things in order."

CHAPTER 32

Boarder Crisis

"Truth is stranger than fiction,
but it is because fiction is obliged
to stick to possibilities; truth isn't."
—Mark Twain

*I*n the aftermath of Addison Leitch's passing, both Walt Shepard and Lars Gren were a great comfort to Elisabeth. But her pain was unremitting. She wrote in her regular column in *Christian Herald* about the fragments, or pieces of the whole, that we see when we consider another human being. When that person dies, what is left are the various impressions of a personality. She likened it to the baskets of small pieces of bread left behind after Jesus fed the multitudes.

"Letters have been pouring in from all kinds of people who had known and been affected by one personality. He was my husband, and five weeks ago, he lost, finally, a long battle with cancer . . . what do you do with the golf clubs, the drawer full of press notices, . . . the Cambridge academic robes and diploma, the leather wallet with his name embossed on it, the monogrammed ring, . . . ? You give some of it away, hoping that people will be able to fathom that you are giving them some of him."

Fragmented pieces of a man, gathering basketfuls of crumbs . . . "He knew that his hands had been committed to ministry of the very Word of Life, the Word that is God, and it was his calling to commit it in turn to faithful [people]." In his tapes of sermons, she noted, his voice was always "natural and vigorous, never tinged with what Spurgeon called the 'ministerial tone.'"

Now Elisabeth was left, collecting the crumbs left behind. "When a man dies it seems that nearly everything is lost, but that is not true. Hundreds, perhaps even thousands, have been fed."

She went on to ponder the difference between Jim's death and Add's.

In Jim Elliot's case, there was little "closure" for Elisabeth, no opportunity to view his remains, no final moment to look upon the face of death. His body was not found until five days after his killing, unrecognizable after its immersion in the muddy Curaray River. The all-male search party had opportunity only for a hasty burial. They interred what was left of Jim, along with his friends, in a muddy hole in hostile territory while Ecuadorian soldiers stood by on alert, nervously cradling big guns and scanning the jungle.

As Elisabeth had pondered Jim's loss, and now in the face of Addison's death, she had thought of one of the shaping events of her childhood. She was nine years old, and Essie, her best and only girl-friend, died. Essie, like Elisabeth, had loved to run and explore, to make secret forts, to climb trees. Now Elisabeth was told that she was gone. Where?

Elisabeth's parents took her to the funeral home to view her departed playmate. There was Essie, lying still in a white dress, hands clasped, her golden curls spread out on a silk pillow.

No one had to tell young Elisabeth that her once-lively, adventurous friend was dead. Elisabeth could see: her spirit had flown.

"It was not a shock. Children are not shocked at things. It is their elders who cannot face reality. I was awed and solemn."

For the rest of her life, Elisabeth noted the day of Essie's death each year in her many journals. Her first experience with a dead body—an empty shell—helped her to accept her loss.

The same was now true of Add. When she had viewed his still body in the casket, his face was in repose, smoothed of pain. He had flown. The physical evidence of the spiritual reality helped her to say goodbye and begin to grieve, a luxury she had not had with Jim.

Socially common euphemisms about the reality of death irritated her. When people would hesitantly approach her and speak of Dr. Leitch's "passing away," she wanted to say, "Oh, no, he's dead, you know." Most of the time, however, she controlled herself.

A missionary in Ecuador—who seemed to specialize in updating Elisabeth about unkind rumors—wrote her that another missionary had told him, "Elisabeth Elliot has certainly got fame and fortune out of her books—wonder what she'll write about this husband's death now!"

As Elisabeth shared this with Val, away at college, she said philosophically, "Well, Val, remember what [the apostle] Paul said, 'Our only defense is a life of integrity.' People are bound to criticize us, no matter what we do, and it is to God that we must answer for our actions. God knows, and you know, that I never asked for the things that have happened in my life, and I can turn them over to God, asking Him to accept and sanctify and use them for the feeding of His multitudes, as He accepted and sanctified and used the little boy's loaves and fishes." (She also noted that she had certainly not "made a fortune" from her books, but had averaged about $5,000 a year.)[1]

By January 1974, Walt and Lars had boarded with Elisabeth for about four months.

As we've noted before, Elisabeth Elliot loved tall, young, well-mannered, and manly men. Walt Shepard was in his late twenties, from a godly missionary family with a compelling story of spiritual transformation, intellectually and spiritually curious, funny, thoughtful, and sensitive. They had an arrangement where he would do household chores in exchange for rent, but she also appreciated their friendship, not just his help. She liked the way Walt's mind worked. Some evenings they'd watch television, the then-popular British class drama *Upstairs, Downstairs*. Walt took to calling Elisabeth "Lady." She loved it. She gave Walt some of Addison's clothes, and cheered on his growth, successes, and interests. She laughed and gave him advice about all the young women who swooned over him, some of whom he tried desperately to avoid.

Lars Gren's story is more obscure than Walt's. When I first met him in 2017 and 2018 I asked him my usual types of questions about his early days, his origins, his vocation, how he came to Gordon-Conwell back in 1973 and met Elisabeth, and his journey with Jesus. No sauce and no story. He told me to put away my laptop and my yellow pad and my black gel pen.

I did, and we talked of other things. We went for a walk by the sea. He cooked me dinner. He urged me to stay longer when I needed to leave. It was companionable, in a controlled way. Lars was not interested in sharing much of his story, though occasionally dramatic pieces of it would pop out, almost against his will.

I later discovered his reticence was not unique to me.

Certainly that's his prerogative, but I wish he had told me more.

Lars was born in 1936 to Norwegian parents who lived in New York. They had a restaurant business and worked hard every day of the year except for Christmas. Lars had a sister a year older, and his parents felt they could not run their business and care for two children. So when Lars was two, his parents traveled to Norway and left little Lars in the care of his grandparents, Far and Jor. He lived with them for ten years.

In an undated letter in the spring of 2001, he wrote several pages about his life, though he asserted that writing and spelling were hard for him. He said that he was the son of his grandfather's old age. "They were modles for true Christyian. He was the church custodien for 37 years."

Then as World War II ended, a small-for-his age Lars was taken to a ship called the *Stavangerfjord* to sail to the United States to be reunited with his parents and to meet his younger brother. He spoke no English. His grandparents had paid a woman to take care of him on the voyage, but she never showed up. Lars was lodged in steerage, a young, blond boy bunking with adult men.

He arrived in America, re-met his family, and worked in the family restaurant. He attended public school, getting zeroes on every assignment for months until he learned English. He had a difficult relationship with his father, as Lars found it hard to love and respect him in the same way he cared for his grandfather. "I was stubborn my Dad was quick to apply the rod but with a temper. Nine difficult years followed. My doing exactly what he said but not out of love rather a 'ill show you I cand do it.' Any talking we did as the bare minimal. Mother was the glue that held the family together."

Lars's 2001 letter is one of the few documents that traces his early path, in his own words and diction. He was a hard worker, washing endless dishes in his parents' restaurant, then graduating to bartending as a teenager. He enlisted in the Navy, then became a women's clothing salesperson.

He eventually settled in Atlanta. According to a local newspaper announcement, on April 9, 1962, he married a young woman named Sherry Anne at a Baptist church in Atlanta.

His wife left him within two years. They divorced, though Lars didn't tend to include that part of his story when he arrived at Gordon Conwell Theological Seminary. He had no college degree, but told friends that Gordon had waived their usual requirements and admitted him based on "life experiences." He was a hard worker but lacking in scholarly, intellectual skills.

After Lars became a lodger in the home of Elisabeth Elliot Leitch, he worked hard, as did Walt, to do anything to help care for their landlady in the hard months after Addison's death. They took out the trash, raked leaves, shoveled snow, split and carried firewood, and cleaned the house, though of course no one could meet their landlady's exacting standards. But Walt and Elisabeth already had a trusted relationship, and it didn't take long for Lars to feel a certain rivalry.

When Elisabeth would go out to the car, Walt would carry her things for her, get her settled, open the garage door for her, and close it after she had pulled out.

Not to be outdone, Lars would sit on the sofa when Elisabeth was out at night so she could see him waiting as she pulled into the driveway, ready to spring into action and open the garage door.

Walt would shine Elisabeth's shoes. Lars noticed and started putting his shoes out for Walt to buff. This did not happen.

Walt would shine at the dinner table as well when he and Elisabeth discussed theology with great fervor. Unable or unwilling to contribute, Lars would simmer, furious, his face gradually turning purple, until he stormed away from the table.

The men were like two young bucks, vying for the female's attention. Or, as Walt put it decades later, each was like a stallion passing gas to mark his territory.

Lars was usually reticent about his past, but at one point he and Walt had been talking, and he shared the fact that he'd been married before. Walt didn't think a whole lot about it, but some weeks later, Lars, Elisabeth, and Walt were sitting at the breakfast table.

They were talking about someone's upcoming wedding, and Lars mentioned wistfully that he'd just love to know what it was like to be married.

Walt choked on his eggs and toast. "Uh," he said. "Don't you think you need to be forthright with our landlady about your situation?"

Lars choked as well. Slowly he admitted to Elisabeth that yes, he had been married, but was divorced. He gave a reason that both his former wife and his brother today deny was the case.

As time went by, Elisabeth mustered her considerable powers to plant the faintest possibility of a relationship between Walt and Valerie. Walt was twenty years younger than Elisabeth, and Val was ten years younger than Walt. Lars was nine years younger than Elisabeth.

Just to add to the mix, there was Van, who had been a compassionate support to Elisabeth throughout Addison's illness and death, and the aftermath, just as she had helped Elisabeth after Jim's death in Ecuador. She was always hovering, always looking for a way back into Elisabeth's domestic life.

Elisabeth and her lodgers would go to parties, dinners, movies, and other excursions. One night, as Elisabeth sat typing a letter to Val, she interrupted herself to note that there had been "a very gentle knock on the study door. It was Walt: 'Thanks for being here, Ma'am. Really appreciate it.'"[2]

During this time Elisabeth traveled regularly for speaking engagements. She had met a friend and gifted retreat organizer named Jan Webb, whom Elisabeth considered to be "the world's funniest woman" who made her "collapse with laughter," but with whom she could share her deeper thoughts.

In June, Elisabeth wrote to Jan, "One year ago tomorrow we learned that Add's cancer had moved to the bone. I look back and can hardly believe what God has done for me in this year. How did I get through last summer? One thing—I hung onto Scripture with my fingernails, as it were, more desperately than ever in my life." She told Jan how she'd stuck a note on her mirror, Jesus's words when His disciples panicked in their fishing boat in a storm. "Take courage. Fear not. It is I."

Elisabeth closed her letter, "I think of you in your uncertainty and longing, and wonder if perhaps those simple words may do for you what they did for me—they gave me spiritual equilibrium. I love you, Jan, and am so glad you're my friend."[3]

In other correspondence, Elisabeth stepped up her comments about Walt in her letters to Val.

She wrote to her daughter, "Lars, Walt and I had supper . . . at Aunt Van's, and Walt saw, for the first time, the serious portrait of you which Aunt Van has on her table. He was rather stunned to silence, and when I told him later that I had that picture too, on the dresser in my bedroom, he said, 'Well, if you find me in your bedroom someday when it's not trash day, you'll know why.'"[4]

Elisabeth watched Walt and fluffy MacDuff playing outside . . . there was a frozen crust on the top of the snow, and "poor little Duffer" could run on top of the crust most of the time, but now and then it would give way, and he would crash through all the way up to his ears. He had to jump and struggle to get out, and then would resume running after Walt, who was galumphing through the snow in Addison's blue and white boots.

Elisabeth sent Val Walt's card with his contact information. Val responded, "What are you trying to do to me?! I love you so much and am praying for you, Val."

Elisabeth wasn't the only one trying to fix Walt up. From the moment he arrived at Gordon Conwell in 1972, long before he ever set foot in Elisabeth's home, most of his friends and the faculty seemed unduly concerned about marrying him off. They set him up with all kinds of dates. Walt didn't have time or money to date, but he still knew that he'd rather stay home and read the encyclopedia or have a root canal than go out with some of those women.

One night he was at a professor's home and saw the book *The Savage My Kinsman,* Elisabeth's vivid account of the first year she and little Val lived in the jungle with the Waodani, on the coffee table. The prof's wife talked about the book's beautiful photography. Walt agreed, the images were stunning.

"What about the little girl in those pictures?" she asked.

"Oh, she's cute as a button," drawled Walt.

"Do you know where she is today?" Mrs. Professor asked him.

"Well, let's see, the cute daughter of Elisabeth Elliot . . . she's probably married to one of Billy Graham's sons," Walt responded.

"Oh, no!" said his hostess cheerfully. "She's actually right down the street, living with her mother when she's home from Wheaton!"

Now, almost two years later, Wheaton student Val was going to concerts, hockey games, retreats, movies, and working harder on studying, even as her mother's letters sang Walt's praises.

In those snail-mail days, Val "debated and debated" over sending a valentine to Walt and "finally decided not to because I didn't want to be one of the many who would send him one! I guess it was my <u>pride</u>! Then I was mad that I didn't. Oh well. <u>Please</u> don't tell him that!"

A week or two later, Elisabeth wrote, "Well, by now you'll have gotten a birthday card from a very fine young man who lives at 746 Bay Road. I had a hard time controlling myself when he came to me on Friday evening . . . and asked me if I thought it would be appropriate for him to send a birthday card! . . . If anyone ever accuses me of attempting to manipulate my daughter's friendships I shall stoutly disclaim any part in such. I only told the young man that I was sure you would not be offended, that you would, in fact, be pleased. Was I right?"[5]

Elisabeth kept it up. Early March: "Guess whose hair I cut this afternoon?? Yup! And he looks <u>so</u> handsome. No, I didn't cut it short. Just a neat trim."[6]

Mid-March: "Dearest Val, These past days I have spent hours talking with Walt. He is really an amazing man, and I thank God for bringing him to me at just the time I needed him. He is kind and thoughtful beyond words . . . One of the great satisfactions of talking with Walt is that nothing is <u>lost</u>. He takes it in, thinks about it, assimilates it."

Walt further secured Elisabeth's affection by loving her dog. He'd take MacDuff out for a run in the evenings. "Duffer loves Walt, and vice versa," Elisabeth wrote. "Walt and I were here alone Wednesday evening. He insisted that he didn't want me cooking for him, since I had had company, so he took me out to dinner. . . . Wasn't that sweet, and so typical of him?"[7]

Val sent Walt a birthday card (wondering if it was too forward of her to do so, and then deciding that birthdays were appropriate occasions for anybody to reach out to anybody). Elisabeth wrote to her daughter that "he was so 'twitched out' (an expression I picked up in Texas!) he couldn't do" his 500 pages of theology reading over the weekend.

Sitting in the Wheaton library for twelve hours one sad Saturday, Val, who was struggling with her grades and "feeling dumb," consulted a book on Gothic architecture. And there, on the library card used for checkouts in that pre-computer age, was a name in ink from October 1945, one Elisabeth Howard. Val smiled before she plunged back into the dreaded paper, thinking how different she was from the young Elisabeth, who Val was sure never struggled with academics in her entire life.

Meanwhile, Elisabeth hosted a birthday dinner for Walt with several seminary couples; they had steak, stuffed mushrooms, and cake. "I had given Walt a pair of navy-blue trousers to match the herringbone tweed coat of [Addison's] which I had also given him. He looks wonderfully handsome in that outfit."[8]

Walt would drive her to local speaking engagements. "It is such a help to have him drive, and so comforting to have him around. How terribly blessed I am in a thousand ways, and I am grateful."

In the yawning gulf of her second widowhood, it was as if Elisabeth was desperately seeking distraction. Walt's reassuring presence seemed to keep her loneliness and pain at bay. For a while. She'd prepare a picnic lunch and stop by the library, find Walt and ask if he could get away. They'd drive to the sea or some picturesque spot and dine al fresco.

Elisabeth wrote to her daughter, "Dearest Doll, Walt and I ate lunch down by the Bass Rocks. Wonderful surf, sparkling sea, whirling and crying gulls, blue sky—just what I needed for 'undisturbing' my disturbed mind!"[9]

It seems Elisabeth took everything she appreciated about Walt and channeled it toward her daughter.

On March 25 Val wrote to her mother, who had invited Walt to say hello to Val during a mother-daughter phone call, "I think Walt was embarrassed to be put on the phone. Did you make him do it? If you did, don't do it again."

Part of Elisabeth's affection was that Walt resurrected her memories of the young Jim Elliot. She wrote to Val that Walt was so excited when he heard that Val was on the phone that he vaulted out of her study and went out to scrub the kitchen floor, and then took MacDuff over to the high school to jump hurdles. "He is so really so terribly sweet and sensitive I can hardly stand it, and he reminds me very much at times of your own father!

"He was, of course, sorry to hear of your being so upset about your grades, and understood just how you felt in wanting to live up to people's expectations. Lars, too, felt so sorry for you when I told him about your grades at breakfast. He has a hard time in school, I think, and would be very sympathetic indeed."[10] (Empathetic about Lars's academic challenges, Elisabeth had asked Walt to help Lars with some of his seminary work.)

Did Val feel manipulated by her mother's Walt campaign? Did she mind that Elisabeth shared Val's feelings of intellectual inadequacy with the two young bucks? "I was absolutely clueless. I was preoccupied with my life in college. I just knew that Mama loved [Walt] dearly, and I was so grateful that he was a comfort to her after my stepfather's death."[11]

And what about Walt? What was he thinking when he wasn't scrubbing the kitchen floor and vaulting over hurdles with Elisabeth's dog?

"I didn't even think about Val in a romantic way back then," says Walt. "I thought, 'you idiot! She's young enough to be a younger sister to you, and she's dating all these hotshots at Wheaton!'"

But still, in 1974, when Val was a young nineteen and Walt was twenty-eight, something did begin to happen that even someone as determined as Elisabeth Elliot could not have orchestrated all on her own.

"I was . . . so excited to get Walt's letter," Val wrote to her mother. "I never would have dreamed that he'd write me a full-fledged letter. Nor did I realize he'd be so nervous about it! I just hope that when I come home we both won't be nervous wrecks."[12]

Walt drove Elisabeth to the post office, bank, and grocery store one warm afternoon. When Elisabeth opened a letter from Val with her picture, Walt "all but drove the car into a ditch. He was 'wiped out'! Then I read him your letter (steady now, relax)—all but the paragraph about him. He kept asking me . . . if he could see that picture 'one more time.' He is a darling, and so exquisitely sensitive it hurts to watch him."[13]

Not to be outdone, at dinnertime Lars was found gazing and exclaiming over Val's photo. "He wished aloud that he were younger."

Lars still had some unsold women's clothing from his retail days. He pulled out a turquoise blouse that he thought would fit Val, and urged Elisabeth to send it to her.

Val wrote asking her mother for any pictures of Walt. She was terribly excited that he "actually wants to write to me!" She wrote him back, though "I couldn't think of very many clever things to say, like he did."[14]

A week later Walt was sick in bed. Elisabeth brought him vitamins, orange juice, and anything else she could think of. She wrote to Val. "Enclosed are two terrible pictures of Walt which were used in last year's and this year's student directories, plus one I cut out of the catalogue, which is nice, but not very clear. . . . He is so very much more handsome than any of these can show!"[15]

By the end of May, Val was feeling disappointed and confused because Walt had not written to her for five weeks. She also felt a lot of academic pressure; in the Howard family, her various cousins seemed to all be high achievers, and she felt she did not measure up. At any rate, she told her mother, "I have not given up hope about Walt. In fact, I'm giving him the benefit of the doubt, hoping that he has grown a lot in the past five weeks."[16]

Elisabeth responded that she and Van were praying for Val and Walt. "Only God knows what is going on in his heart. He has had a great deal of suffering and upheaval in his short life, and he has a list of things to get sorted out, and I can only try to guess what he is experiencing now. . . . I am so thoroughly convinced that the Lord has laid His hand on Walt, saving him repeatedly from violent death, saving his soul from destruction, and I am sure that He which hath begun a good work in him will perform it until the day of Jesus Christ. I hope with all my heart that God will somehow, someday, bring the two of you together if this is His will. Of course I want His will, but it seems so probable to me today that this must be His will! It is good to be able to ask it, and to leave it in the Omnipotent hands."[17]

In May, Walt finished his second year of seminary and returned home to New Orleans.

Val spent the summer taking classes at Wheaton. Because of Wheaton's policy against students taking too many academic terms in a row without a break, this meant that she would need to take the fall semester off, home in Hamilton.

In June, Elisabeth attended the festive wedding of a close friend's daughter. She got home at almost midnight, thinking what a lovely time it had been, "and I realized afresh what a dear friend Mrs. K. is to me. I wished so much that [Add] could have been there—for my own sake, of course, since I hate being in a social situation without a husband—but also for his, because I'm sure he would have enjoyed the parties."[18]

She went on to note that Lars, who was away on summer break, had called to tell her that he was unexpectedly coming to Hamilton. "He arrived at supper time and will be here, I guess, till Tuesday. I told him I haven't got time to entertain him, since I have all those lectures to get together for next week at Wheaton, but I guess he'll amuse himself by mowing the lawn, etc.!"[19]

In July, Elisabeth visited her daughter, staying in her dorm room. By some interesting coincidence, Walt Shepard's parents were visiting Wheaton at the same time, and Walt had suggested to them that they get together with his landlady and her daughter. Mr. and Mrs. Shepard took Elisabeth and Val out to dinner.

Immediately sympatico because of their shared international missions experience, Elisabeth and the Shepards chatted away about Ecuador and Africa. Val contributed, but for the most part felt shy and embarrassed. But that was nothing compared to the end of the meal.

Mr. Shepard, Walt Senior, put his hands, if not his cards, on the table and said, "Well, you know that in the part of Africa where we lived, the tradition is that when a young man finds the woman he wants to marry, his family gives a goat to the bride's family."

Val started sinking under the table. Elisabeth's eyebrows shot up.

So Mr. Shepard continued cheerfully, "We just want you to know that we've got a little goat for you. He's out in the car!"

Elisabeth loved it. Val died. And as they said their goodbyes after the meal, Walt Senior repeated, "Well, that goat will be coming along pretty soon!"

When Walt heard the story, he died too. It wasn't as if he had talked to his dad about any of this. In Walt's mind, Val was just plain off limits. "Dad!" he sputtered. "What were you thinking? There's no way that's going to happen. I'm not worthy! You know my past!"

His dad just looked at him. "What other blessings do you think God's holding back on for you, Son?" he asked. "If you're going to finish seminary and preach the gospel, you'd better get the grace part right! You are forgiven!"

CHAPTER 33

Walking MacDuff

"Father, I know that all my life is portioned out for me
And the changes that will surely come I do not fear to see,
But I ask Thee for a present mind Intent on pleasing Thee."
—Anna L. Waring, one of Elisabeth Elliot's
mother's favorite writers

*B*efore Val came home from Wheaton in the late summer of 1974, she wrote to her mother, "I am getting quite worried about Walt being in the same house with me in the fall. I think it will be a very unnatural way to get to know a guy. It will be like I am on a display all the time and I don't want that. . . . Whether Walt starts anything with me or not, I don't really want him in the same house."[1]

As it turned out, with both Elisabeth's and Val's invitation, Walt did lodge in Elisabeth's house that academic year. He slept in the basement, and Val reclaimed her former bedroom on the main floor. Lars returned to live in one of the other rooms, down the hall.

Walt and Val found themselves spending a lot of time doing chores together. They'd wash dishes after each meal, companionably swirling soap and wielding dish towels, talking about small things. On weekends, he was gone most of the time, working for a catering company.

Every night, Walt would stand up, stretch, and prepare to walk MacDuff the dog. He'd invite Val to come with him. As the nights went by, the walks got longer and longer. "We walked that little dog to death," Walt says. "One night we were talking about reformed theology." Walt pontificated long and hard, laying out grand visions of the complicated doctrine. Val looked at him in the dark, with the little black Scottie pattering away in front of them. "Yes, that's what

I've always believed," she said simply, perhaps thinking back to her discussions with Addison Leitch when she was a young teen.

Many walks later, they were out one early winter afternoon getting groceries for Elisabeth. "When you go back to Wheaton, you're going to date, right?" Walt asked. He felt that she was young and needed to check out her options. Val didn't know what to say. She knew she "really, really" liked Walt. She knew she didn't want to date at Wheaton. The time she'd spent with Walt couldn't even be called dating. Except for one square dance they'd attended together at the seminary, they had spent time just doing errands, washing dishes, raking leaves, and walking poor little MacDuff's paws off.

"What about you?" she asked. "Will you be dating at the seminary?"

Walt smiled. "Oh, no," he said. "I've already found the girl I'd like to marry."

A few days after that, they sat in front of the fireplace, watching the dancing flames. "Do you think maybe thirty years from now we might be sitting in front of a fire together?" Walt asked.

A few days after that, Walt told Val he loved her.

On December 21, Elisabeth Elliot's birthday, she held her usual caroling party, a festive night full of students, professors, family, and friends, all singing Christmas carols around the fire. Late, late that night, Walt and Val sat on the sofa together.

"Val," Walt said nervously, "I'd really like you to be my wife."

Val, as practical as her mother, said, "I can't respond to a statement. Is there a question there?"

Walt backed up. "Will you marry me?"

Val had been raised with certain proprieties. "Have you asked my mother for her blessing?" she asked.

Oh! thought Walt. *I am such an idiot. I'm going at this backwards.*

"No," he told Val, jumping up. "I'll go ask her now."

It was two o'clock in the morning

Walt ran down the hall to Elisabeth's room, rapped on the door, heard a sleepy "come in," and popped into the room as Elisabeth sat up, leaning against the pillows propped on her headboard. She was used to late-night talks with her daughter and young boarders.

"I would like to ask your permission to marry your daughter," said Walt.

Long silence.

"Have you already asked her?" Elisabeth asked.

Walt's heart fell. Clearly he was doomed. He had not followed proper Elisabethan protocols.

"Uh, oh, ma'am, I am so sorry, I've already asked her."

There was a longer silence. Walt prepared himself for the worst.

"Walt," said Elisabeth, "there is no man to whom I'd rather give her."

Walt and Val made their plans. He borrowed money from his dad and got a ring. They would wait until Val finished school—seventeen months in the future—before they married.

In January 1975, a happy Val returned to Wheaton. Happy Walt continued in his last semester of seminary. And happy Lars was thrilled that his self-perceived "rivalry" with Walt was over. Much of the tension in the house dissipated, except when Walt would ask him about his feelings for Elisabeth. "You're carrying a massive torch for her," he said.

Lars blew up and walked out of the house.

Never one to be shy, Walt tried to talk to Elisabeth. "Why is Lars so moody and upset and angry?" she asked.

"Ma'am," he said, "you're so wise, but with men you're so stupid. You're oblivious to what's going on here."

"No," denied Elisabeth. "I can't imagine that he's thinking [in a romantic] way about me."

Later that spring, however, one morning Lars and Elisabeth were in her kitchen, and he may or may not have asked her on what she perceived as a date. He was making something to eat; she was washing dishes. She told him, back still turned to him, that because of his feelings toward her, it was not appropriate that he live in her home. He needed to find another place to live.

Furious, he stormed out without another word, though he says that later he went back to her and remonstrated with her regarding her lack of graciousness. She listened, thanked him, and then that was that.

CHAPTER 34

Depression Lurks

*"Joy is not mere jolliness. Joy is perfect acquiescence,
acceptance, and rest in God's will, whatever comes."*
—Amy Carmichael

By the warm months of 1975, Elisabeth's days were long, leisurely, and unscheduled. She read, thought, walked, and wrote. In June she was entranced by a book called *The Outermost House* by naturalist Henry Beston, a 1928 account of his year's contemplative stay alone in a house on Nauset Beach.

She rented a cottage on Cape Cod. Roses and honeysuckle bloomed, taking her back to her childhood in Pennsylvania. Elisabeth went for a walk alone beside the sea, ending up at the Fish Pier to watch fishermen unload their catch. She bought a piece of swordfish—complaining that it was an astronomical $1.50 for half a pound—from a keen, blue-eyed fisherman who looked like he should be a character in a novel.

She was asked to contribute a chapter to a book for Tyndale House as one of twenty "leading Christians" recounting their "most significant experience with God." Elisabeth declined to be included.

"How can one speak of <u>that</u>?" she wrote in her journal.

Lars called from Atlanta. No reason.

Elisabeth dreamed that she was in a hotel room in San Francisco with Addison.

Her two months alone were punctuated with letters from "dear Walt" and Val, who were "bubbling with joy." Then on August 1 she flew from Boston to London, full of a "deep sense of God's rich blessing" even though the United States was in "a mess. Recession, unemployment, skyrocketing prices (gas is 54 cents now, to go soon to

75 cents, and my Chrysler '72 eats a gallon every ten miles). My food bill (alone—no entertaining, no desserts, <u>very</u> simple menus) was $60 in July." Meanwhile various friends were dealing with cancers, challenges with adult children, and one couple she was close with were on the verge of divorce, as the husband was already living with another woman.

"People are dying of thirst in Africa, of hunger in India. Russia buys our wheat so our cost-of-living rises. Aleksandr Solzhenitsyn [the celebrated Russian novelist and Soviet dissident] is here in U.S. making impassioned pleas that we not help Russia. No one hears. [President] Ford refuses to see him because [Secretary of State] Kissinger says no. Women's Lib advocates the Equal Rights Amendment and compulsory childcare. Mrs. Ford supports this.

"Yet I am contented in my own world, grateful for all I have, conscious of its source, trust Him to do with me, with Val, Walt, with <u>all</u>, what He purposes to do."

Elisabeth went on to Scotland. Everyone she saw was "chewing, drinking, munching, guzzling, or lugging along a basket or thermos flask. Trains are uncomfortable, bumpy, slow, late, and <u>filthy</u>. Toilet paper—as effective as a rake." The scenery, however, was "simply breathtaking and surpassed anything she'd ever seen, including Ecuador and Wyoming. She relished the castles, pipers, kilts, and lochs.

She ended her trip in England with the Crown jewels, Harrads, and a visit at the home of J. I. Packer in Bristol. She could not wait to go home. "It will never have looked more welcome. I am not really tourist material, I fear. I love to stay put. I love peace and productivity—two things traveling provides not at all."

She somehow got back to 746 Bay Road in one piece. "Ah. Bliss to have <u>space</u>, <u>comfort</u>, <u>order</u>, <u>predictability</u> once more!"

Her desk was piled high with writing and speaking requests, which offered a myriad of opportunities to upset her cart and travel some more.

She took Val's antique wedding dress to be altered. It had belonged to Addison's mother-in-law.

"I miss Walt around the house," she wrote in her journal, "—at <u>every</u> turn."

Elisabeth declined *Christianity Today's* invitation to write an article on the twentieth anniversary of the Waodani incident, an invitation to address MIT students, an invitation to "head up women's ministry" at a Congregational church, and a request to debate a "women's lib" proponent. "Good Lord—deliver me from the hands of my oppressors! And show me when to say <u>yes</u>. The day will come, I'm sure, when no one will ask me to do anything. If I am occupied in the will of God, it will be all right. Lord, keep me pressing toward the mark."

She had new renters. She timed their showers, worrying about heating oil and hot water. They both also committed the sin of sleeping later than she thought appropriate.

Lars stopped by to visit Elisabeth. He had a new red sports car.

"Depression lurks around the corner. . . . No heart to take up my tasks of preparing the courses I'm to teach. . . .

"I took almost the whole day off, like a parenthesis, sitting in the sun on the terrace, reading Anne Morrow Lindbergh's Bring Me a Unicorn. Today I can be grateful for the quiet and being alone—yesterday both seemed intolerable . . . but today I am at peace again. Missing Val and Walt does not affect me like pain today. Very aware of how life for one means death for another. I am getting old, not wishing to check off the months and years quite so rapidly . . ."

Val and Walt prayed she'd be kept from loneliness and discouragement. Elisabeth reassured them that she kept herself busy.

She taught her Bible class at church, read, walked her dog, and visited with friends. Still, she had all kinds of bad dreams—blue vampires, worms, herself seven months pregnant, her house robbed, her purse lost, late to catch a plane, her house full of hungry people and the meal unmade.

She felt "greatly agitated" about the women's movement after she attended the first meeting of "Concerned Evangelicals for Women" at Gordon Conwell one evening. She searched the Scriptures for encouragement as she reviewed her own views and the courage it would require her to take her stand on what she fervently believed to be true. "Lord, give me strength to obey. I do not want to be in this arena. But if this is a part of the 'race set before me,' help me to run it—looking to Jesus. I'm repelled by it, I'm afraid, I'm reluctant, but I've been those things before and you've helped me to overcome them. I'm your hands."

She went to a Columbus Day picnic at the beach with people from her church. It was a crisp yet warm autumn afternoon, the water dazzling in the sunlight, sailboats skimming along the blue. There were dogs romping on the beach, her small niece and nephew collecting shells . . . Elisabeth felt, as many of us have in such a beautiful setting, a sense of the fleeting nature of time. She looked around, feeling alone. Everyone else was relaxed, in the moment, and here she was looking at her watch, thinking about the papers she needed to grade, the lectures she needed to prepare, the talks she needed to outline.

"Dr. Anderson said I must cut back on my self-discipline!!! This is BILGE. God, strengthen me to do Your will."

She went on. "But I did not regard the time at the beach as wasted. I tried to practice Jim's words: 'Wherever you are, be all there. Live to the hilt every situation you believe to be the will of God.'" She did not seem to realize that even as she checked her watch and thought about her to do list, she wasn't totally present at the picnic.

Still, these were precious fall days. The sun slanted through the hemlocks on Bay Road. Her house glowed with reflected, rosy golden light from the carpet of fallen leaves in the backyard.

"It was a pleasure this morning to get my hands into hot dishwater, and to clean stove and counters. I love cleaning things!"

But she panicked at her desk. Lectures. Papers to grade. Speeches to prepare. Flights to book. Correspondence. Menus. Oil change for her car. Groceries to buy. Concerns about her lonely, aging mother. Feelings of failure. Duties undone. She didn't have enough time to think. Tired.

She traveled. She spoke. She taught. She read missionary biographies, and felt a heavy responsibility, the notion that human beings who belong to Christ carry "all this treasure" in earthen vessels. She was well aware of the cracks in her own pot. She wondered what people saw. "Do they see this treasure [Christ, in a very ordinary vessel], or do they see only the dull clay—Elisabeth Elliot—missionary, author, lecturer, visiting professor, etc. etc.??"

The King James Version Gideon Bible in her hotel room was open to Psalm 26. "Judge me, O LORD; for I have walked in mine integrity: I have trusted also in the LORD; therefore I shall not slide."

"The claims of Christ," she wrote in her journal, "in mission, in individual daily life (which includes the whole woman question—more and more of an issue and a burden to me for so much that is fraudulent is swallowed so uncritically by Christians): obedience to the Father's will, the laying down of one's life for the life of the world."

At this point Elisabeth had written 112 pages of her new book, which would be eventually released as *Let Me Be a Woman*. "Are they readable?" she wondered. "I can hardly bring myself to find out." The book was essentially a wedding present to Walt and Val, written to Val as "notes about the meaning of womanhood," composed at the height of the women's movement that Elisabeth believed clouded the essential issues, not of biology or equal opportunity, but the elemental nature of femininity and masculinity at the core of God's creation.

She read a book called *The Female Woman* by Arianna (known today as Arianna Huffington.) She "had (at the age of twenty-five!) demolished Women's Lib with a very well-documented and scholarly attack. I am just playing in the shallows."

It's not my purpose to give a synopsis or abstract of Elisabeth Elliot's views on feminism and sexuality, nor to pigeonhole her. Elisabeth's writings and speeches on gender roles are available to anyone who wishes to peruse them for further study. Some revere her, and some despise her, because of them.

What is relevant to our understanding of this human being and her story, though, is how she <u>thought</u> about these issues. As best she could, she did not start with her own preferences that felt comfortable to her. She sought what she believed to be the will and design of God, no matter how it felt. She habitually felt that if one was presented with two options, either in a life choice or a consideration of opposing points of view, it was usually wiser to take the more difficult road. If she believed in a sovereign God whose breath created the universe, an omniscient, eternal Father who had in fact died for her and bought her by His own blood, then the most important element in all of life was not her own comfort or feelings, but His will.

So Elisabeth habitually tried to crucify her own desires, pride, preferences, ambition, freedom, identity—anything that might impede obedience. She felt this way about any life decision, or any issue on which she took a stand based on her understanding of the Scriptures.

When people opposed her points of view, Elisabeth perceived their opposition as suffering for the sake of the truth, though criticism hurt her deeply. She saw herself, as her brother-in-law Bert Elliot had said years earlier, as a "seer." She identified with reviled Old Testament prophets who were dismissed in their own day as crabby kooks.

During a talk with her rector, who'd been surprised when several women at the parish had been angry and offended that he had picked up the check for them at lunch, they explored "the women issue and what's behind it all. I suppose it goes back to a fundamental hatred of authority which is natural to all of us."[1] Elisabeth firmly believed that women were created "<u>for</u>" the man, as noted in the Genesis account, and "that this woman, for one, actually likes it that way!"

Later, at a Gordon College event, she noted in her journal that a "flaming liberationist (though married) was there with all guns blazing challenging the panel as to whether indeed God had actually created woman in an inferior position to man. I said He most emphatically did." She believed that seeing masculinity and femininity were the issues at hand, not mere biological distinctions between genders, and that these essences were a reflection of the arrangement of the universe and the full harmony and tone of Scripture. . . . a glorious hierarchical order of graduated splendor."[2]

When Elisabeth argued these issues with the feminists of her day, it wasn't as if she had an inflated ego and saw herself as God's appointed superhero to proclaim truth. She had a deep-seated sense of inferiority from her family of origin, Jim Elliot's treatment of her during their long courtship, and her own sense of failure as a writer. She also habitually sought humility as a virtue.

But as far as Elisabeth Elliot could tell, she had been given a public platform and she must not let opposition deter her from speaking the truth as she believed it, even though it was painful.

She had felt the same way when her views about God and the evangelical public relations spin on "results" in the mission field resulted in criticisms, withdrawn speaking invitations, and boycotts on her book *No Graven Image*. The rejections hurt. But Elisabeth expected a life of pain, suffering, and rejection. That's what Jesus had promised His followers.

Sometimes this mindset seemed to draw Elisabeth toward decisions that would incur painful outcomes, even if they were unnecessary.

Elisabeth wrote in her 1975 journal, "I am beginning to realize that there is a sense in which I must give my life for this woman question. I did not <u>want</u> to be involved. I did not want to read or hear about it. I did not want to stick my neck out again by espousing an unpopular view. I did not wish to be pitted against Mollenkott, Jewett, Hardesty, Scanzoni, and now Kay Lindskoog. I did not want to be 'crossed off' with a 'there she goes again!'

"But I must take my stand in obedience and faith. This, I believe, can be accepted as 'an act of intelligent worship' (Rom. 12:1). God knows I do it only because I believe I am right. I believe I identify with Christ in this. So help me God!"

CHAPTER 35

Keep Me from Tears

"Measure thy life by loss and not by gain,
not by the wine drunk but by the wine poured forth;
for love's strength standeth in love's sacrifice,
and whoso suffereth most hath most to give."
—Ugo Bassi

A month or two later Elisabeth received a surprise regarding the years when she lived in enormous conflict with fellow missionary Rachel Saint among the Waodani. She received a letter of apology from John Lindskoog, director of Wycliffe in Ecuador. He told Elisabeth, "I think I understand the situation of the conflict with Rachel Saint much better now than I did then or at any time until recently. . . . I was not aware of the severity of certain behavioral problems that R. has . . . [Elisabeth], I want a relation of unhindered fellowship and confidence to prevail between us. . . ."[1]

It was a very gracious letter, Elisabeth told Val and Walt. "Apparently they've been having a terrible time with poor Rachel, and she has been taken out of [Waodani territory] and put in Quito as a disciplinary measure."

In early February 1976, Elisabeth panicked slightly, realizing that Val's May wedding was exactly three months away. "Much to think of. My own state of mind now (probably fairly chronic throughout my life so far!)—guilt at not accomplishing more in less time; apprehension when I think of the Urbana responsibility; hurt and uneasiness about what people say to and about me; and that always underlying, crying, longing." She constantly yearned for a man.

Brent the lodger left and spread unkind, callous, arrogant tales about her. A day or two later she got a letter from Virginia Mollenkott accusing Elisabeth of a "very light (low) view of Scripture. A very upsetting letter." She took heart from her Bible reading that morning, which included God's words to the apostle Paul in Acts 18: "Do not be afraid; keep on speaking, do not be silent. For I am with you . . ." (v. 9 NIV). Meanwhile, sales were strong for her newly released small book about loneliness. She received constant letters from fans who shared their troubles and how she had encouraged them through her writings.

She still had two lodgers, one whom she rarely saw and seemed to fly beneath her radar, and the other who left dirty dishes in her sink, took twenty-minute hot showers, and did not scrub the bathroom tub. For these and other sins she was thrilled when he decided to move in with an older couple who would charge him no rent.

Lars Gren, who was steadily working to make himself indispensable, found a new boarder he had carefully vetted for Elisabeth. He repainted Elisabeth's front hall and showed up "big as life in the very center, all dressed up" at her local speaking engagements. He had Elisabeth and friends from the seminary to his home for supper. He took Elisabeth out to dinner to an upscale restaurant near Bunker Hill. "I had delicious swordfish steak, tender and juicy and covered with butter and lemon," Elisabeth wrote to Val. "Lars is fun to be with, is never pushy, always courteous, and makes me feel like a woman. One needs, now and then, to feel like a woman, doesn't one?"[2]

Lars was very good at making her feel that way. Another time he took Elisabeth to dinner in Gloucester for her birthday, presenting her with "some White Shoulders perfume and cologne—lovely stuff. It is very nice to be cared for. He knows exactly how to treat me, knows what and how to order, knows that I like my salad dressing on the side, that I want [decaf] instead of [regular] coffee, and knows what makes me laugh. I enjoy such company—on a different basis than when he lived here."

Other evenings were not as pleasing. Elisabeth had dinner one night at her brother Tom's home with the editor of a well-known evangelical magazine. "A very strange man, colossally egotistical . . . who talked non-stop. He'll never know that his host was one of the world's most interesting people—he never gave him or anybody else a chance. Oh dear—let's not be that way! Stop me if you see me headed in that direction as a garrulous old woman!"[3]

On another occasion she spoke to students from University of Massachusetts, Smith, Williams, and Dartmouth at a retreat. The kids responded enthusiastically, though Elisabeth was flummoxed by their vocabulary choices. "Wow, that was kinda neat," said one. "I just really really want to thank you, Mrs. Leitch, I mean you know it was just really great to just really learn some really neat stuff that I just never really thought of."

Meanwhile, she sent Val recipes and cooking advice. "Peach melba . . . I included that in my suggested menu on the recipe card. It's just vanilla ice cream with a peach half and raspberries (or thawed frozen raspberries with the syrup). Elegant and easy!"

But the main focus was the wedding planning. "Yes, 500 invitations," she wrote to Val. "No, we won't pare it down. They're already ordered.

"Yes, time to look for and buy a veil when you get home.

"How nice of that old man to send you money!"

Elisabeth was thrilled for their season of young love, Walt's beginnings in ministry as a Presbyterian pastor in rural Louisiana, Val's beauty, freshness, and excitement about all that lay ahead.

Elisabeth thanked God for their joy and love. She prayed earnestly that "the sickness of longing (which floods me as I see their happiness and thank God for it) may not have power over me. This is the thing to pray. It is a human longing—humanly speaking it has tremendous power at times. The Lord can reduce that power, can give me dominion over it, and turn it into 'something beautiful.'"

Ah. But "maturity is the ability to accept with equanimity the changes in role that life requires. My relationship to Walt has run a strange gamut—landlady to mother-in-law. Am I mature enough for this?"

She thought about dyeing her hair for the wedding but decided to just go with her gray. A tooth broke—just "gave way" while she was chewing. She felt old, and very conscious of her solitude. No matter how many people she entertained in her home, or how many listeners applauded her after a speech, she was exhausted with the business of making reservations, responding to piles of correspondence, looking ahead to a life of more of the same. Alone.

Elisabeth reread notes she had made in preparation for the writing of *No Graven Image*, years earlier. She was "surprised to find thoughts which I would have said are of more recent origin, insights I have by now forgotten, and an understanding (it seems) of concepts I am now trying to understand! O Lord—how slow I am, how forgetful. I haven't time to think."

Val came home for spring break. Elisabeth mailed out wedding invitations, steeling herself to spend $72.11 for postage. Lars hosted a dinner at his apartment for Elisabeth, Val, Van, Elisabeth's lodger, Ken, and two others. Van made no secret of the animosity she felt because of Lars's interest in Elisabeth. Elisabeth wrote in her journal, "An undercurrent of bitterness runs through everything that

Van says to either Lars or me. She really was rude and cutting to me, glum and uninterested in others. And I had just written an article on forgiveness!"

Elisabeth attended a trustee/board meeting at Stony Brook School in New York. She was the only woman. "Very interesting men. 19 of them."

At the end of April, Gordon College inaugurated a new president, and Corrie ten Boom came to speak and receive an honorary doctorate. She spoke using "much Scripture, poetry, epigrams, and an overwhelming impact. The conviction on all of us—here is greatness, here is truth, spoken out of the deep knowledge of suffering."

"You don't know me," Corrie told Elisabeth later. "But I know you!"

Ah. To be known. At 1 a.m., Elisabeth reflected on it all in her journal, "I'm in bed, remembering the nights, the love, the ecstasies—

'The moon is up
And I lie alone!'

"But I am absolutely sure that in His will is my peace—and ultimate joy, and I've given it all over, once again."

To Elisabeth's delight, Corrie invited Elisabeth and Val to tea. They talked about suffering. Elisabeth had been intrigued by Corrie's book and the movie, *The Hiding Place*. Corrie told her that the film showed .01 percent of the cruelties and hardships of the concentration camp. Elisabeth asked her if she ever got tired of telling the same story, over and over, to audiences around the world.

"No," said Corrie, whose wisdom informed a deep sense of simplicity in Jesus. "This is the story God gave me to tell. Sometimes I think, 'Oh—I must have something new!' But no. It is humbling to have to say the same thing. The donkey that carried Jesus was not proud; he knew the shouts, applause, and hosannas were for Jesus."

They discussed suffering, the mysteries of why God allows children and other "innocents" to endure awful things, as well as the depths of Christ's own agonies. Corrie told Elisabeth that American Christians, while eager and welcoming to her message, had no understanding of how Christians in repressive nations routinely suffer. Corrie told Elisabeth that "Christians in [tyrannical and hostile] countries are much happier—they have to be genuine because of the terrible price they must pay." And they had prepared for suffering, which can only happen by soaking oneself in the Word of God.

In spite of her own horrific losses at the hands of the Nazis, Corrie told Elisabeth she'd had "a very happy life." She had told the Lord that she was His. He had chosen a single life for her. She had prayed for "victory over sex life—and Jesus gave it."

Tremendously energized by this "true saint and prophet" and her victories in similar struggles to her own, Elisabeth wrote in her journal, "Thank God for this great encouragement on my road. Very special messenger for me just now at a crossroads—Val leaving, my life to change, what next?"

She mulled over "strange weaknesses and temptations" in herself. Where was the victory over "sex life" that Corrie had received? (By this she meant ongoing preoccupations, not actual sexual activity.)

She prayed part of her hero Amy Carmichael's poem,

> *Lord crucified, O mark Thy holy Cross*
> *On motive, preference, all fond desires,*
> *On that which self in any form inspires*
> *Set Thou that sign of loss.*

She found, as the days ticked down to Val's wedding on May 1, that she had a subtle yet constant desire to remind others that she was soon to be alone. Here she was widowed again, feeling old and stuck, even as fresh young Val was about to set out on new adventures with her strong, caring husband, leaving Elisabeth in a dry, solitary life. This was "one of those damnable things inspired by Self. Forgive me, Lord, and keep me from tears, please."

Elliots, Howards, Shepards, and friends arrived. Elisabeth fixed her jammed garbage disposer with a crowbar. She served mushrooms stuffed with crabmeat and chocolate mousse to the bridesmaids. On the last day of April, Val slept with Elisabeth, as the rest of the beds were occupied by Jane, Jean, Beth, Marion, and Add's daughter Katherine.

"Lord," Elisabeth prayed over her daughter, "You know my gratitude."

The next day, May 1, 1976, her hand trembled as she wrote in her journal, two hours before the ceremony. The bride had had her bubble bath, the bridesmaids were dressing, and all Elisabeth could pray was, "Lord—keep mine eyes from [visible] tears!! Please."

Why was she so concerned about friends and family seeing her cry?

The wedding was glorious, with all the usual last-minute snafus that annoyed the mother of the bride but were noticed by no one else. Lars, who had catering experience, was immensely helpful with its planning and execution. The bride and groom took off for their honeymoon in the Virgin Islands, with, of all things, a copy of the newly released *Let Me Be a Woman*, which Walt had promised to read.

Elisabeth got a telegram. "Luxurious privacy. Your book makes strong Walt weep. We love you. Val and Walt."

After the honeymoon, Walt and Val set up house in Walt's small apartment in Centerville, Louisiana. There were no curtains. "What's with this?" asked Val, concerned about privacy. "We just duck and run," said former bachelor Walt.

Soon they moved into a little house in a sugar cane field, from which Walt, full of youthful energy, simultaneously pastored three small churches. They were happy.

Elisabeth carried on. She traveled. She spoke. She wrote. She thought. Her new book went into its second printing; Jim Packer wrote her a cheering letter extolling it.

In August 1976, Elisabeth returned to Ecuador. Val's marriage had created a new season for her. She had felt many changes inside. "The pull to come and live here is surprising to me, and surprisingly strong. Lord, work Your will in my life, at any cost. My house, my work, my ministry . . ."

She traveled with old missionary friends. There was a mud avalanche that blocked the road to Shandia, but they eventually arrived, and she found herself sitting in what had been Val's room in the Elliot's old home in Shandia, the house that Jim had built. "What memories flood over me. Jim is everywhere. Val is a baby and I sit in this room, by candlelight as now, feeding her at my breast at 2 a.m., Jim asleep in the next room."

She went through all the books still on the shelves and dug through her old files that had been stored in a barrel in the attic. There were Waodani language files, Quichua files, notes and stories jotted on scraps of flimsy paper in the jungle.

"Shall I come back here, Lord? Let me say again all that Betty Scott Stam said in her prayer—but you know, Lord, how my flesh and heart fail here at the prospect. My beautiful house in Hamilton in contrast to this. My car, as compared with the hideous trail we covered today on foot from the end of the road. My 'fans,' as compared with these Indians [who, Elisabeth felt, often found her mildly amusing and could not care less about what she had to say]—forgive me, Lord, and give me grace to obey whatever You direct.

"Val's marrying must be for me a juncture. I have to face the possibility of coming back to Ecuador. I left for her sake. My job with her is done. What now, Lord and Master?"

She visited Puyupungu, where she and Jim had lived after they married. She spent time in Tewaeno with the Waodani, discovering that Rachel Saint had left just the day before. She gripped hands of old friends like Mincaye, Dabu, Kumi, Wiba, and Dayuma, along with many downriver Waodani who she'd never met. Dabu, whose life she'd saved so many years before, told her, "I cried very hard when I heard your husband died."

After her time in Ecuador, Elisabeth went on to Colombia and the home of her hero, Katherine Morgan, who ministered for a fruitful lifetime in the highland town of Pasto.

Returning home, Elisabeth spoke to 2,700 young people from the Evangelical Covenant Church of America. Her topic: "Taking the Next Steps: The Future."

She wrote in her journal, "Feeling isolated, baffled, inadequate. Also, much in need of guidance myself, regarding:

1. What to say here

2. What to write for [an upcoming magazine article]

3. My novel

4. Ecuador???

"If I am to assure these kids of the Shepherd's care, I must rest in that assurance myself."

But still. Underneath it all, there was that flaming desire. "Huge hungers still threaten to paralyze me—to think that nearly at age 50 I'm still having to pray, 'Breathe thru' the heats of [my] desire, Thy coolness and Thy balm."

She longed for a man. During a conference at the Wisconsin church of Stuart and Jill Briscoe, whom she liked and admired greatly, she found herself almost speaking out loud to "'Darling,'—wanting my man to be with me, to bear with me the responsibilities" she felt whenever she spoke to an audience, but wanting most of all that "consciousness of another consciousness that is conscious of me! Wanting to matter to someone. The fact that 950 women have signed up for today and another 700 for tomorrow—that I do, in a sense, 'matter' to them—does not fill the space."

Not yet concerned about her own sanity regarding the invisible "Darling," she took 2 Peter 1:1–11 seriously: 'Set your minds, then, on endorsing by your conduct the fact that God has called and chosen you.' That means my conduct alone in a motel room as much as my conduct in the midst of [nearly] 1000 women. . . . Do I trust the One who called me to fill the void or to enable me to embrace my loss for His glory? By Thy grace, Lord."

She was taken to the airport for her flight to her next engagement in Kansas. Another takeoff, that strange sense of accelerating into oblivion. "My thoughts go, always, to the Man. Where is he? Does he, in fact, exist?" On this airplane, she was a nameless passenger.

"No one knows me. Not really. A name. A speaker. A slot on a program. . . . Check it off. Check her off. I check them off."

And away she would go to the next engagement.

"If only I had someone on a trip like this, to share it all with. Impossible. I couldn't have a husband and be doing this. I don't want a 'traveling companion!' I suppose it is a consort, a lover, that I want, and that is not an option. The very want gives me the chance to deny myself and take up the Cross. Thanks, Lord. Bless these kids here. Let me be poured-out wine for them."

Aloft on another flight, toward another speech. In Wichita, she was charmed by her hotel room with its "king-sized bed, basket of fresh fruit, bouquet of glorious pink peonies, and patio by the sparkling swimming pool. I love it. The anonymity, the quiet, the isolation, even though I want HIM!"

CHAPTER 36

It's Too Much

*"The cruel chisel destroys a stone with each cut. But what
the stone suffers by repeated blows is no less than the shape
the mason is making of it. And should a poor stone be
asked, 'What is happening to you?' it might reply, 'Don't
ask me. All I know is that for my part there is nothing for
me to know or do, only to remain steady under the hand
of my master and to love him and suffer him to work out
my destiny. It is for him to know how to achieve this. I
know neither what he is doing nor why. I only know that
he is doing what is best and most perfect, and I suffer
each cut of the chisel as though it were the best thing for
me, even though, to tell the truth, each one is my idea of
ruin, destruction and defacement. But, ignoring all this, I
rest contented with the present moment. Thinking only of
my duty to it, I submit to the work of this skillful master
without caring to know what it is.'"*
—Jean Pierre de Caussade, *The Sacrament of the
Present Moment*, carefully saved in Elisabeth's
worn notebook of favorite quotes

*E*lisabeth went on to Portland, Seattle, Denver, Boston, and then New
Hampshire for a time of writing and reflection. She had recently read
books by Erica Jong (*Fear of Flying*, which Elisabeth called "brilliant"), Jill Briscoe ("not brilliant, but cheerful"), and Father Robert
Capon, an Episcopal priest, theologian, and chef. Now she read Judith
Rossner's *Looking for Mr. Goodbar*, the 1975 *New York Times* #1
bestseller. Elisabeth wrote in her journal, "Will the God who fur-
nished Rossner (and Erica Jong) with the vision and the imagination

and the brains to depict a life of despair help His humble servant Elliot to depict a life which shows some Christian hope??"

Again, she jotted themes for the novel she desperately wanted to write. "A good one, this time!

"<u>If</u> I am to write a novel, as Jim Packer is absolutely persuaded I must do, I must have the courage to ignore what people will think—especially how they will read it as my autobiography. . . . Jim has promised to 'cover' this matter in prayer.

"Second, I must receive the <u>vision</u> which now tarries. The pictures I must show must first be shown to me.

"I must not try to write for the Mennonite booksellers or the Baptist ladies or for Jill or Dr. Ockenga or Mother or my seminary students or Hattie or Vic Oliver, and I must not be distracted by what I imagine their opinion will be."

She jotted cryptic notes about her novel. On one hand they're just fragments, indecipherable crumbs of her creative yearnings. On the other, they are almost like a code, or a metaphysical poem, by which we might get insight into the mysteries of some of Elisabeth's decisions over the next year or two, which would in fact determine the narrow riverbanks of the rest of her life.

- Forbidden love . . . obedience to the Will. Suffering and death. Fear. These were not <u>problems</u> to do something about, but <u>gifts</u> to do something with.
- A habit of sadness.
- An offered grief.
- Fulfillment—not through "self-realization" but through self-giving.
- "Control" of one's dating—ends by becoming victim.
- Spiritual motherhood—reception, bearing burdens, dying to give life, self-giving to nurture, pride, an act of faith (who knows what child she'll bring forth?). Woman who sees herself as unsuited to this man . . . deliberate act of will: surrender him.
- Transcending one's own disasters. Being obedient to will of God (e.g., resisting temptation) for the sake of the world.
- Forgiveness—the healing of memory.
- Death: the Gate of Life.

"I must put forth every ounce of intellectual, emotional, and imaginative <u>energy</u> that I can summon. (And that's really too hard—too much trouble.)" She determined to tell no one what she was writing.

"I must <u>see the truth</u>. O God—I know I can't do it without that elementary condition: 'If ye continue in My Word.'

"The book must be earthed—strongly incarnational, flesh and blood and bone and nerve. Harnessed to light, spirit, eternity, the foundations of the world, the Word."

She could sense this cosmic, towering, titillating creative project before her. But it was overwhelming. Intimidating.

She concluded, "Well—it's too much. Too big for me."

She read secular writers who stirred her deeply with archetypal truths about humanity and the universe. But sometimes she felt she could only write in stereotypes. This realization that she could not write in the way that she desired was another stark, yawning loss of this season of her life, one that's not commonly recognized. From the time Elisabeth Elliot returned to the United States from Ecuador in the early '60s, she had devoured classic and modern literature that evoked the human condition against the backdrop of God's mysterious universe. She wanted to write great novels. She wanted to engage and stir urbane New Yorkers. She wanted to call into being essential human truths through the power of story. She wanted pages that she had written to stir people's hearts in the same way she was so deeply stirred, her heart and eyes lifted up, by well-crafted literature, visual art, and music.

"In order to write a novel you have to have a power of concentration which enables you to live in the story. If one could operate on two levels simultaneously it would be possible to be a novelist and a housekeeper, teacher, speaker, hostess, etc. I don't seem able to do this. I spend most of my energy on the secondary roles, then try (usually futility) to thrust myself into the story for a couple of hours at a time. How can I get to <u>know</u> Erica and Ann [two of her characters] with so many distractions?"

It was easier, of course—though still painful, as any writing is excruciating—to write articles and non-fiction books and teach classes and speak at Christian conferences and retreats. It kept her busy, it paid the bills, and perhaps this lifestyle was all she could do.

Even as Elisabeth Elliot made this unusual concession of failure, it fit with her mindset in the early fall of 1976. She was at a critical juncture. She had been torn apart by the horrific suffering and disintegration of the man she loved. Twenty years afterwards, she would, with tears streaming down her face and Lars standing nearby, call it the biggest trial of her faith.

At the same time, she deeply desired to be a truly great writer expressing universal, primal, visceral human experiences in the context of unseen eternal realities. The fact that she could not do this deeply bruised her and caused her to fall back on what she *could* do. What was safe.

It was not so much the death of a dream as much as it was the disturbing realization that the dream was impossible to achieve because of what she regarded as confines in her own talent.

Like all of us, she was quite conscious of our own limitations, and was well familiar of the dynamic of depending on Christ's sufficiency to do what we cannot.

"One of the aspects of my vocation is the repeated experience of weakness, the knowledge that I can't do the thing that is asked, I cannot meet expectations. For the strength of Christ is 'made perfect' in weakness. The painful discipline of preparation gives occasion for the recognition of this weakness, and it is something I must endure alone, since to speak of it is to invite comments—'A lot you have to worry about! Look what you did at _____.'"

The feeling induced one of her earliest vulnerable memories. "In the first and second grades at Henry School I was terrified of failure, and woke at night in tears. I remember (Aunt) Anne sitting with me in the rocking chair by the front window, trying to help me with arithmetic and assure me that I would be able to learn it just like the rest of the pupils. Mother, concerned at last by my tears, went to the teacher and was told, of course, that I was near the top of the class."

As we've said, Elisabeth's one novel caused more consternation than contemplation among Christian readers, and secular readers had no interest in reading a story about the spiritual awakening of a young missionary trapped in the constraints of her evangelical subculture.

During her marriage to Addison, she was perhaps too happy or distracted to write fiction, though he often referred in casual correspondence to his wife busily "working on a novel." At one point she had envisioned a story in the Gothic, surreal environment of the legalistic boarding school where she had spent her teen years.

Though Elisabeth would continue to write fiction pages here and there over the years to come, another Elisabeth Elliot novel was just not to be. She felt she could not do it.

Elisabeth could have written great novels, but she gave up and wrote other things instead because of weariness, time constraints with her speaking schedule, and, once she married Lars, the push to make money.

Of course the choice was hers to make, and tens of thousands of readers have testified to how their lives were influenced and changed for the better because of Elisabeth's nonfiction writing and speaking ministry in the late 1970s, '80s, and '90s.

Personally, though, it was another loss. Not as great as Addison's death, of course, but a fundamental loss to who Elisabeth was. Her literary dreams, goals, and hopes created a high bar that she could not scale.

This, like the other losses in her life in the mid-1970s, brought Elisabeth, I think, to an unstated point of concession. *If I can't do what I yearn for, then I will do what I can. Another death to self. Good.*

And maybe she could not live life "to the hilt," as Jim had said so often. Free and full, reveling in experiences, confident in the presence of God.

And youth, to be sure, was gone forever. She mourned over the wrinkles next to her eyes, the folds in her neck, the strange thin crepe that had snuck into her once supple skin. She mourned the loss of her intimacy with her departed husband, and yearned, each day, for that which she'd been forced to give up, though she did not act on those desires.

Though she was thrilled about Val and Walt's marriage, she saw in them the fresh beginnings that her own season in life denied. She missed them; they were far away, occupied with their own new life and ministry. She wistfully remembered her early marriage with Jim. But she forged on, traveling, speaking, writing . . . with crowds, fans, and even friends and family, she felt alone.

As we've seen, she constantly longed for the smell and feel and camaraderie of a man. She looked for him constantly. "I only want to think of The Man," she moaned in her journal, knowing that her next step would be to kick herself in the pants and do the Next Right Thing. "Can't I just wallow for a minute?"

During the autumn of 1976, Elisabeth continued teaching her Bible class at her congregational church. She had Gordon students over for dinners and rousing hymn sings. She got as involved in the lives of her four lodgers as they would let her. These young people boarding in her home provided a magnetic, sometimes melodramatic distraction. She genuinely cared for them and wanted the best for them, even as she wrung her hands over their habits that drove her crazy. She missed them when she traveled and felt unseen and alone. "They acknowledge me," she wrote in her journal.

Still, back at home, the kids' busy comings and goings, their youth and passion and sense of limitless opportunities ahead reminded her acutely of her own advancing age and her feelings of diminishing options.

Elisabeth's journal overflows with drama snippets. "Sunday. The usual sullenness on Van's part because Lars was here for dinner. Should I simply refuse to have her when I want to have Lars?"

One female boarder became engaged. She and her fiancé sat on Elisabeth's couch one evening, "radiant, excited," Elisabeth wrote in her journal. But ". . . I—separate. Longing."

Elisabeth's longing was not for a specific person. She longed for someone, she knew not who, who could stir her with the mighty passion and oneness that she had known with Addison.

Meanwhile, Lars sat there longing for *Elisabeth*. "It is a wonderful thing to be loved. It makes my days and nights shine a little." She felt that the longing of unrequited love was like a "pain [that] binds [people] round tightly like a chain and fetters. I am not now chained."

But oh, the nights were long!

"The peach tree is getting down to its last leaves outside my study window. Winter and death come again." She remembered the sodden leaves on a hillside outside Addison's hospital window when his cancer was first discovered.

"The love that I had—not possible again," she wrote. "Nearly 50 years old."

One day a boarder sat with Elisabeth shedding "storms of tears" because her parents wanted her to live at home for one quarter.

"You're acting like a 12-year-old," said Elisabeth, who just may not have been the most gifted counselor of her day.

"Can't I express my feelings now and act like a Christian tomorrow?" wailed the girl.

Elisabeth felt mystified by the lack of duty, diligence, discipline, determination, denial, and all the other D virtues that had been the very pillars of her own upbringing. But she *loved* all the young people whose lives intersected with her own. Their gaffes made her all the more conscious of her own failings. She wrote after,

"Misgivings, always, about my right to speak as I do when I myself am so selfish. What blind spots, what hoard of gold do I cherish, Lord? I'm afraid to ask. Afraid, also, to be discovered in some gross inconsistency, 'terror of the weakness and mutability of oneself,' as G. K. Chesterton puts it.

"There is a price to be paid if we will be God's mouthpiece. It is self-denial at every point. No to my desire to preserve my self-image. No to my fears of failure and discovery. No to each separate thing shown to be inspired by self. No to the comfort of not taking a hard, clear look at the truth."

Elisabeth's "Just say no" to sin, fear, and self is admirable. But I find myself wishing for a flip in her thinking, for "just say 'No'" is not strong enough a mantra for most of us. It is only our great "Yes" to God, yes to His will, yes to His love, over and over, at each point and each temptation in our broken journey that can eclipse and diminish the power of sin and temptation.

By Christmas 1976, Elisabeth glumly noted it would be her first Christmas season without Val around.

Just before Christmas, Lars took Elisabeth to the *Nutcracker* ballet, then to an elegant dinner. He gave her "a beautiful dinner ring. We talked of the impossibility of any future. No illusions. No false hopes. But it is so comfortable to be loved and cared for. He knows I am grateful but can offer no more."

He told her the things he imagined people saying about him. "He's chasing after a rainbow. Where does he get the crush? Why doesn't he stay in his own backyard?"

"No answers. All I know is I'm glad he's around."

At one point Val asked her mother if she had any feelings for Lars, and in the next breath wondered if Elisabeth had ever thought of her own life as good material for a novel.

As 1976 ended, Elisabeth returned to speak at the Urbana missions conference. She talked at some length with Billy Graham, and was astonished to find that students overflowed her sessions just as they did his. People told her of dedicating their lives to God's service because of her talk. Others, already on the mission field, told her how her books had influenced their decision to go. She felt humbled. Amazed.

And then there were conversations like this, in which a young woman called her.

"Mrs. Leitch, I was just wondering if I could talk to you for a minute?"

"Yes—on the phone."

"Okay. Well, um, I was just wondering if you knew 'Sam' and 'Constance.'"

"No, I don't believe so."

"Okay. Well, um, I was just wondering because they knew your husband [Jim] really well. They worked with him in the jungle."

"Oh?" said Elisabeth. "And where was that?"

"Contemana. They really know him well down there."

"Where is Contemana?"

"It's where he was—in *Peru*. That's where they work, and they wanted me to tell you hello."

"Oh," Elisabeth said. "Thank you."

After this strange interchange, Elisabeth closed her year, and her journal. She thought about Billy Graham's amazing ministry, and of the team he had to help him. She felt alone. During his invitation to the students to be willing to go anywhere God might asked, she accepted it for herself. "He is Your servant, Lord. So am I. Let me do Your work, in Your way, in the place You choose. Here? Ecuador? Where?"

CHAPTER 37

The Fence

"Some things may legitimately be alleviated,
others necessarily endured. May God give us
wisdom to know the difference."
—an unattributed, underlined entry in Elisabeth Elliot's
well-worn notebook of favorite quotes

The emotional centerpiece of Elisabeth Elliot's life story from 1963, when she returned to the United States from Ecuador, and late 1976 was her marriage to Addison Leitch and his harrowing death. Her second widowhood was an ironic season of pain, loss, distraction, yearning, and seeking God's will. After Add's death and Val's marriage, did the Lord want Elisabeth to go back to Ecuador? She wondered and prayed about it. What was once unthinkable was now on the table.

But she did not return to live in the Ecuadorian jungle.

1976 was a year of primal, almost unbearable loneliness. Elisabeth knew there would never be another Addison Leitch. Or Jim Elliot. The desirable, appropriately aged men she knew of were few, far between, and married. But then she read *A Severe Mercy*, the account of a young atheist couple's shining, intentional love, their friendship with C. S. Lewis, their journey to faith, and then the horrific death of the wife at age forty. Something fluttered inside Elisabeth. She identified with the deep love, suffering, and loss that the author, Sheldon Vanauken, evoked so well. Vanauken had his master's from Yale and was a much-loved professor of history and English literature at Lynchburg College. He seemed like a kindred spirit, and Elisabeth found herself thinking repeatedly of this man she had never met.

Elisabeth wrote in her journal that her brother Tom had informed her that Sheldon was "not yet remarried, is middle-aged and at once my heart leaps up! His story is of a great love, and he can <u>write</u>. Lord, Thou knowest!"

Some pages later Elisabeth related the great news that Tom had shared further, crucial information for the height-conscious Elisabeth: yes, Sheldon Vanauken was "very tall." He was corresponding with Tom. Perhaps he would come to the Boston area in the springtime. . . . "What would we talk about if we had opportunity?"

But nothing ever came of that brief, fluttering hope. Where, then, was The Man God had for her? Perhaps he didn't exist.

But there <u>was</u> a man in Elisabeth's life who was utterly devoted to her. He appeared at every opportunity, solicitous, helpful, opening doors, complimenting her looks, always ready to do whatever she needed.

She noted in her journal on September 2, 1976, "Dinner with Lars in Portsmouth. Excellent French onion soup, deviled crab, Danish ice cream and unutterably boring conversation. No. Lars cannot express himself. He is a bundle of inhibitions. He does things for me constantly—he just re-laid all the terrace flagstones. But I cannot give him anything but an evening now and then, with only half my attention. Fell asleep while he was talking coming home in the car."

But Lars was always there. Trimming the lawn, painting the hall, picking her up from the airport. His conversation made her snooze. But he took her to nice restaurants. He knew her preferences and needs and he wanted to take care of her. She felt like a woman with him, not just a speaker and writer. And he was tall.

As time went on, Elisabeth settled for a different writing life than the one of which she dreamed. She settled for a different man as well. She had to have a man. And here he was. Perhaps she had just overlooked all Lars's sterling qualities. Perhaps he was God's perfect provision for her.

At first, Lars was just not an option. They are not well matched. But he was in her life. She spent a lovely evening with him and his mother in Palm Beach. She pondered, constantly pondered. At the end of January 1977, she wrote,

"Turmoil in mind and heart. One week ago I was telling [a friend] there was not the remotest possibility of my ever marrying Lars, even if I fell in love with him. 'It's preposterous. Out of the question.' Next day I was wondering if it was possible for me to love him. Now I wonder if I could marry him. <u>Is</u> it preposterous?

"Yes.

1. I'm too old for him. It would be unfair to him.
2. He is not in the Jim Elliot and Addison Leitch league.
3. What is he going to do for his life work?
4. How should we arrange a life together?

"But does the idea appeal to me, in spite of all odds? Yes.

1. He takes <u>care</u> of me. I love it.
2. He appreciates me.
3. He has loved me selflessly for three years.
4. I am perfectly at ease in his company.

"But:

1. What would people say?
2. What of the 'image'?
3. What of his life—oughtn't he to have children?
4. He would have to be 'outshone' upstaged, take a back seat—if I were to continue my 'public' life.
5. Money?"

She wondered if she should ask for a sign. And as always, Elisabeth prayed for God's will to be done, whatever the cost.

On January 30, Elisabeth wrote, "When it comes to love, <u>anything</u> can happen. But what is this falling-in-love business?"

She thought of her own advice, that when two alternatives seem equal, one should choose the harder one. The problem was that she just didn't know which would be harder, staying single or marrying Lars.

Elisabeth gave a casual dinner party for some friends, with "Lars acting as <u>host</u>. Genial, efficient, dependable. Makes me feel like a total woman, at ease, cared for. What am I to do?"

A few days later, her doorbell rang and she jumped, finding herself hoping it was Lars. It was. They had tea and hors d'oeuvres in the study.

Elisabeth told a friend about Lars. The friend "was not shocked nor did she think the possibility absurd. Encouraged me to think of the real man apart from the 'image' or what he would do to my own image. That, I'm beginning to think, is the real crux. Am I thinking wholly secularly in my concern for my image?"

Elisabeth was at a point in her writing and speaking life when offers and opportunities poured in from around the globe. "You are at the zenith now," her friend told her, "so you are being tested as to whether you will choose the bright lights or a 'nobody' who humanly speaking will not enhance your public reputation. It may well be a spiritual issue—and it comes just at the peak, when it must be most difficult for you to make that choice."

The next day Lars put his arms around Elisabeth and said, "I want to take care of you."

"How greatly I long to be taken care of!" Elisabeth wrote in her journal later.

"Obstacles:

1. El que diran [her concerns of what people might say]
2. Money—the Addison Leitch trust is to be dissolved
3. His career
4. This house
5. Taking yet another name
6. The comparisons—Jim, Addison
7. Val, Walt?
8. My lodgers (it ought not to seem a problem, but it does)
9. Age"

Two days later, Elisabeth's brother Tom Howard talked with her in metaphysical terms about "courtly grace" and Lars "steady, persevering dauntless devotion—the most stunning datum."

The older one is, Elisabeth thought, *the fewer things matter in marriage.* "Companionability and love are tops. A month ago, marrying Lars was an impossibility." Now, she wondered, was it an "inevitability"? She felt like she was being moved toward one possibility and only one. "Holding onto my widowhood does not appear to be an option, yet relinquishing it was remote a few weeks ago."

She felt like God was opening her eyes. "Perhaps I have sought only joys of my own definition. And now, what if the universe offers me another kind? Shall I refuse it? Or shall I, in humility, accept the gift? (Gifts are not of one's choosing!) I must be purified in order to do so—purged from the self-love which is at the root of my hesitation."

She jotted Charles Williams's severe words in her journal. "The approach by love is the approach to fact; to love anything but fact is not love." Was her journey not so much about loving Lars as loving the "fact"—the principle of dying on the altar? Here, at last, was something tangible she could get hold of—the sacrifice of her own self-image. Toppling "graven images" had been her theme since the early 1960s. Did this notion, then, draw her toward Lars as the means by which she might lose her idolatrous perceptions of self?

Wondering this, I for the first time got a glimpse into why, on principle, Elisabeth may have married a man who was so unsuited to her. Perhaps all might have gone swimmingly if he had not had such rage and control issues, which she did not yet know.

"Love," Elisabeth wrote, "is, I suppose, passage. It is a Valley (of the Shadow of Death, in some ways), but like the Great Valley, not one in which I walk alone The Lord is beside me—He's been here before, seen and known it all, leads me for His name's sake, says to me, 'Don't be afraid. I've _led_ you this way. I see the end from the beginning, and all that troubles you now. Just walk with Me.' To walk with Him means, I know, to leave behind things I cherish and cling to. It won't do to lug them along—my name, Add's name, my money, Add's money, this house, my lodgers, my class—they are to be turned _in_. Lars is not to fit into _my_ life. I am to fit into _his_. And so far, I have no idea of the shape of his life, so can't be arranging myself to fit that shape."

After Elisabeth Elliot wrote those pensive words, the doorbell rang, Lars stood at her door. She opened it. He stayed for four hours. "If ever a man made a woman love him . . ." wrote Elisabeth later.

A few days later Lars drove Elisabeth to a speaking engagement of 550 Campus Crusade [CRU] women. It was another example, she thought, of his willingness to do anything at all to make things easy for her, but it does leave one wondering if his life had any "shape" at all except for Elisabeth's.

She felt a "moment of truth" at the podium. "He, dressed in navy suit, wearing glasses, pacing back and forth slowly on the periphery of the crowd, waiting for me. It seemed a paradigm . . ."

Later she heard a sermon on obedience to God—"willingness to do what one doesn't want, forgetting one's own plans."

Still, Lars knew her strong personality. He didn't want to be jerked around. "You mustn't think you've got the string of a yo-yo on your finger," he said. He put his arms around her. "I just want to take care of you. . . . I've never loved anyone, never _wanted_ anyone, the way I want you."

Elisabeth thought of the confidence, the steadfastness, the courage that Lars had shown for years, even when rebuffed, ignored, even scorned. "I owe him many apologies," she thought.

She gave a speech to yet another packed house full of eager listeners. She found herself choking a bit on one of her standard lines: "My first marriage was a miracle, my second was unbelievable, and I don't really expect God to solve my 'problems' by giving me a third husband. The odds against that would be astronomical."

Now she wondered. Would they?

On Valentine's Day, they had dinner in his apartment. He gave her a romantic card and a bottle of her favorite perfume. "He makes me feel like a woman. Is anything more important in a man-woman relationship?"

"Well, *yes*," I think to myself, sitting in my office decades later.

The next night, they sat "like teenagers" at a movie, Lars's arm around Elisabeth, "his hand holding mine. Bliss!

"He makes me feel like a woman," she repeated in her journal. "Is anything higher on the list of what matters? Christ loved the Church—took the initiative loved Her when she would not love him, wooed her, won her, gave himself for her, cherished her, held her, comforted her . . . accepted all indifference and rebuff, ultimately conquered her hardened heart. The analogies are stunning."

"But Elisabeth!" I want to whisper to her across the past. "Lars was no Christ!"

Then, in February 1977, Lars said the words that went to the heart of Elisabeth's most deeply felt need at the time.

"I'm the one who's going to build the fences around you," he told her, "And I'm going to stand on all sides."

"What a thing to say! Inspired!" Elisabeth wrote. "It keeps ringing in my mind."

Elisabeth's journal from that point on roils with doubts, lists of her concerns, primarily about finances and Lars's lack of a job, as well as her determination to be true to the will of God, and as always, her willingness to die to self to do so. Meanwhile, she wrote steamy love notes to Lars, like a giddy young woman full of passion.

In November, Lars presented her with a ring, his mother's small diamond solitaire. She accepted. They married on Elisabeth's 51st birthday, December 21, 1977. And he did indeed build fences around her. On all sides.

Within nine days, she told her closest friends and family members that she had made the biggest mistake of her life.

PART THREE

Believing

CHAPTER 38

Who Was She?

"Read Christian biographies so you can see
the hand of God in all the ups and downs,
the sorrows and joys, the perplexities and dangers,
the disasters of one individual life It will
help you to trust Him."
—Elisabeth Elliot

As any author knows, when you write a book, whether fiction or non-fiction, you enter the lives of your characters. They talk to you. You mourn over their losses, hope for their best, lose patience with their gaffes, and dwell in a strange in-between world that sometimes merges your subject matter and your own conscious experience. During such times, your family tends to avoid you.

For me, however, there was a strange plot twist in my own life that echoed Elisabeth Elliot's emotional journey in such an eerie way that it made my head spin.

I said earlier that the emotional centerpiece of this book is its account of Addison Leitch's battle with cancer and his subsequent death. When I was writing that long, sad part of Elisabeth's story, I lived in her anguished journals. Writing such intense episodes, word by word, channeling her constantly spiraling emotions, required me to live experiences I had not yet had. Elisabeth's intimately personal flow of fears, hope, and pleas to God recurred in my waking life and in my dreams. I walked through her past with her.

Then her past became my present.

Within just weeks of weeping as I wrote the story of Addison's death, I raced with my own beloved husband of thirty-seven years to an emergency room. Lee had courageously battled a rare brain cancer for a decade. He had had massive cranial surgeries, and nearly died. We had been through a lot, but Lee's cancer had been in remission. Life had been halfway "normal" for several years.

Now he suddenly had new symptoms. The ER brain scan revealed a big, fast-growing, radiation-induced tumor that had not been there three months earlier. It was a brand-new, different type of cancer. It extended into his brain. The proton radiation that had saved my husband's life ten years earlier had caused an expanding, voracious, ominous malignancy that was now rapidly consuming everything in its path.

Life "as usual" screeched to a halt. I shoved my Elisabeth Elliot manuscript, and all else, aside.

Lee was admitted to the hospital. He had a million tests, and then a palliative brain surgery to debulk the tumor and get a biopsy. One of his surgeons called me from the operating room. Nothing could be done, medically. The pathology reports would soon confirm that Lee did not have long to live.

Elisabeth Elliot's intimate, awful journey immediately became my own. Metastasis, morphine, and caregiving on a whole new level. There were many blessings, such as the incredible help of hospice, which did not exist when Addison Leitch was dying. Our adult kids gathered in our home. Our young grandchildren understood that Gramps would soon leave for Heaven. Friends and neighbors brought food, hugs, laughter, and memories.

Lee was brave, funny, and full of faith in Jesus. Within three weeks of the actual diagnosis of the new tumor, he breathed his last, which was a mercy. We told him what a great race he had run; we sang and cheered him on in that final journey. We held him and watched him slip from this world of shadows to the unseen but real and eternal world of light, power, freedom, joy, and the presence of Christ. We exulted. We wept.

There was, and is, nothing unique or special about my own pain. We of the sisterhood and brotherhood of Christ all go through dark, difficult, and painful losses of all kinds in our earthly journey. All I know is that the Rock that held Elisabeth Elliot in her much-loved husbands' deaths held me as well. It holds me still.

As I have emphasized repeatedly in these books about Elisabeth Elliot, the stories of Christ-followers on this broken planet do not all end with a victorious, triumphal flourish from which readers may draw a tidy syllabus of life lessons. The question for ardent Elisabeth Elliot fans has never been, "What would Elisabeth do?" or how to "be like her." It is, as for all of us, that we seek to be like Jesus, and take both comfort and warning from the stories of His flawed friends who have gone before us.

After Lee's death, in my own bereavement, I eventually returned to my writing commitments. I picked up with Elisabeth's story where I left off. As I traveled in time through her journals, I saw clearly that her story in the years covered by this book could not end tied with a perky Pinterest bow. Yes, she heroically weathered the wretched grief of Addison's death. But then, day by day, page by page, I was chilled to the bone by some of the decisions Elisabeth made in her second widowhood, particularly her gradual choice to marry Lars Gren.

I had been warned about aspects of Lars's character from the beginning. Elisabeth's friends and family, as well as people who had watched him at events or book signings, deluged me with unsought observations of his behaviors. I had not known quite what to think and had reserved judgment. I still reserve judgment. It's above my pay grade. As I've said elsewhere, I've personally experienced both sides of Lars—his charming, funny, engaging self, and his cold, controlling, angry self. I bear him no ill will. We're all messed up people.

But grief concentrates the mind, and perhaps it causes one to call things as one sees them, not as others might wish they were. In the painful after-grief of my own husband's death, as I reread Elisabeth's sometimes too-frank journals, and breathed in her experience in the four years of her second widowhood, all I could see was that Elisabeth's understandable loneliness, deep need for affirmation, physical hunger, weariness, and desire to be "protected" gradually, insidiously, led her, step by cajoling step, into a difficult third marriage that confined and controlled her for the rest of her long life.

Lars courted her lavishly, faithfully, and cleverly. Though he was "a bundle of inhibitions" who could not express himself and was so "unutterably boring" that she could not stay awake, gradually, eventually, he wore her down, and she convinced herself that he was God's will for her life. His earlier divorce was not an obstacle.

Many who revere Elisabeth Elliot do so because of the many books she wrote during her decades of marriage to Lars. Under his strong control and shrewd management, Elisabeth spoke all over the world and for twelve years hosted a radio program called *Gateway to Joy* that had an enormous influence on thousands of women. She wrote bestselling nonfiction books for her evangelical audience. She was well-loved and respected in the 1980s and '90s, as she is today, by many Christians because of her uncompromising views on biblical obedience, suffering, and eternal priorities, as well as her perspectives on sexuality and women's roles. Because of Lars's management, that body of Elisabeth's work exists today for all who wish to access Elisabeth's strong teachings.[1]

Others did not agree with some of Elisabeth's opinions and had no interest in her books or speeches, but still admired her gutsy missionary service so many decades earlier. She became an admired evangelical icon. She was not well-known in the "secular world" she had once longed to influence. But she had incalculable influence on students who credited her with their decisions to go into international service work, and women who sought to shape godly homes and become more like Jesus.

In all of this, Lars was by her side. He was often charming and friendly to those who attended Elisabeth's conferences, balancing the fact that Elisabeth could sometimes be abrupt and withdrawn when she signed attendees' books. He worked hard, and could be quite funny and amiable, poking fun at himself as "the third Mr. Elliot." He and Elisabeth developed, if not a partnership, an often-loving alliance that stayed in place for almost four decades.

But it was not "a great love story," as some writers or interviewers wanted to spin it. The truth would not fit the picture that fans wanted to hear. Even as I was anguishing over this part of Elisabeth's story, some wanted me to keep everything tidy. "You wouldn't want to write anything that would reflect poorly on Elisabeth," one Christian leader mused.

Well, no, I wouldn't *want* to, and I don't think I have.

But this aversion to human complexity is exactly the type of thinking in Christian circles that vastly frustrated Elisabeth Elliot. She would have been the first to encourage me to speak the truth, however gnarly it might be. Except Elisabeth would not have said "gnarly."

Elisabeth was quick to admonish her audiences not to put any Christian leader on a pedestal. "Pedestals are for statues," she would say. Elisabeth was not a marble effigy, but a flesh-and-blood woman with strengths and weaknesses, like us all. In the season after Addison's death, she was not yet the woman she would become in her later years of teaching, writing, and the often-painful crucible of her relationship with Lars. That pain, in fact, may well have led to her deepest season of growth and productivity as a follower of Christ.

Again, we cannot typecast the marriage. There were many seasons of sweetness, laughter, and love. There were also many instances when her husband's rage, control, verbal abuse, and abrupt departures broke Elisabeth's heart. Lars would physically leave for a while, or he would not speak to her for days. In my first interview with one of Elisabeth's brothers, Dave, he did not mention any of this, but then called me an hour later, conscience-stricken, to relate what he had left out: that Lars would be subsumed by irresistible tides of anger, his face becoming "purple with rage." Every day.[2]

Elisabeth had chosen a relationship that certainly enhanced her own suffering. Perhaps she felt it kept her in a constant posture of offering herself on the Lord's altar, or it was a thorn in her side to keep her humble.

So for me, her chosen yet sometimes miserable biographer, there came a great challenge. I'm a pessimist, though I prefer to call that being a realist. I've always seen and celebrated the mess of true human stories, having lived my own. They enhance my wonder at the grace of God.

We can't paint Elisabeth's story with lovely pastels and blurred edges, pretty and placid. It is through the sharp edges and cracks in the veneer that God's grace, no matter what, shines through.

Nor can we probe and weigh out the story with an either/or mindset, like a melodrama. Lars was not a one-dimensional evil villain. He evidently thought he was a follower of Christ, but his life did not show evidence of that fact. Nor was Elisabeth not a guiltless and guileless heroine. We must instead see their story, and all our stories, with a both/and mind. Yes, there was viable good and strong ministry, and happy hymn sings around the piano in Lars's and Elisabeth's home. Yes, there was also brokenness, anguish, and sin. Just like in our own lives. Many people today love Elisabeth's books, radio programs, speeches and letters that came from the very season of life where she was living with discord, control, and pain at home. Elisabeth could write viable truths about freedom in Christ even as her husband checked how many miles she put on the odometer and unpredictably denied her access to the daughter, son-in-law, and grandchildren she loved. Lars could be both charming and boorish. So could Elisabeth. She purposed to honor her husband, but she did not always succeed. Her tongue was a formidable weapon. Good, bad, glory, pain, tedium, hope, and despair were all mixed together in her life's tale.

There is no question that Elisabeth Elliot was a woman yoked by duty, obedience, and fidelity to God's commands. At the same time, she was essentially a person, in the 1960s and '70s, who loved freedom. She loved the sense of liberty in people she admired, like the widowed Katherine Morgan, who served God with humor and reckless abandon, and seemed so free in her own skin.

Elisabeth gloried in the beauties of untrammeled nature, hiking with her dog running free up the paths and woods ahead of her. She refused to leash her dogs at home, regardless of highway danger—"oh, how I love to watch them <u>run</u>!" even though that meant the premature death of three of them.[3]

As we've seen, she resonated deeply with writer Isak Dinesen, who told a story of the time, when her property manager in Africa was trying to break an ox so it could be yoked for use in the fields. The manager tied up the ox for the night, and the next morning it was found grievously wounded, attacked, while helpless, by a leopard. The ox had to be destroyed.

But perhaps he'd really gone free. Isak Dinesen wrote with great understatement, "he would not be yoked now."

If anyone knew what it was to take Christ's yoke, it was Elisabeth Elliot. I am not suggesting the freedom she desired was freedom *from* Him. But something in Isak Dinesen's quote reverberated in me. I saw the 1960s, early '70s-era Elisabeth Eliot as a woman who loved not the wanton self-flow freedom of that hippie era, but the true biblical liberty found in obedience. One need not be leashed, because one will return to the Master out of love and fealty.

When she was young, Elisabeth wasn't managing herds on a farm in Africa, but she had been that woman running through the South American jungle to deliver infants and save tribal women in the throes of difficult childbirth. She had sat, helpless, when some died. She had lived in the wild, eaten charred monkey fists, bathed in rivers with people who could have suddenly turned and killed her as easily as they had speared her first husband to death. She had grinned at the throbbing energy on the streets of New York, and walked, tall and resolute, through the alleyways and warrens of Jerusalem, circa 1967. She had resisted the seductive offers of the likes of Ecuadorian admirers, European professors, and her old friend Cornell Capa.

She had tried, with a growing sense of despair, to write stories that captured truth in a way that skeptics might see it. Like Amy Carmichael and other gritty heroes who came before her, she railed against the image-conscious habits of the Evangelical Machine, whose every story must end with glorious conversion and coherent happy endings, lest God look bad. She never got over those who did so with the deaths of Jim Elliot, Nate Saint, Ed McCully, Pete Fleming, and Roger Youderian.

She wanted to live life to the hilt, and in Addison Leitch, she found a soul mate toward that end. They may not have been swinging on vines through Latin American jungles, but in his intellectual capacity, spiritual care for his students, love of God, wit, sexual zest, and humor she found a likeminded adventurer.

But in the aftermath of Addison's death, that Elisabeth Elliot began to change. Her love and passion for nature, music, literature, and the Bible was still there. But there was now an exchange, a deal she must have struck with herself in which she gave up freedom for security. This woman who would not even leash her dogs because she loved for them to run free, regardless of the danger, became a person whose highest value was the desire to feel *secure*. So Lars's words about fencing her in, with him somehow standing on each side, did not repel her. They drew her in.

President Dwight Eisenhower once said, "If you want total security, go to prison. There you're fed, clothed, given medical care and so on. The only thing lacking . . . is freedom."

Surely such words are too harsh. But there is the nub of a point there. Like many women to whom she spoke, Elisabeth found herself in a marriage characterized by control. Her husband dictated the thermostat setting, listened in on her conversations, interrupted her time with others, criticized her habits, and often pulled her away from people she enjoyed. Elisabeth did what she counseled other women to do: she submitted. She saw Lars as her head. But she suffered.

"My darling," she wrote to Lars in an undated letter written at the height of her travel and speaking ministry, "Something is surely wrong, as that other time, when 11 days went by with zero communication. . . . It is hard to be on these [speaking] trips, trying to give, asking to be allowed to be God's mouthpiece, yet aware that if my listeners knew the standoff that exists between us, the constant irritation I cause you (posture, thumb, attitudes . . .) they would find my words hard to swallow. And I nearly choke on them myself sometimes."

She went on to humbly tell Lars that his criticisms of her habits and behaviors "are <u>often</u> right, and I am aware of your pleas and corrections and suggestions. I know that you are God's gift to me, my head, my lord, my cherisher (i.e., husband) and according to Ephesians 5 you are to make me without 'spot or wrinkle.' I want to be the sort of woman you can <u>love</u> and be <u>proud of</u>—I am working on it.

"I almost feel schizoid when we are on a trip like this—people speaking so appreciatively and gratefully on the one hand, and on the other the painful awareness that nothing (almost nothing?) is the way you would like it. You were very particular about my expressing appreciation to [someone for a paid advertisement of one of Elisabeth's books]; perhaps it is more important that we begin at home.

"I love you, darling. I am thankful for you. I am sorry this weekend has been such a miserable one for you. . . ."

After every speech, she'd head back to the hotel room she shared with Lars and gauge his response to her presentation. If he was happy with it, all was well. If he thought she had done a poor job, he would not speak to her and remove himself from her physically.

Certainly, Elisabeth could have alleviated the suffering of her third marriage by not entering it in the first place. She exercised choice. I believe, as she said, that she made a mistake. But once she had made her bed, so to speak, she was committed. She endured for thirty-eight years until God took her Home in 2015. Being Elisabeth Elliot, she had no choice but to do so. In that context she strove, in her discomfort, to yield herself to her heavenly Father.

When she was diagnosed with Alzheimer's in the late 1990s, Lars prohibited the use of what he called "the A word" and kept her on the speaking circuit. She was tired and did not want to travel any more. But she had to submit to her husband. She complied.

Gradually she came to the point where she could no longer remember the lyrics of her often-quoted hymns, or the date that Jim Elliot was killed, or she would lose her place in the notes she was now dependent on. Lars kept booking her for events, even as there were whispers in the audience and people wondered if Elisabeth was ill. Always meticulous about her dress, she now appeared on platforms looking disheveled, her blazer misbuttoned. On at least one occasion, Lars had Elisabeth sit in a chair on the stage, mute beside a large tape recorder that played one of her messages given back in the day when she was strong and well.

Her family and closest friends were worried that Elisabeth's once-strong spirit had been crushed. She needed rest. She expressed fear and confusion. The family staged an intervention, removing Elisabeth, who had agreed, to an undisclosed location outside the United States. They pleaded with Lars. But over time, Elisabeth herself begged to go back to Lars. "He is my husband," she said. "He is my head."

Gradually Elisabeth Elliot, brilliant linguist, lost language itself. She spoke in gibberish, then, bit by bit, retreated into silence. Much of her private voice was lost as well, as Lars burned most of her journals from the years of their marriage, a choice he now regrets, as he actually gave his life to Jesus in 2019. Lars and a cadre of faithful young female caregivers met Elisabeth's daily needs as her health declined.

Elisabeth's death in June 2015 was, in fact, eerily reminiscent of what Elisabeth herself had written about the subject of her 1968 biography, Kenneth Strachan. "Far from crowning with glory a life of earnest endeavor to be a faithful servant," she wrote, that servant's death "seemed like the last mock-cry." There was no glorious summation, no last triumphal words from the great leader. No deathbed clarity regarding all that had gone before. Just a last, long, quavering breath.

"Can we ever for an instant contemplate a life as God sees it, without sentimentality? Or will we, the instant we see clearly, lacerate ourselves either for looking through rose-colored glasses, or for judging without charity? Sentimentality is not compassion, for it is blind and ignorant. Compassion both sees and acknowledges the truth and accepts it, and perhaps God alone is wholly compassionate.

"And God alone can answer the question, who was he?"

The same can be asked about Elisabeth Elliot. *Who was she?*

I would say she was a woman who lived imperfectly, as we all do, loved God, and sought to serve Him with everything she had.

But one thing we know is that Elisabeth would prefer to answer in her own words, not mine.

"The answer is beyond us. Here are the data we can deal with. There is so much more that we do not know—some of it has been forgotten, some of it hidden, some of it lost—but we look at what we know. We grant that it is not a neat and satisfying picture—there are ironies, contradictions, inconsistencies, imponderables. . . ."

"Here, then," Elisabeth Elliot concluded, as do I, "is as much of the truth as one biographer could discover about a [person]. Let the reader find as much of its meaning as he [or she] can."[4]

The Truth *Is* Love

*"Nobody has seen the trekking birds take their way
towards such warmer spheres as do not exist, or rivers
break their course through rocks and plains to run into
an ocean which is not to be found. For God does not
create a longing or a hope without having a fulfilling
reality ready for them. But our longing is our pledge, and
blessed are the homesick, for they shall come home."*
—Isak Dinesen

There has been much loss since I first leaned back against Elisabeth Elliot's gravestone back in 2018. So many graves have been added to the ranks of the dead. It's so odd, I think now, that my own kind husband should be one of them, though Lee has not yet been interred. His ashes rest in an upright black box on the mantel in the home we built so many years ago.

In many of Elisabeth's writings, she'd describe the view from her office in her last home, where the strong, cold waves of the Atlantic Ocean would break on the massive rocks of the shoreline beyond her window. Now I sit at my own desk, a new widow and freshly acquainted with death, pondering with enhanced insight the life and death of Elisabeth Elliot. The woods beyond my home office windows are winter-frozen, their leafless, black branches soaring into a dull gray sky.

I know far more about Elisabeth, Lars, Addison, Jim, and the other friends whose story I've told in these pages. But there is no need to tell all, nor would it be possible. Elisabeth's legacy is far more than the sum of her choices in the time frame covered by this book and the work she created in her later years. In writing this much of her story,

I've sought to follow the guidance I sensed years ago, as I leaned on the irregular stone of Elisabeth Elliot's grave.

The truth, in love. Ah. So often we hear that phrase as a dialectic. As Tim Keller has said, "Love without truth is sentimentality; it supports and affirms us but keeps us in denial about our flaws. Truth without love is harshness; it gives us information but in such a way that we cannot really hear it."[1]

Surely, in the body of Christ, today as in the first century when the apostle Paul exhorted Christ-followers, we need both truth and love in our dealings with one another. Those of us who write books must seek to incorporate both in our observations of our subjects.

But in the end, there is a deeper mystery in the very nature of truth and love, and the gospel itself. These are not only propositional actualities to be academically studied and exercised in our dealings with one another, excellent as that is. There is more to be found in the person of Jesus Christ Himself. He does not just speak these powerful, multi-dimensional words. He is Truth. He is Love. The Word became flesh and dwelt among us. His mercy is our salvation and assures our resurrection. His mercy is also our legacy, that which we pass on to those who follow.

In winter's chill, the days are short, and the nights are long. Last evening I went for a walk. The cold moon rose before me. The wind tossed the branches of the leafless trees. Desolate, but the icy night seemed by its very bleakness to stir with a great secret. God is with us. What looks dead will live again. The wind blows where it will. The great dance goes on . . . life, death, the turning of the seasons and the pages of not just Elisabeth's, but of all our journals, day by day, year by year, until our earthly voice is stilled by the One who has ordained each page in our book, before even a one of them came to be.

We can choose to look only at what we see, and live accordingly. Or we can know: dancing beneath the frozen surface, life still flows. Vast blue-green vistas lie ahead. That which was dead will live again. He who is both truth and love has assured it. Spring, the ultimate spring, is coming.

With Gratitude

If there was ever a season in which I experienced the incredible support, love, and help of our community of friends old and new, it was while I wrote this book. My husband's final illness and death eclipsed the writing process, of course, but the immense care I received during Lee's departure mingled with my professional responsibilities. For a writer, as for all creative vocations, there's no tidy dividing line between life and art. They mingle, informing and enriching one another. My "personal" friends and my "professional" friends all contributed to who I am and what this book came to be.

Valerie Elliot Shepard and Walt Shepard, lifelong EE friends Arlita and Joe Winston, and Kathy Reeg of the Elisabeth Elliot Foundation: thank you, first for your friendships, trust, and prayer support, and for sharing the wealth of Elisabeth's journals, letters, notes, jottings, notebooks, lists, dreams, and hopes. Thank you all for reading the manuscript. Thank you, Kathy Gilbert, for sharing your EE letters and papers, and for so graciously reading the draft manuscript as well. Thank you, Peter deVries, for your memories and insights about your Aunt Betty, Addison, and your mom, Ginny.

Joni Eareckson Tada, thank you for your rich friendship, prayer support, and solidarity in writing this book's foreword, as well as your openness to the next project God may have for us!

Patti Bryce, Royden Goodson, Ellie Lofaro: thank you for sharing your thoughtful and witty insights regarding the draft beginning and end of this tome.

Thank you to Bob Schuster at the Wheaton College Archives, for originally helping me access all those stuffed boxes of EE correspondence a few years ago, and Anthony Solis, for your willingness to dig up arcane details.

Andie and Jim Young, Kelly and Rob Stuckey, Carey and Steve Keefe, Janice Allen, and Laura and Jim Warren: I am so blessed to have dear, wise, generous, and faithful friends who just happen to have homes on the water or in the mountains, giving me soul-enriching habitats in which to write.

Robert Wolgemuth, my longtime friend and agent, and Nancy DeMoss Wolgemuth, thank you for your generous support. Erik Wolgemuth, thank you for your solidarity and for so ably carrying the ball down the field and across the goal line on this project.

To Lifeway's Devin Maddox and Clarissa Dufresne, thank you for your support, expertise, and flexibility, particularly when this book demanded that it become something it wasn't originally designed to be!

Enormous thanks to: Supper Club, Church Group—particularly my fellow elves Connie and Sam Shabshab—HSM, Medium Group, ICM colleagues, and my many other friend groups that don't happen to have official names.

Thank you to the brothers and sisters of McLean Bible Church and McLean Presbyterian Church—particularly pastors David Platt, Ryan Laughlin, and Steve Smallman. Thank you to the army of friends and family who prayed for us, laughed and cried with us, and fed us. Thank you for doing life with me still, though I can't help but miss all those great meal deliveries during Lee's journey Home!

To my amazing adult children and funny grandchildren: Emily, Haley, Ben, and Walker; Brielle and Daniel: I love doing life with you, and I am so thankful that we could all pull together in such love and unity as we bid your dad and Gramps farewell. (For now.)

Now, friends—since only friends read a book's acknowledgments—I'm not just tying up these pages with a nice Christian bow, but I really am robustly grateful to God. Thank You, God, for giving me work that I love. Thank You for Your extraordinary provision of all the above relationships and blessings. I am overwhelmed most of all by the sure sense You have given me of Your grace, presence, and indescribable provisions for eternity. Thank You.

Ellen Vaughn
Reston, Virginia
March 29, 2023

Notes

CHAPTER 1

1. Not wanting to clutter the text, I have not footnoted Elisabeth Elliot's many journal entries in this book. I've also routinely made small grammatical adjustments in those entries, such as spelling out some of her abbreviations, to make a smoother reading experience. In addition, to avoid confusion, I've called my subject "Elisabeth" throughout this volume, though family and close friends called her "Betty." She preferred the more formal "Elisabeth" in public, and often used it in private from 1969 on, since that is how Addison Leitch referred to her.

2. As in *Becoming Elisabeth Elliot*, I've chosen to call the tribe "Waodani" throughout this book, both in my own writing and in my quotes of others' words from the time period when the slur "Auca" was routinely—and innocently—used by many.

CHAPTER 2

1. Elisabeth Elliot, *Who Shall Ascend: The Life of R. Kenneth Strachan of Costa Rica* (New York: Harper & Row, 1968), xi–xii.

CHAPTER 3

1. Michael Marshall, *Gospel Healing and Salvation,* quoted by Elisabeth Elliot in http://www.reformedsheology.com/2008/01/feminin-ity-by-elisabeth-elliot.html.

2. Some of this descriptive material about the 1960s originated in *Jesus Revolution*, which I coauthored in 2018 with Greg Laurie. It was released by Lionsgate as a feature film in 2023.

CHAPTER 4

1. EE to "Dearest Family," October 8, 1963.

2. Laura Ingalls Wilder, *Little House in the Big Woods* (1932; repr., New York: HarperCollins, 1971), 44.

3. EE to "Dearest Folks," February 19, 1963.

4. EE to "Dearest Folks," October 8, 1963 (Jim's birthday and her anniversary).

5. EE to "Dearest Family," September 30, 1963.

6. EE to "Dearest Mother and All," February 3, 1964.

7. EE to "Dearest Mother," October 10, 1964.

8. EE to "Dearest Family," September 30, 1963.

9. EE to "Dearest Family," November 11, 1963.

10. EE to "Dearest Family," November 20, 1963.

11. EE to "Dearest Folks," December 10, 1963.

12. EE to "Dearest Folks," December 10, 1963.

13. EE to "Dearest Folks," December 3, 1963.

14. Account of Elisabeth's dad's death to her siblings Phil, Dave, and Ginny, January 10, 1964.

15. EE to "Dearest Mother," January 8, 1964 (the 8th anniversary of Jim's death).

CHAPTER 5

1. EE to "Dearest Mother," April 3, 1963 (written while she was living in Shandia).

2. EE to "Dearest Family," February 3, 1964.

3. EE to "Dearest Family," March 27, 1964.

CHAPTER 6

1. EE to "Dearest Ones," February 14, 1964.

2. Ironically, a number of people interviewed for this book who ended up in ministry said that God had used Elisabeth Elliot to motivate them to do so.

3. EE to "Dearest Family," February 25, 1964.

4. She noted that this "is how non-Christians feel . . . simply a soul to be 'won,' a statistic on a missions report."

5. EE to "Dearest Folks," March 9, 1964.

6. EE to "Dearest Folks," March 9, 1964.

7. Note that these questions made enough impression to be jotted in her journal.

8. EE, notes, Lectures on Job.

9. EE to "Dearest Mother," March 10, 1964.

CHAPTER 7

1. This is a paraphrase of early twentieth-century journalist H. L. Mencken's famous description of Puritanism.

2. EE to "Dearest Mother," March 10, 1964.

3. EE to "Dearest Ones," February 14, 1964.

4. EE to "Dearest Folks," February 25, 1964.

5. For one example among many of Elisabeth's position on this topic, see https://elisabethelliot.org/resource-library/gateway-to-joy/take-a-stand-for-jesus-on-homosexuality/.

6. EE to "Dearest Mother," March 10, 1964.

CHAPTER 8

1. See Romans 1:14, Amplified Version.

2. J. I. Packer, foreword to *No Graven Image* (Wheaton, IL: Crossway Books, 1982), ii.

3. Elliot, *No Graven Image*, 58–59.

4. Elliot, *No Graven Image*, 59.

5. Elliot, *No Graven Image*, 106.

6. Elliot, *No Graven Image*, 136.

7. Elliot, *No Graven Image*, 189.

8. Elliot, *No Graven Image*, 190.

9. Elliot, *No Graven Image*, 223.

CHAPTER 9

1. EE, notes, Lectures on Job.

2. Elisabeth Elliot, *These Strange Ashes: Is God Still in Charge?* (Grand Rapids: Revell, 1998), 96.

3. Elliot, *These Strange Ashes*, 125.

4. Elisabeth Elliot, *No Graven Image*, (Wheaton, IL: Crossway Books, 1982), 242.

5. Elliot, *No Graven Image*, 242–43.

6. EE to "Dear Ones," October 25, 1966.

7. Harold Lindsell, "One Doesn't Tell God," *Christianity Today*, July 8, 1966, https://www.christianitytoday.com/ct/1966/july-8/books-in-review.html.

8. As quoted in Elisabeth's journal, June 2, 1966.

9. EE to "Dear Ones," October 10, 1966.

10. As quoted, back cover, 1982 British edition, *No Graven Image*.

11. As quoted by David Swartz, "Elisabeth Elliot, Missionary Rebel," Patheos, Anxious Bench, August 28, 2019, https://www.patheos.com/blogs/anxiousbench/2019/08/elisabeth-elliot-missionary-rebel/.

12. Timothy Keller, *Walking with God through Pain and Suffering* (New York: The Penguin Group, 2013), 172.

13. As quoted in Elisabeth's journal, February 4, 1967, quote is from C. S. Lewis, letter to Owen Barfield, September 12, 1938.

CHAPTER 10

1. EE to "Letter to Family," May 4, 1964.

2. EE to "Letter to Mother," December 9, 1964.

3. EE to "Dearest Mother and All," May 28, 1964. Names in the letter have been changed.

4. Harold Lindsell, "One Doesn't Tell God," *Christianity Today*, July 8, 1966, emphasis added, https://www.christianitytoday.com/ct/1966/july-8/books-in-review.html.

CHAPTER 11

1. Robert William Service, "The Blood-Red Fourragere," https://www.poemhunter.com/poem/the-blood-red-fourragere/.

CHAPTER 12

1. EE to "Dearest Ones," November 22, 1966.

2. Philip Gefter, "Cornell Capa, Photographer, Is Dead at 90," *New York Times*, May 24, 2008, https://www.nytimes.com/2008/05/24/arts/design/23cnd-capa.html.

3. EE to "Dearest Folks," February 25, 1961.

4. http://artdaily.com/news/24409/Cornell-Capa--Founder-of-International-Center-of-Photography--Died-at-90#.XXZ3zF2JI_4

5. EE to "Dearest Folks," May 15, 1961.

6. This account mingles Elisabeth's journal entries, jotted right after the conversation, and her letter to "Dearest Ones," November 22, 1966, in which she shared some "quotes from Cornell" with her family.

CHAPTER 13

1. EE to "Dear Ones," December 19, 1966.
2. Elisabeth Elliot, *Who Shall Ascend: The Life of R. Kenneth Strachan of Costa Rica* (New York: Harper & Row, 1968), xi–xii.
3. Elliot, *Who Shall Ascend*, 11.
4. Elliot, *Who Shall Ascend*, 27.
5. Elliot, *Who Shall Ascend*, 99.
6. In 1971, committed to the belief that the future of the gospel in Latin America must be vested in the Latin Church, with missionaries serving under Latin leadership, control of all LAM ministries was legally transferred to Latin partners. In 2014, LAM became part of United World Mission, which, according to their website, presented synergistic opportunities for advancing global Kingdom work through partnering for leadership development, church planting, and holistic ministry, helping more than ninety nations, seeking to help leaders establish and build up the indigenous body of Christ.
7. Elliot, *Who Shall Ascend*, 93.
8. Elliot, *Who Shall Ascend*, 117.
9. Elliot, *Who Shall Ascend*, 118.
10. EE to "Dear Ones," October 25, 1966.
11. Elliot, *Who Shall Ascend*, 152–53.
12. Elliot, *Who Shall Ascend*, 160.
13. Elliot, *Who Shall Ascend*, 161.
14. Elliot, *Who Shall Ascend*, 161.

CHAPTER 15

1. Robert Mcg. Thomas Jr., "Eugenia Price, 79, Romance Novelist, Dies," *New York Times*, May 30, 1996, https://www.nytimes.com/1996/05/30/arts/eugenia-price-79-romance-novelist-dies.html.
2. https://www.legacy.com/us/obituaries/dispatch/name/david-redding-obituary?id=18565495

CHAPTER 18

1. Elisabeth's quotes about Jerusalem in this chapter are from her book, *Furnace of the Lord: Reflections on the Redemption of the Holy City*, Hodder and Stoughton, reproduced from the U.S. edition by arrangement with Doubleday and Company, New York, 1969.

CHAPTER 19

1. http://www.nybooks.com/articles/1967/04/20/report-from-vietnam-i-the-home-program/
2. EE to "Letter to Family," January 1968.
3. EE to "Dearest Mother and All," February 26, 1968.
4. EE to "Letter to Family," January 1968.
5. EE to "Letter to Family," May 1968.
6. EE to "Letter to Family," May 1968.

CHAPTER 20

1. EE to "Dearest Mother and All," October 1, 1968.
2. Quote from Elisabeth's journal: Amy Carmichael, *Things as They Are: Mission Work in Southern India* (1903; repr., Pantianos Classics, 2016), 30.
3. Elisabeth Elliot, "Furnace of the Lord: In Support of the Arabs," *Christianity Today*, October 6, 1978, https://www.christianitytoday.com/ct/1978/october-6/furnace-of-lord-in-support-of-arabs.html.
4. See Jeremiah 7:3–7 (RSV).
5. This is quoted from Elisabeth's 1968 journal, not Cornell's letter itself.
6. EE to "Dearest Mother and Others," May 28, 1968.

CHAPTER 21

1. Elisabeth Elliot, "Furnace of the Lord: In Support of the Arabs," *Christianity Today*, October 6, 1978, https://www.christianitytoday.com/ct/1978/october-6/furnace-of-lord-in-support-of-arabs.html.
2. EE to "Dearest Mother, Mom, Dad, [Mr. and Mrs. Elliot, Jim's parents], and everyone," Christmas 1968.
3. Tom Howard to "Dear Addison," December 17, 1968.
4. EE to "Dearest Mother," December 9, 1968.
5. EE to "Dearest Mother," December 19, 1968.
6. EE to "Letter to Mother," December 9, 1968.
7. Addison Leitch to "Dear Katharine," December 15, 1968.
8. EE to "Dearest Mother," December 11, 1968.

CHAPTER 22

1. Tom Howard to "Dear Mother and Family," January 7, 1969.
2. Dave Howard to "Dearest Mother and Family," January 6, 19698.
3. Richard K. Kennedy to "Dear Elisabeth," December 23, 1968.

4. "Addison Leitch Weds Elisabeth Elliot," *Christianity Today*, January 31, 1969, https://www.christianitytoday.com/ct/1969/january-31/women-ministers-marry.html.

5. Hans Bürki to "Dear Elisabeth," December 1967.

6. Hans Bürki to "Dear Elisabeth," January 1968.

CHAPTER 23

1. https://www.gordonconwell.edu/about/history/

2. Ellen Vaughn interview, one of many, with Walter Shepard, Southport, North Carolina, May 2018.

3. Eleanor Vandervort to "Dear Elisabeth," March 6, 1950.

4. Eleanor Vandervort to "My Sweet Bet," Tuesday night, March 1965.

5. Obituary for Eleanor Chambers Vandervort, *Gloucester Times*, November 4, 2015, https://obituaries.gloucestertimes.com/obituary/eleanor-vandevort-772532331.

6. Addison to "Dear Richard," November 15, 1969.

7. EE to "Dear Families," January 13, 1970.

8. Addison to "Dear Boyd and Nelle," August 2, 1972.

9. Ellen Vaughn interview with Peter deVries, September 4, 2021, Charlotte, North Carolina.

10. EE to "Dear Family," June 26, 1970.

CHAPTER 24

1. Addison to "Dear Boyd and Nelle," August 2, 1972.

2. Addison to "Dear Joe," August 24, 1970.

3. Addison to "Dear [Mrs. Woodruff]," March 28, 1972.

CHAPTER 26

1. "Key Statistics for Prostate Cancer," revised January 12, 2023, https://www.cancer.org/cancer/prostate-cancer/about/key-statistics.html.

2. William J. Catalona, "History of the discovery and clinical translation of prostate-specific antigen," *National Library of Medicine*, April 16, 2015, https://www.ncbi.nlm.nih.gov/pmc/articles/PMC5832880/#bib5.

3. Addison to "Dear Daughters of the Dispersion," November 15, 1972.

4. Ibid.

5. Addison to "Dear Bess," February 26, 1973.

6. Addison to "Dear Glenn and Margaret," March 2, 1973.

CHAPTER 27

1. Corrie ten Boom with Elizabeth and John Sherrill, *The Hiding Place* (Grand Rapids: Chosen Books, 1971), 165.

2. Addison to "Dear Ramez and Becky," March 29, 1973.

3. Robert Welkos, "Dean Burk, Supporter of Laetrile, Dies," *Los Angeles Times*, October 11, 1988, https://www.latimes.com/archives/la-xpm-1988-10-11-mn-3603-story.html.

4. Addison H. Leitch papers, archives of the Presbyterian Historical Society Philadelphia, Pennsylvania.

CHAPTER 29

1. Tom Howard to "Dear Kinfolks," September 22, 1973.

2. "He Leadeth Me," Words: Joseph H. Gilmore. Music: William B. Bradbury. Public Domain (1862).

3. EE to "Dear Family," September 26, 1973.

CHAPTER 30

1. Tom Howard to "Dear Kinfolks," September 22, 1973.

2. Tom Howard to "Dear Kinfolks," September 22, 1973.

3. From *The Book of Common Prayer*, https://www.bookofcommon-prayer.net/burial_of_the_dead_rite_I.

4. Tom Howard to "Letter to Family," September 1973.

CHAPTER 32

1. EE to "Dearest Val," January 6, 1974.

2. EE to "Dearest Val," February 11, 1974.

3. EE to "Dear Jan," June 14, 1974.

4. EE to "Dearest Val," January 21, 1974.

5. EE to "Dearest Val," February 25, 1974.

6. EE to "Dearest Val," March 7, 1974.

7. EE to "Dear Val," March 18, 1974.

8. EE to "Dearest Val," March 11, 1974.

9. EE to "Dear Val," March 1974.

10. EE, "Dear Val," March 27, 1974.

11. Ellen Vaughn phone interview, one of many, with Valerie Elliot Shepard, January 12, 2023.

12. Val to "Dearest Mama," March 31, 1974.

13. EE to "Dearest Val," April 4, 1974.

14. Val to "Dearest Mama," April 22, 1974.

15. EE to "Dearest Val," April 29, 1974.

16. Val to "Dearest Mama," May 2, 1974.
17. EE to "Dearest Val," May 26, 1974.
18. EE to "Dearest Val," June 4, 1974.
19. EE to "Dearest Val," June 23, 1974.

CHAPTER 33

1. Val to "Dearest Mama," July 21, 1974.

CHAPTER 34

1. EE to "My Two Darlings," November 24, 1975.
2. Elisabeth Elliot, *The Essence of Femininity, A Personal Perspective*, Council on Biblical Manhood and Womanhood, https://bible.org/seriespage/25-essence-femininity-personal-perspective.

CHAPTER 35

1. EE to "Dearest Val," February 21, 1976.
2. EE to "Dearest Sweet Val," February 9, 1976.
3. EE to "Dearest Val," February 12, 1976.

CHAPTER 38

1. Check out the Elisabeth Elliot Foundation's extensive resources, elisabethelliot.org.
2. Ellen Vaughn interview with Dave Howard, Ft. Myers, Florida, February 8, 2018.
3. Zippy had to be put down because he kept running away and getting into the neighbors' chickens or something, and Muggeridge and MacPhaerce were hit by cars.
4. Elisabeth Elliot, *Who Shall Ascend: The Life of R. Kenneth Strachan of Costa Rica* (New York: Harper & Row, 1968), 162.

EPILOGUE

1. Tim Keller, *The Meaning of Marriage* (New York: Penguin Books; reprint edition, 2013).

ELISABETH ELLIOT

Elisabeth's first husband's life was cut short when he attempted to bring the gospel to the Waodani people of Ecuador. In spite of the hardship, Elisabeth lived a life of faith. But, her life's message reveals that her suffering was actually the greatest gateway for joy. Learn more about Elisabeth and her life in these three books.

ELISABETHELLIOTBOOKS.COM

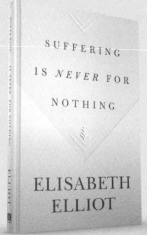

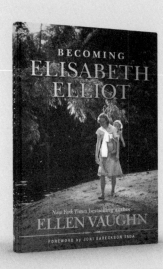

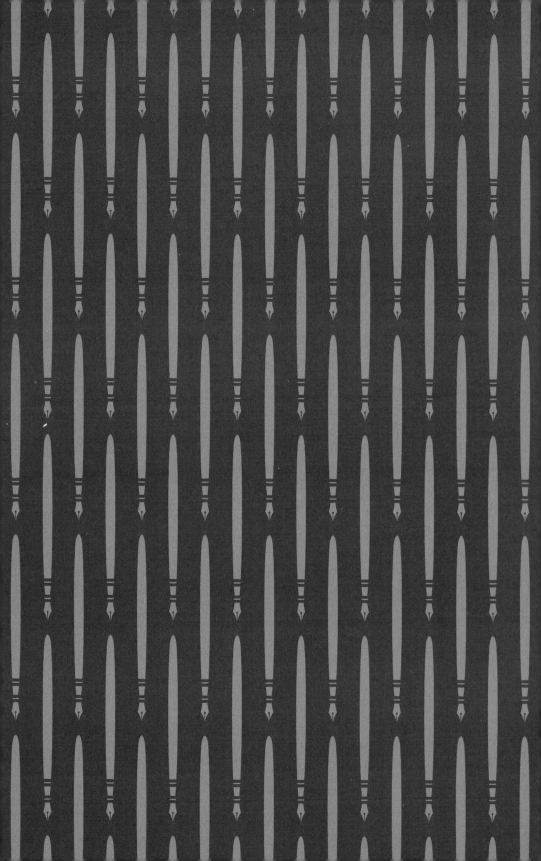